Making Their Place

Making Their Place

Feminism After Socialism in Eastern Germany

Katja M. Guenther

Stanford University Press
Stanford, California

Stanford University Press
Stanford, California

Printed in the United States of America on acid-free, archival-quality paper.

Library of Congress Cataloging-in-Publication Data

Guenther, Katja M., 1975-
  Making their place : feminism after socialism in Eastern Germany / Katja M. Guenther.
    p. cm.
  Includes bibliographical references and index.
  ISBN 978-0-8047-7071-2 (cloth : alk. paper)--ISBN 978-0-8047-7072-9 (pbk. : alk. paper)
  1. Feminism--Germany (East) 2. Post-communism--Germany (East) I. Title.
  HQ1630.5.G84 2010
  305.4209431'09049--dc22   2010004845

Typeset by Bruce Lundquist in 10/14 Minion

Contents

Illustrations

Maps

Acknowledgments

While working on this book, I have benefited from the intellectual, emotional, and financial generosity of many people and institutions. Dr. Heike Kahlert of the Institute for Sociology and Demography at the University of Rostock and Theresa Wobbe of the Institute for Gender Research at the University of Erfurt and their colleagues were gracious hosts while I conducted fieldwork. Christine Wild always gave me the feeling of having a home away from home, as did my many hosts in Rostock and Erfurt. My uncle, Fritz, offered a level of logistical support of which most fieldworkers can only dream. My mother, Adelheid, shared her good cheer and insider advice on navigating various aspects of daily life in Germany.

The German Academic Exchange Service (DAAD), the National Science Foundation (#0402513 with Robin Stryker), and the University of Minnesota, including the Department of Sociology there, enabled me to dedicate the necessary time and effort to this project. The findings reported here do not necessarily reflect the opinions of any of these institutions. I thank the staff and fellow visiting scholars at the Minda de Gunzburg Center for European Studies at Harvard University during the spring of 2008 for their intellectual hospitality and for affording me the time to write.

Some passages of text in this book originally appeared as part of journal articles. "Understanding Policy Diffusion Across Feminist Social Movements: The Case of Gender Mainstreaming in Eastern Germany," *Politics & Gender* 4, no. 4: 587–613. Copyright © 2008 The Women and Politics Research Section of the American Political Science Association. Reprinted with the permission of Cambridge University Press. "'A Bastion of Sanity in a Crazy World': A Local

Feminist Movement and the Reconstitution of Scale, Space, and Place in an Eastern German City," *Social Politics: International Studies in Gender, State, and Society* 13, no. 4: 551–75. (c) 2006 Oxford University Press. Reprinted with the permission of Oxford University Press.

I have been fortunate to receive spirited guidance from Ron Aminzade, Elizabeth Heger Boyle, Erin Kelly, and Mary Jo Maynes. I am especially indebted to Robin Stryker for her enduring support. Daphne Berdahl, Barbara Einhorn, Myra Marx Ferree, Eileen McDonagh, Sherry Martin, Marilyn Rueschemeyer, and Kathrin Zippel kindly reviewed drafts of chapters as they evolved or sparked new directions of inquiry through their comments on presentations or conversations. At Stanford University Press, Kate Wahl and the anonymous reviewers stimulated my thinking.

Writing a book requires more than just financial and intellectual resources. Dana Collins, Deirdre Kiely, Karolyn Lord, Molly Talcott, Eve Watson, and Kathrin Zippel have been especially generous in sharing their empathy, humor, and encouragement with me. My nephews Fox and Orson provided reliable comic relief during moments of stress, and I eagerly look forward to their feminist futures. My sister, Barbara, first imagined this project and exhorted me to pursue it. My wife, Tuppett, resiliently withstood my long absences and frequent distraction, and she has always kept me on the path of this project with her confidence in both me and in the book. Her determination and commitment, and her sense of fun and mischief, are constant sources of inspiration for me.

Most importantly, I am indebted to the women in Rostock and Erfurt who took the time to welcome me and to share their stories with me. Collecting, recording, analyzing, and disseminating their stories for almost a decade has been a profoundly challenging, moving, and satisfying experience. I thank all of the participants for sharing themselves with me and for showing me the many rich possibilities of feminism.

Abbreviations

ABM	Arbeitsbeschaffungsmaßnahmen (Employment Creation Measures; see also SAM)
ASF	Arbeitsgemeinschaft Sozialdemokratische Frauen (Working Society of Social Democratic Women)
CDU	Christlich Demokratische Union Deutschlands (Christian Democratic Union)
CDU-FU	FrauenUnion der Christliche Demokratische Union (Women's Union of the Christian Democratic Union)
DFB	Demokratischer Frauenverband (Democratic Women's Association; postunification name of DFD)
DFD	Demokratischer Frauenbund Deutschlands (Democratic Women's League of Germany, East Germany); see also DFB
EU	European Union
FRG	Federal Republic of Germany (West Germany)
FTZ	FrauenTechnikZentrum (Women's Technical Center)
GB	Gleichstellungsbeauftragte (Gender Equity Representative)
GDR	German Democratic Republic (East Germany)
LFR-MV	Landesfrauenrat Mecklenburg-Vorpommern (State Women's Council of Mecklenburg-West Pomerania)
LFR-TH	Landesfrauenrat Thüringen (State Women's Council of Thuringia)

PDS   Partei des Demokratischen Sozialsmus (Party of Democratic
             Socialism)

RFI   Rostocker Frauen Initiativen (Rostock Women's Initiatives)

SAM   Strukturanpassungsmaßnahmen (Structural Adjustment
             Measures; see alsoABM)

SED   Sozialistisches Einheitspartei Deutschlands (Socialist Unity Party
             of Germany)

SPD   Sozialdemokratische Partei Deutschlands (Social Democratic
             Party of Germany)

UFV   Unabhängiger Frauenverband (Independent Women's
             Association)

Making Their Place

The Place of Feminism
After Socialism

THE COLLAPSE OF STATE SOCIALISM in eastern and central Europe in 1989 transformed the world. International leaders hailed the dawning of a new era in which formerly socialist states were to flourish socially, economically, and politically. In spite of these optimistic predictions, struggle has marred the road toward long-term stability. Citizens of formerly socialist states have faced a plethora of problems including interethnic conflict, political division, economic meltdown, and soaring unemployment.

In much of the region, women disproportionately shoulder the burden of the challenges of life after socialism. Women were typically better represented among workers in socialist states than in the capitalist West, but they have been consistently overrepresented among the un- and underemployed in many parts of eastern and central Europe since 1989. While postsocialist transformations have created new opportunities for women, especially for those with specific skills (see, for example, Ghodsee 2005), women overall have witnessed the loss of state support for their economic activity, the curtailing of their reproductive rights, and the rise of traditional gender ideologies that value women primarily as mothers and wives rather than as active participants in the labor market and political life.

Across eastern and central Europe, women have resisted these changes. The most visible feminist mobilization in the region was the East German feminist movement, which worked to integrate women's issues into the calls for a reformed socialism during the tumult of 1989. Yet the national-level mobilization of the East German feminist movement survived only a few months after the collapse of the Berlin Wall in November 1989. Since that time feminist activity in both eastern Germany and other parts of postsocialist Europe has largely disappeared from public view.

Still, in eastern Germany—as elsewhere in eastern and central Europe—women continue to organize. Cities and towns throughout eastern Germany are home to feminist organizations that address issues like violence against women, women's un- and underemployment, women's political representation, and family and childcare policy. The eastern German cities of Rostock and Erfurt, for example, have each given rise to more than a dozen women's organizations since 1989. These local women's organizations—and the local feminist movements they comprise—emerged when forty years of state repression ceased and the sudden installation of democracy created new arenas for activism and engagement.

Both the local feminist movements in Rostock and Erfurt formed around a fundamental concern for the well-being of women. They offer social services while also engaging in political advocacy and public awareness campaigns to increase women's status and challenge gender inequalities within a range of institutions such as the family and the state. Both movements started out seeking to help women cope with the sudden rupture as socialist East Germany unified with the democratic, capitalist, and less gender egalitarian West Germany. The feminist organizations in the two cities address the same issues, including women's unemployment and violence against women. Both operate in the same political structures and the same national political climate and culture. Even the cities that are home to these two movements are uncannily similar in terms of their sizes and population characteristics.

Yet while the feminist movement in Rostock has been a startling success in many ways, the movement in Erfurt has struggled. The two movements have embraced different feminist ideologies and divergent strategies for effecting change. More recently, they have taken dissimilar positions vis-à-vis the rise of the European Union (EU) as a source of gender equality policy.

How has this happened? Why were the paths of the feminist movements in Rostock and Erfurt after unification so different? Given shared experience with socialism and German unification, and common political structures and institutions, shouldn't these movements be relatively similar? This book examines local feminist movements after socialism and explains why these feminist formations vary across places, even within the same national state. I draw on interview, observational, and archival data to analyze the central differences, as well as important similarities, between the feminist movements in Rostock and Erfurt. I chronicle the continued resistance of women in the former German Democratic Republic (GDR, or East Germany) to the new expectations for gender and gender relations introduced in eastern Germany as a consequence of German unification in 1990. What emerges is a story not just about two feminist movements but also an analysis of how the people and structures in two cities struggle to define themselves, their values, and their understandings of gender in a period of monumental social, economic, and political upheaval.

While the national-level feminist mobilizations during the immediate unification period of 1989–90 garnered significant public and scholarly attention, interest in women's organizing in eastern Germany largely disappeared when national-level mobilization ceased. This shift gives the impression that the feminist movement in eastern Germany is a thing of the past, and that the spate of problems women faced as a consequence of unification was resolved. In reality, feminist organizing after 1990 has been widespread and remains important precisely because of the stubbornness of many of the gendered social problems resulting from unification, including high rates of un- and underemployment and outmigration among women.

I focus on feminist organizing at the local level both to bring postsocialist feminism to light and to incorporate localized social movements into scholarly discussions of social movements. The relative neglect of local social movements within the rich literature on social movements obscures activism at the nonnational level as apolitical or as less meaningful than activism targeting the national state. This in turn renders much of women's social movement activity invisible or unimportant as women are often more active and visible as social movement actors at the local level (Eschle 2000; Ferree and Mueller 2004; Klawiter 2008; Ray and Korteweg 1999; Taylor 1999).

A framework centered on place illuminates why local movements develop differently. Place is typically conceptualized as occurring along three dimensions (Agnew 2002). First, place refers to locale, or the site of daily, routine life. Second, place invokes a geographic location that expresses relationships and connections among different spaces and forces, including political, social, and economic processes. Finally, place summons a sense of collective identity and of belonging through bonds that individuals and communities develop for the settings in which they lead their lives.

Places are not static; they change and can be changed, over time and in response to internal and external pressures (Guenther 2006; Paulsen 2004). Places are in a constant state of reproduction and reformulation, reflecting social relations and practices and involving struggles over power and meaning. Local social movements are both the outcomes of, and participants in, the project of making places. While the specificities of place can limit possibilities for social action, local movements can also mobilize place and its attendant identities to redefine the logic of a place, to align their interests with those of other actors working to build and maintain local identities and ideologies, and even to create their own political and discursive opportunities. Thus, place is an evolving project, the exact contours of which are an accomplishment rather than a given.

The concept of place—which cultural and social geographers largely developed—is especially useful as a lens through which to examine social movements because it allows for the synthesis and expansion of political and cultural perspectives on social movements. Political process theory typically focuses on the importance of political opportunities for movement success and privileges the state as the central target of movement activity. Political process perspectives explore how states contribute to the formation of social movements and their outcomes, often focusing on political opportunity structures like the presence or absence of political allies and shifts in the political balance of power as critical in giving rise to social movements, and in shaping organizational dynamics, activities, and outcomes (see, for example, Kriesi 1995; Minkoff 1999; Tarrow 1994, 1998). Cultural perspectives, which stem from the new social movement tradition, elevate issues of identity and solidarity and have been especially widely utilized in studies of feminist and women's movements (Taylor 1996; Whittier 1995). While both perspectives offer useful sensitizing concepts for understanding the development and outcomes of social movements, they also provide partially obscured views of social movements. Previous efforts at addressing the importance of the local for social movements (Hellman 1987; Ray 1998, 1999) have stressed political, institutional, and organizational dynamics to the exclusion of considering the historic trajectories of place and the intersections between local cultures, identities, and politics.

A framework organized around place recognizes the salience of *both* a place's structures of power *and* cultural practices for the emergence of social movements. Different levels and units of governance have their own rules of political engagement, distributions of power, and political leanings. Likewise, cultural practices and norms vary across locales. Thinking about place attends to both of these dimensions in trying to understand the emergence and outcome of social movements.

Understanding feminism in eastern Germany requires attention to politics and culture. Not only did women experience changes in both of these domains, but they also participated in efforts at changing both of these domains. Women's issues like violence against women, for example, involve political and cultural norms and problems. Movement goals include effecting policy outcomes and cultural changes. Rather than seeking to separate or compartmentalize politics and culture, I integrate them in my analysis, recognizing their distinctive and common parts in unraveling the roots of the variations in feminism after socialism.

Thinking about place also enhances knowledge about gender for, as Doreen Massey (1994) argues, places vary in their expectations of femininity and masculinity and the relationship between them. Although the sociological literature on gender widely recognizes gender as context-specific, sociologists have yet to fully engage with how or why specific gender systems surface in particular places. In examining the feminist movements in Rostock and Erfurt, I uncover important differences in how gender is understood in these two places, and I trace these understandings to specific mechanisms and features within the cities' place characters.

Place and the politics of place character—or how different social actors struggle to define a place and its significance—have been crucial to the development and outcome of the local feminist movements in Rostock and Erfurt. The specificities of any given place help explain the feminist formations within that place. Local contexts shape various aspects of social movement organization, identity, strategy, and outcome. As cultures, traditions, and networks differ across specific locations, women's movements may utilize location-specific tactics, including framing strategies (Benford and Snow 2000), have access to unique, local cultural (Swidler 1995) and organizational (Clemens 1993) repertoires and sources of collective identity (Melucci 1995; Taylor and Whittier 1992; Thayer 1997), and be able to offer participants different types of selective incentives (Heckathorn 1996; Knoke 1988).

Because different levels of the state vary in their practices of, and ideas about, gender, women's organizations working in different geopolitical spaces face different political constraints and opportunities. Simultaneously, feminists mobilize to reinforce or reinterpret how they understand the places to which they belong. In both Rostock and Erfurt, the local feminist movements have sought to participate in how the place of the cities is defined, but the extant contours of the cities' place character, or specific combinations of politics, economy, geography, history, culture, and organizations that interact and endure over time, presented these two feminist movements with different constraints and opportunities. Ultimately, the feminist movement in Rostock has been more successful in participating in the process of making place than that in Erfurt since German unification in 1990.

Local places are situated within nested arenas of social action, and local social actors capitalize on—and manipulate—relationships with other levels of action to promote specific understandings of their local place. In a complex global environment, this means that diverse social actors—including feminist movements—can attempt to participate in the process of making place and of defining the linkages between places. For example, policymakers in Rostock largely reject the federal unified German state as a legitimate source of identity or politics, but embrace the EU as a meaningful and important partner in the development of the city and its sense of place character.

Even in an increasingly global world, local places also shape how people experience life. Local norms and identities serve as filters for understanding processes of globalization. Through "glocalization," local places moderate the demands and effects of global processes.[1]

Given the multiple scales of action available to social movements in eastern Germany, the women's movements in Rostock and Erfurt have the possibility of jumping scale, or strategically targeting one level of social action over another (Masson 2006; Regulska and Grabowska 2008). For example, many feminist organizations in Rostock bypass the federal state as a site for meaningful social action and instead focus on the EU. Sometimes, what appears to be a constraint at one level of action creates an opportunity for meaningful change at another.

Three interrelated aspects of the places of Rostock and Erfurt have been especially crucial to the ideologies and goals of local feminist movements, the nature of state responses to demands made by these movements, and the paths of movement development (see Figure 1.1). The seeds of these forces took root well before unification. However, their power became evident only after democratization opened new pathways for political participation and protest.

First, political forces include the political climates of the two cities and their respective states, the distribution of political power within these locales, and the dominant goals and strategies of policy actors. Political forces also include the balance of power between state organs and the feminist movement. Particularly important politically are the degrees of legitimacy and capacity of feminist actors and organizations.

Political Dimensions

Distribution of
political power

Political culture

Goals of the state
regarding inequalities

State responsiveness to
feminist demands

Cultural Dimensions

Local histories and
traditions

Cultural repertoires

Community identities

Expectations of women
and gender relations

Spatial Dimensions

Geopolitical
positioning

Spatial alliances with
other areas/regions

Influence of different
scales of activity

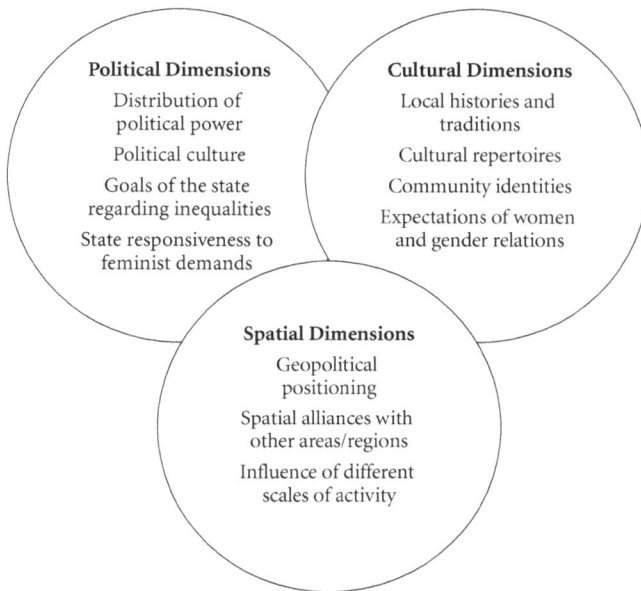

Figure 1.1 Dimensions of Place Salient for Local Feminist Movements in Rostock and Erfurt

Second, cultural forces involve specific local histories and cultural repertoires that create different possibilities for feminist movements to expand, reposition, or come into conflict with, existing traditions, social norms and expectations, and community identities. Especially critical here are socialist legacies, or the memories and (re)interpretations of the socialist past that shape responses and attitudes toward the postsocialist present and future. In the western imagination, socialist legacies are too often represented as archaic anchors to a dismal past, as retardants to progress and the full ascendance of democracy and capitalism. However, as I demonstrate in subsequent chapters, socialist legacies are not just sources of retardation, regression, or nostalgia. They may also serve as innovative strategies for maintaining individual and group identity and survival (Berdahl 2000a). Rather than being regressive, under specific conditions, socialist legacies may actually be progressive, *enhancing*, instead of limiting, the efforts of feminist movements to achieve gender equality. To illuminate the relationship between socialist legacies and specific outcomes for gender relations, my analysis of the feminist movements in Rostock and Erfurt attends to how, why, from where, and under what set of circumstances feminist activists and community leaders draw on socialist and/or postsocialist rhetoric and practice, and to what effect.

Finally, spatial forces encompass the geopolitical positioning and fictive geographies of the two cities. Fictive geographies refer to spatial alliances, or social constructions of space that bridge multiple geographic locations, allowing inhabitants of one location to claim membership in geographically and geopolitically bounded areas to which they do not ostensibly belong. Spatial alliances are highly relevant for the project of constructing places because who or what a place is aligned with contributes to the character, identity, and practices of that place. Spatial forces also involve dynamics of scale and opportunities for movement across levels of governance to effect change.

Feminist Formations in Rostock and Erfurt

Stretched along the mouth of the Warnow River until it reaches the Baltic Sea coast, Rostock is a city marked as much by wide, open expanses as by crowded, more typically urban cityscapes. Rostock is part of a German periphery that occupies a liminal space between two different Europes: eastern and western. The city is located in the poorest and most rural of the so-called new German states that were once part of GDR. When I first visited Rostock in 2000, the city was still reeling from the changes accompanying the end of state socialism in 1989 and the unification of East and West Germany in 1990. Like so many other cities in eastern Germany, Rostock was being rebuilt and renovated. Scaffolding swathed the majority of the picturesque Baroque and Gothic buildings in the city's historic center. The sound of hammers echoed along every street. A reinvention was underway.

Although only a short ride away on the street car, the Südstadt, or South City neighborhood, feels a world apart from the charming downtown district that has developed over centuries around the University of Rostock, the oldest university in northern Europe. In the Südstadt, the unsightly cinderblock highrises, or *Plattenbauten*, that characterized East German urban planning stretch in seemingly endless rows. The lawns around the *Plattenbauten* are overgrown and pocked with dandelions. Local youth have spray painted various social and sexual commentaries on benches and trash cans; one wall of a building reads, "Only the pig says capitalism is inevitable."

I follow a sagging footpath to a small cement office building that is wedged between two apartment buildings. A bright purple sign announces that I have found the Beginenhof, Rostock's women's center. The Beginenhof houses several local feminist organizations that offer an array of services and opportunities, including counseling and advocacy for survivors of physical, sexual, and emotional violence, job training and placement, language instruction, cultural enrichment through art and dance, and political organizing.

The women who work at the Beginenhof are mostly in their forties and fifties. These are women who worked in a range of occupations before unification, holding jobs as diverse as ship's engineer and teacher. Their commitment to gender equality and their need for work led them to women's organizing in 1990. They sit with me in the small café on the first floor where we drink coffee and smoke cigarettes as they share their stories of life in East Germany before and after German unification.

Located in this building since 1994, the Beginenhof is named for the Beginen, or Beguines, a colony of pious women dedicated to altruism and religious mysticism who founded largely self-sustaining communities, mostly in the Low Countries, Germany, and France, between the thirteenth and eighteenth centuries. First recorded as residents of Rostock in the thirteenth century, the Beguines ran a hospice and orphanage until the end of the sixteenth century on a central street still named Beginenberg (Beguines' Hill).

According to its publicity materials, the Beginenhof models itself on a set of underlying principles that governed the medieval Beguines. First, the Beguines lived free from male violence, religious and secular structures of violence, and ideological dogmas. Second, the Beguines fostered a free, solidary society in which women and their children could live and work in an alternative to hierarchically organized guilds and without being forced into isolation from the world at large. Third, the Beguines practiced "social engagement," seeking to interact peacefully and cooperatively with each other and with members of other communities. Finally, the Beguines strived to create communities in which women's diverse life experiences, living arrangements, and thinking could be harmoniously united.

In adopting the name and mission of the Beguines, feminist activists in Rostock successfully co-opted an important local legend to frame their mission as a natural progression of Rostock's history rather than as an abrupt deviation from the city's traditions. As one volunteer at the Beginenhof noted, "This name does not suggest the bra-burning lesbians of the West, but instead a local tradition of women's autonomy." Indeed, in many of its efforts, the feminist movement in Rostock has been able to capitalize successfully on local traditions, norms, and legends, as well as on the city's leftist political culture, to embed itself as a natural part of the city and to further its aims. In so doing, the feminist movement feeds back into the city's place character. The feminist movement reinforces positive identities and boosts community self-esteem during a period in which the city has suffered a great deal from the overwhelming changes accompanying the end of state socialism and the introduction of capitalism.

In Erfurt, feminists have had fewer opportunities to capitalize on place. Situated in southeastern Germany, Erfurt lies in a politically and socially conservative region. As in Rostock, feminists have actively organized there since 1989. In fact, although the GDR had functionally collapsed several months earlier, many feminists in Erfurt take pride that in July 1990, Erfurt became the first city in the GDR to support a municipal women's center.[2] The feminist movement in Erfurt had an auspicious start, drawing national media attention when a group of feminist dissidents stormed the local headquarters of the East German secret police in Erfurt, setting off a domino effect of similar citizen takeovers in cities across the GDR.

One of my earliest interviews in Erfurt was with the city's Gender Equity Representative (Gleichstellungsbeauftragte, or GB), a political appointee charged with overseeing gender issues in the city and supporting women's organizations. Erfurt is an architecturally austere city with the exception of the charming area around the Krämer Bridge, a 120-meter-long bridge that, with thirty-two houses built on it, is the world's longest inhabited bridge and the only bridge of its kind in Europe. The GB's office sits in the upper floors of what appears to be a former mill not far from the bridge. A tall woman with an imposing stature but a warm smile, the GB glowed like a proud mother as she rattled off the names and goals of the feminist organizations in Erfurt her office has supported over the years. She cheerfully described amicable relationships with the men who have served as mayor during her time as GB. Her enthusiasm for her work was clear as she described her involvement with the first feminist organization in Erfurt, which ultimately gave rise to both of the city's women's centers.

Yet when I asked her about the challenges the feminist movement in Erfurt has experienced, her face darkened. Although appropriately diplomatic, she admitted that Erfurt is not necessarily a city that embraces feminism. After an initial wave of support for feminist and women's causes among city leaders in 1989–90, the political climate of the city and of the local state became increasingly closed to feminist interests. By the late 1990s, as funds earmarked to support social services related to unification dried up, the city sought to minimize its commitments to feminist organizations. City leaders decided to merge the GB's office with the office dedicated to issues of immigration and ethnic diversity in 1997. Women's organizations operating as municipal institutions were terminated and handed over to independent nonprofit organizations. In a political and cultural environment generally hostile to feminist concerns, feminists have struggled to establish a firm foothold in the city. Feminism—and especially the radical strand of feminism adopted by one branch of the local feminist movement in Erfurt—simply didn't align with city's understanding of itself as a place where family and church reign supreme.

In this place, ideological and tactical disagreements emerged both within and across feminist organizations. Groups skirmished over limited resources. Fresh wounds aged into old grudges, inhibiting collaboration and cooperation across organizations and undermining the movement's external legitimacy. Ultimately, feminists were largely excluded from the project of making place in Erfurt after 1989.

Women in eastern Germany experienced the collapse of state socialism as an opportunity—and in many cases even as an obligation—to organize and mobilize as women, for women. Yet such efforts have not been unilaterally successful. When the federal state did not present long-term possibilities for successful agitation by feminist organizations, eastern German feminists focused on subnational levels of the state instead. Here, they perceived greater chances for achieving success and felt more comfortable and capable. Still, not all local places provided optimal conditions for feminists to participate in defining the values, identities, and practices there. Differences in place have created divergent opportunities for women to organize to address the problems and issues stemming from the transformation from state socialism to democratic capitalism.

Gendered Transformations After Socialism

The collapse of state socialism in 1989 and the unification of East and West Germany in 1990 created both problems and possibilities for women living in the former GDR. Unification quickly followed the collapse of the GDR and the ousting of its ruling party, the Socialist Unity Party of Germany (Sozialistische Einheitspartei Deutschlands, or SED). The victory of a conservative alliance of political parties, led by West German Chancellor Helmut Kohl, on March 18, 1990, signaled the GDR's acquiescence to move ahead rapidly with unification.

German law provided two options for how unification might progress. One route would have involved the dissolution of the governments of both East and West Germany and the creation of an entirely new constitution. Instead, unification proceeded under the provisions of Article 23 of the West German Basic Law, which called for the accession of eastern Germany into the existing Federal Republic of Germany (FRG, or West Germany). The inability of the Soviet Union to support the interests of the GDR and the SED ensured that the unification process would follow terms set by the FRG.

Consequently, rather than adopting East German policies about welfare and gender relations, the West German system was introduced in East Germany. While the debate about abortion rights, which pitted the GDR's liberal policy against a far stricter policy in the FRG, received more public attention than any other unification issue, other key policy arenas affecting women, including employment, child care, pensions, and divorce regulations, were radically revised after unification in ways that have been largely detrimental to eastern German women.

The western German expectation of a male breadwinner family model in which good women stay home to raise their children is reflected in social policies that make it difficult for women to combine mothering with paid employment. For example, while municipalities may be able to allocate funds for child care, the national state does not guarantee child care for children beyond public schooling, and day care is in notoriously short supply in Germany.[3] Women who choose to be mothers in the unified Germany face the dilemma that their earnings may not cover the expense of child care, a conundrum that is especially salient for solo mothers. Mothers, especially those with young children, regularly report employment discrimination (Rudd 1999). Simultaneously, cultural representations of the *Hausfrau* maintain that the ideal mother stays at home throughout her children's time at home, thereby reinforcing state ideology that good mothers are stay-at-home mothers (Rinke 1994). This image is in stark contrast to West and later western German representations of East German mothers as *Rabenmütter*, or raven mothers, who abandon their helpless infant children in unsafe day-care facilities and care more about their work than their family.[4]

Coupled with soaring unemployment, changing gender ideologies and social policies pushed eastern German women out of the workforce and into the home. While both men and women in eastern Germany have felt the overall contraction of the labor market in the new eastern states, women have been disproportionately affected. In 1994, women comprised two-thirds of all those unemployed in the new eastern states (Brown, Jasper, and Schröter 1995).

Women are also less likely to receive services from state unemployment offices. For example, one study of job referrals made by the state unemployment office in East Berlin in 1991–92 found that women received 57 percent fewer referrals to job openings than equally qualified men (Adler and Brayfield 1997).[5]

Loss of employment was accompanied by a loss of state services in eastern Germany. Most detrimental for women who need or want to work outside of the home, day care is no longer guaranteed for children of any age.[6] The reduction in state support for child care, as well as a reduction in how much time employers are required to provide for paid maternity leave, suggests that the unified Germany is less concerned with women's workforce contributions and more concerned with their maternal contributions (Meyers, Gornick, and Ross 1999).

Other social welfare programs have also been revised in ways that disproportionately undermine women's economic independence, thereby increasing women's reliance on a male breadwinner. Pension plans have been pared down and now hinge on previous earnings, placing women at a disadvantage when compared to men who earn more and have fluid work histories. Taxation favors two-parent, married families, and a special tax benefit for families in which one spouse earns significantly more than the other is especially advantageous for those following the traditional family model. Furthermore, many expenses assumed by the GDR, either in whole or in part, are now the responsibilities of individual eastern German citizens. As prices for everything from real estate to food staples skyrocketed through the elimination of state controls and subsidies, incomes dropped just as quickly (Dodds and Allen-Thompson 1994; Meyer and Schulze 1998).

Eastern German women discovered that their primary value lies in their usefulness as mothers and consumers rather than in their capabilities as active participants in the labor market. Increased personal freedoms and decreased protection from the market characterize the so-called emancipation of East Germany. The simultaneous introduction of democratic rights, massive state retrenchment, and a new gender ideology essentially inverted the type of state eastern German women lived under for forty years.

Eastern Germany in the Unified Germany

Women in eastern Germany experience an intersecting marginalization as both women and as eastern Germans. Certainly, eastern Germany's postsocialist experience deviates from those of other post-Soviet states, and many of the problems that plague nations further to the East, such as major interethnic conflict, complete economic collapse, and struggles to rebuild the state, have not been as pronounced in the eastern German case. Yet an additional challenge for eastern Germany is its unique position as a postsocialist state annexed by an existing democratic superpower. The "wall in the head" is the continued cultural and psychological separation between eastern and western Germans, who often regard one another with animosity and resentment. The unified German government has pumped more than a trillion dollars into the former East Germany with mixed outcomes. Although a few key cities like Dresden and Leipzig are success stories, much of eastern Germany has remained in a consistent economic slump after unification. Eastern Germans have become scapegoats for a range of social and economic problems in Germany, including racist violence and neo-Nazism and a shrinking economy. Western Germans discourses routinely complain that eastern Germans were damaged by communism, rendering them lazy and welfare dependent.

Eastern Germans resent their political marginalization and the denigration of all aspects of the GDR. They also face a heightened sense of relative deprivation vis-à-vis their neighbors in the West (Offe 1997). In East Germany, approximately 50 percent of the population had neither a car nor a color television, 25 percent of dwellings were without indoor plumbing, less than half of dwellings had central heat, and only 16 percent of homes had a telephone (Jarausch 1994). In June 1990, German Chancellor Helmut Kohl promised that the new eastern German states would soon be "blooming landscapes . . . where people will want to live and work." Placing their hopes in such promises, many eastern Germans expected that they would soon share the same standard of living as their western counterparts. Yet eastern Germany continues to lag behind western Germany in terms of infrastructure and basic living standards (Deutsche Bundesregierung 2003, 2004). As much as 12 percent of the population has left the new German states, as Germans call the former East German states, leaving behind empty cities and towns with aging populations. As one eastern German friend told me only half-jokingly, "The only thing Easties can beat Westies at is the number of our unemployed and the size of our welfare rolls."

Eastern Germany constitutes less than one-third of the total population of Germany; the combined population of all of the eastern German states is still less than the population of western Germany's most populous state, North Rhine-Westphalia. This difference in population renders the eastern part of the country more politically vulnerable as it represents proportionately fewer voters. The size of the eastern German population has been one reason for the struggles faced by the Party of Democratic Socialism (Partei der Demokratischen Sozialismus, or PDS, or, since their merger with the Labor and Social Justice Electoral Alternative in June 2007, Die Linke, or The Left), the postunification reincarnation of the SED, in trying to establish itself a major player in the politics of the unified Germany.[7]

Conveniently dropping the "n" from the German word for nostalgia, *Nostalgie*, creates a word beginning with the German for East, *Ost*. The media has capitalized on *Ostalgie* through the creation of hit game shows on East German trivia and talk shows that specialize in where-are-they-now profiles of East German celebrities (Bach 2002). The Little Green Man, a cartoon figure who alerted East Germans when to cross the street at intersections, is the star of his own trademarked product line featuring t-shirts, backpacks, household items, and key chains emblazoned with his image. East German consumer goods, such as the faux coffee distributed by the SED, have set new sales records, and the GDR's state-manufactured vehicle, the Trabant, or Trabi, has become a prized collector's item (Berdahl 2000b). While the eastern Germans I met and worked with are overwhelmingly grateful for the end of socialism and for unification, they also see many aspects of life in the GDR as superior to life in the unified Germany. Economic insecurity, depopulation and the migration of young eastern Germans to western Germany and other parts of Europe, individualism and a corresponding lack of concern for community well-being, and the symptoms of increased social strain, including neo-Nazism, crime, and drug addiction, are just some of the problems eastern Germans see as the direct outcomes of unification.

What I witnessed in my daily life in Erfurt illustrates some of these problems. I sublet an apartment from a young eastern German woman who moved westward for a job. The apartment was small and cheaply furnished, located at the outer fringe of the city's downtown area in a recently renovated building with nine units. Reflecting the tenant composition of a typical apartment building in Erfurt, a young student couple lived in the apartment below me, three of the units upstairs were inhabited by retirees, and four of the units apparently remained empty.

Each day, I walked one block to an underpass that burrowed beneath six lanes of traffic and a greenbelt to connect my neighborhood to the heart of the city. I didn't especially enjoy this experience: the underpass is dark, dirty, and, especially at night, made me slightly nervous, in part because it attracted a group of men who would stand at its mouth drinking beer and occasionally issuing lewd comments. Yet I quickly found that passing through the tunnel was an important ritual in that it served as a sobering reminder of the magnitude of postunification transformations. Walking through the underpass transported me from the Thälmannvorstadt, or Thälmann suburb, a bleak neighborhood comprised of a mixture of old brick buildings and cinderblock high-rises, most of which had not been renovated since unification, to the sparkling center of Erfurt. In the underpass, the wind blended the city's various elements—a baby's pacifier, a few empty beer cans, pieces of a Russian-language newspaper, and dozens of leaves and cigarette butts—into unique sculptures. My gaze invariably switched between the heaps of trash and the tunnel walls, which are caked with layers of graffiti. I was walking through an urban art project, appropriately illuminated by the flickering twitches of failing fluorescent lights.

When I reached the other side, I crossed another street, passing a kabob restaurant that was always empty and scurrying down one final narrow road into the city center. Finally, I entered the attractive, albeit somber, core of the city, leaving behind its unsightly, decayed fringes. As the state capitol of Thuringia, Erfurt is a bustling city, and the city's pedestrian zone, anchored on each end with a large plaza, is consistently crowded. While the plazas are large to the point of being overwhelmingly vast, the streets connecting them are tight, narrow, and pretty. Many of the buildings in this area have been beautifully restored since unification. Canals from the Gera River cut through downtown, bringing the cheerful notes of ducks and running water into the mix of sounds that comprise the city's auditory fabric: church bells, the screeching brakes of street cars, the drone of voices, the sizzling Bratwurst on a street vendor's grill.

Here, freed from the smoky convenience stores and dreary second-hand shops in my neighborhood, a world of clean, bountiful consumer opportunities lay at my fingertips. I could browse through the neatly arranged apparel and house wares at one of Germany's more popular and higher-end department stores, Karstadt. I could stock up on scented bath gels or colorful toothbrushes at one of the three gleaming drugstores within a three-block radius, or parade through the aisles of the spacious supermarket. If I got tired, I would find a comfortable place to rest along the large fountain in the middle of the city's shopping mall. When hunger became an issue, the bakery tucked between the boutiques had, by my count while waiting in a long line, seventeen different types of cake available. I could have my cake and eat it, too, all the while listening in on the dozens of mobile phone conversations around me, or to the happy chimes of Euro coins being placed onto the cashier's tray.

All of this, of course, is new. Twenty years after the collapse of socialism in eastern Germany, the memory of the GDR is obliterated in the new shopping arcades of Erfurt. Especially for the city's older people, the changes are overwhelming. I accompanied an acquaintance in Erfurt, Marta, who celebrated her fiftieth birthday in 1989, on an informal tour of downtown in which she pointed out to me what new stores used to be in the GDR. She was amazed by the rapidity of change in the city since unification, and she joked that she barely recognized her hometown anymore. Marta has mixed feelings about the free market system. On the one hand, she is grateful for the availability of basic consumer goods and the overall improvement in the quality of life. On the other hand, she is troubled by what she sees as a materialist obsession, especially among younger people. So many items that were rationed or substituted in the GDR—sugar, flour, coffee—or that were only available after years on a waiting list—like cars and most household appliances—were suddenly abundant. In Marta's view, the glossy stores and their gleaming wares are part of a "cover up, to distract us from what is really going on." Indeed, after walking around downtown, I have largely forgotten the decay of my outlying neighborhood, the continued crisis of un- and underemployment evidenced by the groups of men that congregate on my street corner, and the flight of young people, disproportionately women, to the West. When dusk falls and Marta and I say good-bye for the evening after a dizzying walk through the shopping mecca of downtown, I head back to the tunnel with a sour taste in my mouth.

Ostalgie is but one piece of a complicated puzzle. Certainly, many eastern Germans are grateful for the support they have received from western Germany. They have also widely embraced their entrance into a new and unfamiliar international system. The collapse of the GDR and its fellow Soviet states marked the end of the cold war, and eastern Germany experienced a significant shift in its alliances as the state reoriented itself from East to West. Unification led eastern Germany out of the protectionist Soviet bloc and into the North Atlantic Treaty Organization (NATO) and the European Union, shifts that have created unique paradoxes for citizens of the former GDR. In many respects, the gender ideology of the EU is more congruent with that of the GDR than with that of the unified Germany, and insofar as the EU supports gender equity policies, it has become a potential resource for feminist activists. Participation in the EU, and democratization more broadly, have also enabled feminist activists in eastern Germany to build networks and coalitions with women from other countries.

Yet the shift in alliances also repositioned eastern Germany from the top of the status hierarchy in the Soviet bloc to the bottom of the status hierarchy in the EU. While once the most economically powerful of the Soviet satellite states, eastern Germans lived in an economically and politically marginalized region of the EU from the time of unification until the accession of new member states further east in the former Soviet bloc into the EU in 2004. Unemployment in many parts of eastern Germany is at 25 percent with no signs of lessening. Eastern Germans move westward by the thousands in search of improved economic opportunities such that some eastern German areas have lost as much as one-third of their total populations since unification; both Rostock and Erfurt shrunk from cities with populations of more than 250,000 in 1989 to slightly fewer than 200,000 in 2005.

In organizing to respond to the shifting landscape of postsocialist eastern Germany, women, as well as the broader institutions and communities of which they are a part, have mobilized socialist legacies, or the experiential histories of individuals, organizations, and institutions during the socialist period. Although western observers especially tend to think of socialism and postsocialism as monolithic conditions, certainly within the same national state, if not across huge swaths of central and eastern Europe, socialism and postsocialism are distinct across specific geopolitical and temporal contexts. How people experienced socialism, and how they experience postsocialism, isn't necessarily the same in one place or context as it is in another. Rather, these are context-specific experiences, and they are an integral part of local communities and individual lived experience; that is, socialist legacies, too, are a part of place. Variations across contexts have meaningful implications for women's political mobilizations because these variations shape the frames, strategies, and ideologies available to activists and to other social and political actors. In Rostock, for example, the socialist past is often revered, while in Erfurt it is more often rejected and feared. These responses have significant implications for the political cultures of these two cities and their respective regions and for the feminist movements that struggle there.

Furthermore, postsocialist transformations are gendered processes. Discourses and practices of gender are deeply interconnected with postsocialist transformations (Gal and Kligman 2000a), as becomes visible by listening to political rhetoric (Young 1999), observing interactions between clients and social workers in welfare offices (Haney 2002), discussing the balance of work and family with men and women (Nash 1997; Rudd 1999; Sandole-Soroste 2002), and following debates about abortion and reproductive freedom (Maleck-Lewy 1995; Zajicek and Calasanti 1998). Discourses about gender are not limited to local or national debates; they also reflect international pressures. During the cold war, Soviet bloc states viewed themselves as in competition with the West, and social policy decisions were one area where Soviet states could assert their superiority over the West. The GDR, for example, introduced its liberal policies governing abortion in response to a confluence of factors (Harsch 1997), including in anticipation of the demands of the feminist movement in West Germany (Einhorn 1992; Maleck-Lewy 1995). West Germany, however, pointed to its ability to support a nuclear family model with a stay-at-home mother as a significant symbol of its prosperity and superiority over East Germany.

The competition today is typically less about beating the West and more about catching up to it. Policymakers in eastern Germany closely follow developments in western Germany and in the EU and its member states, and they often adopt external discursive strategies made available through these new resources to advance policy reform and fashion an eastern Germany that looks and feels like western Germany. Still, responses to the shift in alliances from the Soviet Union to western Germany and the EU and its member states vary. Communities negotiate international pressures, models, and resources in divergent ways, with some even rejecting western ideas and strategies. Local actors harness the complex cultural, political, and economic shifts resulting from unification to redefine gender relations in postsocialist eastern Germany in different, and often competing, ways.

Utilizing the term "postsocialist" in and of itself presents an analytic and ethical conundrum that warrants mention here. As numerous scholars of formerly colonized states have argued, the language of postcolonialism may obscure colonial relations that continue to shape the experiences of citizens in postcolonial states. Labeling people as "postcolonial" also contributes to their "othering," rendering them exotic, unequal, and different. Parallel problems emerge in using the term "postsocialist." The discourse of postsocialism conceals the role of both socialism and of cold war politics in these societies. Rather than recognizing continuities, the conversation around postsocialism all too often focuses on ruptures. At the same time, the language of postsocialism marks eastern and central Europeans as distinctly different from western and northern Europeans because of their socialist history. This "othering" has been especially pronounced in public debates about EU expansion, and in Germany it has helped maintain the "wall in the head" dividing eastern and western Germans.

While sensitive to these issues, I continue to employ the concept of post-socialism in this work. My intention in doing so is not to imply a monolithic socialist past or postsocialist experience, nor to contribute to the continued "othering" of the inhabitants of formerly socialist states. Rather, I view postsocialism as conceptually significant for drawing attention to how socialist ideologies, methods of governance, intergroup conflicts, and strategies for organizing and controlling society continue to inform certain aspects of individual, organizational, and institutional experiences after socialism.

Constructing the Analysis

Women's organizations in eastern Germany clearly respond to an array of complex issues, but *how* women's organizations, and the local feminist movements that they comprise, tackle these issues varies across locales. The subsequent chapters trace the development of the local feminist movements in two cities in eastern Germany, Rostock and Erfurt, from 1989 through 2004. In examining how feminist mobilizations developed during fifteen years in these two cities, I focus on the interactions between these movements, the places from which they emerged, and multiple, nested levels of action, including the local, statewide, federal, transnational, and supranational.

My account of the development of the feminist movements in Rostock and Erfurt is based on fieldwork conducted in these cities during multiple periods between 2000 and 2004 with continued contact through 2009. Rostock and Erfurt lie three hundred miles apart with Rostock perched at the edge of the Baltic Sea and Erfurt snuggled in the rolling hills of the famous Thuringian Forest. The cases of Rostock and Erfurt represent a strategically matched pair (Paulsen 2004), deliberately selected to control for population size and characteristics, while offering variation along several other dimensions, including movement outcome, namely greater success in Rostock and more struggle in Erfurt.

I collected four types of data in the two cities. First, I engaged in ethnographic observations at women's organizations in the two cities. This included attendance at various special events hosted by women's organizations and relevant state offices, as well as observations during routine, daily operations. Second, I conducted in-depth interviews with sixty-three feminist activists and elected or appointed politicians and administrators in the two cities. These women represented a total of thirty women's organizations, four state offices, and all three of the major political parties in eastern Germany. Third, I collected archival documents from women's organizations, including materials such as press releases, fliers, brochures, newsletters, funding applications, meeting notes, position papers, and recruitment materials. At some organizations, I was able to access comprehensive files dating back to the inception of an organization, although in many cases, record keeping was somewhat erratic. In a few instances, respondents also shared their personal files, photographs, and other mementos from their careers as activists. Fourth, I gathered government materials, including annual reports on the statuses of the two cities, policy proposals, and passed legislation. The methodological appendix offers a detailed discussion of the research strategies, data sources, and methodological considerations of conducting the fieldwork and analysis.

Drawing on these data, I construct a comparative analysis of the feminist movements in Rostock and Erfurt to illuminate how the movements in these two cities shape, and are shaped by, the places of the cities. To contextualize the development of the feminist movements in Rostock and Erfurt, I begin in Chapter 2 by presenting a comprehensive background of the history of women's organizing in eastern Germany since German unification. I also introduce a typology of feminist ideologies in eastern Germany that emerged from the data in the course of analysis.

Chapters 3 through 6 focus on the cases of the feminist movements in Rostock and Erfurt and their relationships to the places from which they emerged. Although aspects of place are interrelated and reflect multiple scales of action, I dedicate the first chapter on each case (Chapters 3 and 5) to exploring feminist organizing within the contexts of the two cities, while the second chapter on each case (Chapters 4 and 6) considers the influence of broader scales of activity. Between the chapters, I share short reflections from my fieldwork that provide a fuller picture of life in the two cities. In Chapter 7, I present a systematic comparison of the two cases. I discuss why the place character of Rostock has been more amenable to feminist interests than that in Erfurt and also how the tactical decisions made by feminists in Rostock to make a claim on place have been more effective than the strategies used by feminists in Erfurt. I analyze how the local feminist movements in Rostock and Erfurt are not only shaped by, but also have actively shaped, emerging understandings of place since unification. I elaborate on the differences and similarities between the feminist movements and their relationships to the places and spaces in which they operate.

Specific mechanisms at work in each city influence the ideologies and practices of women's organizations in how they offer services, how they approach the state, and how they legitimize their goals within their communities. Still, this is not a one-sided or unidirectional process. Instead, these two local feminist movements actively struggle to influence and change the cities of which they are a part, working to reconstitute the character of these places. The cultural legacies of German and East German history, as well as local political and cultural traditions and norms, explain the differential development of the place characters of Rostock and Erfurt. Local feminist movements also work to reinterpret these legacies, traditions, and norms to create places accessible, available, and amenable to them.

Lifelong Residents

During my first summer in Rostock, I am so cold that I think I may never be warm again. Every day it rains. My accommodation in the basement bedroom I am renting from an elderly couple exacerbates the cold. The room is almost entirely underground, and it never gets warm. The lone window is at ground level with a view into the roots of bushes. It lets in plenty of cold and damp and very little light.

Herr and Frau Kübler live in a single family brick home with an expansive backyard. Their terrace is netted in so that their beloved pet parrot can have free reign of the house and join them outside. They periodically invite me upstairs to sit with them. They had retired within a year of unification, feeling forced out of the labor market.

Their sons live in the West, and they do not visit often. The Küblers seem starved for company, yet they are awkward in it. They appear puzzled by my interest in Rostock, and they share stories about their lives there in halting narrative. Ten years after German unification, they are still in a state of shock that the German Democratic Republic is no more. History has played a trick on them.

The Küblers are not ones to voice strong opinions. They rarely issue decisive verdicts on anything pertaining to German unification. Everything is a "mixed blessing." Socialism offered them security and solidarity; capitalism brought them a big-box home-improvement store that allowed them to complete the patio for which they collected materials for nearly a decade in the GDR.

Frau Kübler marvels that women work at all in Rostock anymore. She can't figure out how they do it given both the lack of jobs and the lack of child-care

*resources in the city. She treats this as a great tragedy as she believes that chil-
dren benefit from having parents who are engaged in the world around them
and who don't confine themselves to the domestic sphere. "Staying home all
the time is not good for women. It is too isolating, too confining," she declares;
this is one of the few strong statements of opinion I hear from her. Herr Kübler
agrees. "All members of a family must have passions and interests outside of the
family to bring back to it, to make it richer."*

*Returning from a field site one rainy afternoon, I run into Frau Kübler on
the street in front of the house. I am dripping wet and freezing cold. She invites
me to join her for a cup of tea, and I quickly accept, enticed by the thought of a
hot drink and cookies. I make my way upstairs and join her on the netted terrace where we are sheltered from the rain that pours down around us in sheets.
The sunflowers in the back yard have their heads down, and the lawn is looking
swampy.*

*Frau Kübler brings out a pot of tea and sits down beside me. We laugh about
my bad luck with the weather. I've been in Rostock more than a month and have
yet to put so much as a toe into the Baltic Sea. Frau Kübler watches me drink my
tea with her pale blue eyes. Suddenly, she reaches over and puts her hand on my
arm. "What you are doing is very important," she says. "There needs to be more
attention to what is happening here, to the good things Rostock is trying to do,
and to the problems that it make it so difficult to do them."*

*"Thank you," I reply, startled by her uncharacteristically impassioned state-
ment. "I hope that I can do it justice."*

*"I never thought my status as a woman would matter much," she replies.
"Even though I experienced things only women experience—childbirth, violence,
discrimination, motherhood. But now that I am older and have witnessed all
these changes, I realize how important it is to organize for women, as women,
especially in this new Germany. We need to make sure that the good things about
the GDR—and a lot of them had to do with women—don't entirely fall apart."*

*I nod my head in agreement. She smiles and pats my hand. We take a sip of
tea. The rain lightens, and we see the sheen of the sun behind the gray clouds. We
sit on the damp terrace and watch the bright parrot fly against the net.*

2 Feminist Organizing Under Socialism and Capitalism

THE FEMINIST MOVEMENTS IN ROSTOCK AND ERFURT operate within the broader context of postsocialist eastern Germany. The specific features of this context are highly relevant for feminist activity on several fronts. First, German unification created the issues and problems to which feminists in eastern Germany have responded. Second, the collapse of state socialism and the unification of East and West Germany produced particular political structures and discourses, thereby creating specific opportunities and constraints for feminist actors and shaping their strategies and possibilities. Third, feminist resistance existed before unification, and certain structures and experiences from socialist-era organizing and mobilizations in 1989 influenced local movements after the collapse of socialism.

Understanding these features of the context of postsocialist eastern Germany is critical for making sense of local feminist movements in eastern Germany after socialism. Both the rich secondary literature on eastern German feminism, as well as data from my own field work, illuminate the social structures and shifts that gave rise to the spike in feminist mobilization and activity in 1989–90, the subsequent demobilization of feminist organizations targeting the national state, and the proliferation of women's organizations operating at the local level in eastern Germany. They also reveal the key issues addressed, and the major contradictions faced, by women's organizations operating in postsocialist eastern Germany, as well as the feminist ideologies that emerged there after 1989.

The Status of Women in East, West, and Unified Germany

A gendered analysis of the German unification process, and the changes that accompanied it, illuminates how the East German, West German, and the unified German welfare states approach gender relations and women's issues quite differently. Multiple layers of social change gave rise to the problems and possibilities that feminist movements faced and responded to during and after German unification. Initially most critical among these was the tremendous shift in state policies regarding women's status in society and gender relations. With almost incomprehensible suddenness, women in eastern Germany witnessed the complete inversion of East German gender policy. Rather than combining policies from East and West Germany, unification resulted in the introduction of West German policy in the former East Germany beginning in 1990. The East German state promoted women's participation in wage labor, whereas the West German state emphasized the preservation of traditional family units in which women's primary contributions are through the labor of social reproduction within the family.

As reflected in its social policies, the German Democratic Republic (GDR) was substantially more interventionist on women's issues than the West German state was.[1] Already the GDR Constitution, the founding document of the nation after the Second World War, established the state's interest in women, specifying that "the promotion of women, especially in employment, is a societal and state responsibility" (Trzcinski 1998: 78) and guaranteeing women pregnancy and maternity leaves, children's allowance, material and financial assistance with the birth of a child, and equality for married and unmarried mothers in the workplace. The Family Law Code, enacted in 1965, formally abolished women's economic dependence on men in the home and, while rarely enforced, required that men and women divide housework equally (Spakes 1995). The GDR's guarantee of a job for all citizens of working age provided ample opportunity for women to work outside of the home, and because of labor shortages in the GDR, the state actively encouraged women to participate in paid labor. In fact, at the time of unification, East Germany was the international leader in women's labor force participation (Brown, Jasper, and Schröter 1995).[2]

In addition to guaranteeing jobs for both men and women, various social policies in the GDR made the combination of paid work and motherhood feasible for East German women. In response to dropping fertility, the GDR enacted several laws during the 1970s that supported women's abilities to combine paid employment with motherhood. The *Babyjahr*, or baby year, first introduced in 1976, allowed women one full year of paid maternity leave for the birth of second and subsequent children.[3] During each month of employment, women were entitled to a mother's day, one day off of work to take children to appointments or to run errands that could not be completed on weekends. Paid leaves were also guaranteed for either parent in the event that a child became ill. Day care was practically free and guaranteed for children aged three months and up, and it was also provided for children after school. These day-care centers were often operated on factory grounds so that parents had easy access to their children during the day.

Although the East German state encouraged childbearing through its support of women who wanted to combine motherhood and paid employment, marriage was not viewed as a necessary component of family life, nor did state policy promote marriage. During the last ten years of the GDR, 30 percent of all births and 70 percent of first births were to unmarried women (Ferree 1993). By contrast, fewer than 10 percent of all births occurred outside of marriage in the FRG where religious and cultural values, as well as state policies, strongly emphasized the nuclear family model (Le Goff 2002). In the GDR, heterosexual relationships also were not presumed to focus on reproduction. Birth control was widely available to single and married women and couples. Beginning in 1972, abortion was legal through the first trimester for any reason and could be performed thereafter in cases of endangerment to the health of the mother or the fetus. Abortion, along with all forms of birth control, was paid for entirely by the state medical plan, although abortion remained somewhat taboo (Maleck-Lewy and Ferree 2000; Wuerth 1999).

In spite of these seemingly progressive policies toward women, the gender regime of the GDR remained inequitable in many important respects (Trappe 1995). The GDR is often described as practicing "mommy politics" (*Muttipolitik*) through social policies that at once encouraged women to work outside of the home while also maintaining women's responsibilities in the home as caregivers for husbands and children (Ferree 1993; Kolinsky 1999). Married and cohabiting women completed significantly more housework than their male partners even when both were employed full-time outside of the home (Kolinsky 1999; Quack and Maier 1994; Rudd 1999). The maternity policy and mother's days further established that mothers, rather than fathers, were responsible for child care and household labor.

Women were also overrepresented in traditionally female occupations like teaching and nursing, and women dominated low-status industries, such as clothing manufacture, factors which helped maintain a slight wage gap between men and women (Adler and Brayfield 1997; Trappe and Rosenfeld 1998). Furthermore, while the *Babyjahr* provided women with a generous maternity leave, it created reluctance among employers to hire or promote women for fear that they would become pregnant and leave the job for a year (Lane 1983; Szepansky 1995). Many employers regarded women as unreliable and unstable long-term employees, thereby hindering their chances of advancement. Women were noticeably absent from positions of power in both workplaces and in politics, finding the glass ceiling was often quite low. Thus, while East German women's resources for combining motherhood with paid employment exceeded such opportunities in West Germany, women were still subject to gender-based ideologies that inhibited their occupational mobility and frequently limited them to jobs that were regarded as drawing on women's natural talents as mothers and nurturers. Furthermore, women in the GDR were subject to the double burden of paid employment and household service, and were given little freedom to decide how to prioritize these roles.

Nevertheless, women's opportunities for economic participation and independence were substantially greater in the GDR than in the FRG. In contrast to East Germany, where women were valued as workers *and* mothers, the West German model of gender relations emphasized women's roles as mothers and wives and men's roles as breadwinners. Table 2.1 provides a comparative overview of social policy arenas affecting women in the GDR and the FRG.

State policy and public discourse in the FRG assumed that women would work briefly before marriage, then drop out of the paid workforce to raise their children and perhaps return to work once their children were in their teenage years (Daly 2000; Schulenberg 2000). Although the West German Basic Law guaranteed equal rights to all citizens, social policy has done little to ensure women's equal participation in the workforce. Beginning with the reconstruction following the Second World War and lasting through the mid-1960s, the conservative Christian Democratic Union (CDU), which heavily emphasized the importance of the nuclear family and the stay-at-home mother, dominated the West German federal government. During this time, labor policy in the FRG took on the role of protecting women and the government enacted laws that blocked women from working at night, after 5 p.m. on Sundays and holidays, and in certain high-risk jobs, such as mining, and jobs that require lifting more than ten kilograms (Trzcinski 1998).

The 1960s ushered in major changes in West German politics, culture, and society. A wave of feminist activity during the late 1960s and early 1970s drew significant public attention toward issues like reproductive rights, domestic violence, and women's underrepresentation in elected office. The center-left Social Democratic Party (SPD) won control of the national government in 1969. Yet in spite of a ruling party more sympathetic to feminist concerns, and feminist

Table 2.1 Comparison of social policies affecting women in the German Democratic Republic and the Federal Republic of Germany at the time of unification*

Policy Arena	German Democratic Republic	Federal Republic of Germany
Maternity Leave	One year of maternity leave paid at sick-leave rate for each child; guarantee of return to previous position at the end of the leave.	Law requires eight weeks maternity leave with a monetary allowance; additional leave at the discretion of employer. Mother's job protected for four months.
Child Care	Guaranteed, state-funded (albeit not necessarily available) day care and after-school care for all children over three months of age.	Responsibility of parents to locate and pay for child care. Minimal state assistance available for single parents.
Employment	Guaranteed for all citizens of working age.	No guarantee for men or women of any age.
Divorce	No-fault divorce available quickly, usually official within a month of filing. However, because of housing shortages, many divorcing and divorced couples continued to cohabit.	Divorce proceedings require mandatory waiting period of sixty days. Divorces are more expensive and time-intensive if couples have not been separated for at least one year prior to divorce.
Taxation	Taxes assessed largely independently of marital status; income exclusions vary by family size, with largest exclusions for "child-rich" families, or those with two or more children.	"Splitting" of taxes creates the greatest tax benefit for married couples where one member earns significantly less than the other.
Child-Care Subsidies	Financial incentive for every child with exponential increases for "child-rich" families, regardless of parental employment.	Erziehungsgeld, or child-raising assistance, available during the first two years of a child's life only if one parent is the full-time caregiver of the child. Additional subsidies available with demonstrated need.
Social Security/ Retirement	Based on time spent in the paid workforce and calculated independently of marital status. Time spent mothering counted as participation in the workforce.	Male breadwinner model in which women's retirement benefits are closely connected to those of her husband.
Reproductive Rights/ Abortion	Abortion legal in first trimester for any reason, thereafter in cases of medical necessity to protect the mother or child. Abortion and birth control paid for by the state.	Abortion illegal except in cases of demonstrated medical or social need, as verified by a doctor, and with a waiting period. Imprisonment possible. Except in cases of medical necessity, abortion not covered by state insurance plan. Birth control available at discount.

* Most of these policies were developed over the course of forty years; this table reviews policies in effect at the time of unification.

activity that contributed to a cultural shift toward more egalitarian attitudes about women's roles in society, little changed in terms of state policy. Policymakers continued to understand women primarily as mothers and wives, even as the public came to be more accepting of working women and unmarried mothers.[4] Inadequate child-care opportunities, coupled with half days for most kindergarten and elementary schools, created a substantial barrier for mothering women who wanted to work full time.

In the absence of state-sponsored programs to promote women's participation in the labor force, women in the FRG were far more likely to stay at home than their counterparts in the East, and they were often forced to make the choice between mothering and career. By the mid-1980s, 83 percent of East German women were employed outside of the home and women constituted 49 percent of workers, making the GDR the world leader in women's labor force participation (Duggan 2003; Einhorn 1992: if including full-time students and apprentices, as well as women on maternity leave, women's labor force participation is higher than 90 percent). In contrast, between 1966 and 1983, the employment rate for women in West Germany rose a measly 4 percent, from 34.4 percent to 38.9 percent, and at the time of unification, barely half of women in West Germany worked outside of the home where they constituted 38 percent of the labor force (Duggan 2003; Spakes 1995). The work histories of East and West German women were also notably different. Virtually all East German women worked full time, while part-time employment was the norm for West German women. East German women participated in the work force for an average of thirty-five years, while women in West Germany worked an average of eighteen years (Lane 1983; Ostner 1994). In the late 1980s, East German women's income comprised 40 percent of the total income in households with both male and female earners; in the West, women's income contributed only 18 percent to total household income (Ferree 1993). While more than 90 percent of children under age three were in state-funded child care in the East at the time of unification, only 3 percent of children under age three were in state-supported programs in the West (Rueschmeyer 1998). Not only were West German women less likely to work outside of the home, but they were also less likely to be mothers. Ninety-one percent of East German women were mothers at some point in their lives, compared to 80 percent of West German women (Duggan 2003).

Through the unification process, West German policies and discourses about gender became dominant. Most East German state policies that supported women's efforts to combine paid employment with mothering were dismantled. The restructuring of the eastern German economy sent unemployment rates skyrocketing to as high as 50 percent in some regions in eastern Germany in the early 1990s. Such high unemployment, emerging in tandem with the introduction of a male breadwinner model, pushed many eastern German women out of the paid labor force entirely, where they disappeared from unemployment statistics because they stopped actively seeking work or unemployment benefits through state agencies. By 1992, the unemployment rate for women was twice as high as that for men in the former GDR. Public attention to this disparity, as well as gradual economic redevelopment, helped narrow this gap over the course of the 1990s, but women remain overrepresented among the un- and underemployed in eastern Germany, especially among the long-term un- and underemployed.

Women's employment woes are compounded by the dismantling of other structures and services. The unified Germany has not maintained the East German commitment to day care, thereby making employment less feasible for women. Various positive action programs for women in education and employment were discontinued. Important changes in state programs for retirement savings and in maternity leave are less favorable to women in the unified Germany than they were in East Germany. After a heated public debate, eastern German women's right to abortion was also curtailed in the unified Germany. Women in eastern Germany organized—sometimes together with women from western Germany, as well as with men from eastern Germany, the majority of whom also supported the GDR's abortion policy—to resist these changes in 1989–90, but with limited success.

Joining the Reform Movement: Women's Organizations and the Collapse of the GDR

The rise in women's mobilization in eastern Germany began in 1989 as women sought to participate in the reinvention of the GDR. In its fortieth year, the GDR collapsed in the autumn of 1989 as a consequence of economic problems, international pressures and shifts, and a mass domestic movement (Maier 1997; Pfaff 1996). Women's organizations did exist in the GDR prior to the mass mobilizations that ultimately helped unseat the SED, however. The official women's group of the SED, the Democratic Women's League of Germany (Demokratischer Frauenverband Deutschlands, or DFD; since unification, Demokratischen Frauenbund, the Democratic Women's Association, or DFB), dominated women's organizational efforts in the GDR and continued as a core organization for women into the early 1990s and, in some regions, thereafter. With 1.4 million members in the GDR, the DFD was the only formal and officially recognized women's organization in East Germany (Miethe and Ulrich-Hampele 2001). Originally charged with increasing women's participation in the labor force in the postwar period, the DFD came to serve as an organization dedicated to women's dual roles as mothers and workers. The DFD also automatically received representation in the government, creating an avenue through which women could participate in political life, however much the SED constrained their ideas and agendas.

Although the DFD offered women opportunities in leadership and political participation, as an organization that was created and controlled by the state, the DFD was not a social movement organization. The DFD rarely, if ever, challenged the SED's position that feminism was a bourgeois, western import (DiCaprio 1990). Instead, as a state-controlled entity, the DFD was invested in supporting the SED's gender policies and the socialist ideals of community building and service. Still, the DFD created social opportunities for women as they worked together to improve schools and parks and their own skills in both the domestic arts and the trades. *Für Dich* (For you), the women's magazine produced by the DFD, provided women with information intended to help them balance the demands of career and family, while also serving as an outlet for SED propaganda targeted at women.

Beyond the DFD, women participated in informal groups, many of which were sheltered by churches, one of few sites where groups could convene with minimal state surveillance. While a significant number of these groups were religiously oriented, often focusing on themes related to women and theology, many addressed topics beyond the immediate interests of the church or state. Prominent among these were social groups for women on maternity leave, as well as support groups for sexual minorities that emerged in the early 1970s. Still others were groups of only women that focused on issues not specific to women, such as nuclear proliferation, militarism, and environmental degradation (Miethe 1999a, 1999b). Lesbianism, while taboo, was not illegal in East Germany, and lesbian groups and their members, who often hosted small cultural festivals and published underground newspapers, were not generally persecuted by the Ministerium für Staatssicherheit (MfS), or the Ministry for State Security, commonly known as the Stasi. Because they were able to build networks through the hosting of public events, lesbian groups laid important pieces of the foundational networks for feminist activity in 1989 and later.

Unfortunately, relatively little is known about the women's groups of the GDR in terms of their numbers and membership. One of the more comprehensive histories of women's groups in the 1980s (Kenawi 1995) identifies approximately 120 women's organizations in twenty-three cities in East Germany. The vast majority of these groups were founded in 1988 or later, suggesting that before the development of visible instability in the GDR, women's organizations, outside of the DFD, were relatively rare.

In May 1989, a group of approximately two hundred women met in Jena, a city in Thuringia, to discuss how the state could reduce women's double burden of child care and paid labor. In the autumn of 1989, some of these women were among the first participants in the Unabhängiger Frauenverband (Independent Women's Association, or UFV), which quickly became the most visible organization of feminists in eastern Germany and the only organization of eastern German women with a reach across eastern Germany other than the DFD (Hampele-Ulrich 2000; Hampele 1993). When, during the upheavals of the fall of 1989, one of the most prominent dissident groups in East Germany, Neues Forum (New Forum), organized around the slogan, "The country needs new men," feminists in East Germany mobilized around the alternate motto, "No new state without women." In November 1989, a group of feminist activist academics and the editorial board of *Für Dich*, by then largely beyond SED control, published a joint statement in that magazine titled, "Is the Revolution Passing Women By?" Pointing to recent events in Poland and Hungary as examples of social upheavals devoid of women's voices, the authors of this widely disseminated article urged East German women to seize the opportunity to participate in the reformation of the GDR.

Drawing on this momentum, the UFV convened a national meeting in Berlin in December 1989, attracting twelve hundred participants from across East Germany. Here, the UFV developed a political agenda focused on women's increased participation in governance and an improved status of women living in socialist Germany.[5] At this time, it was not expected that East and West Germany would unify, and as such, the UFV focused on how to reform socialism to better meet the needs of women. Among the demands set forth were greater representation of women in government and gender-neutral language in family policy. At this stage, women in the GDR reasonably expected expanded rights in a reformed socialist state.

The UFV's foray into national politics was short-lived, as were its demands. In March 1990, the GDR held its last independent election. Joining forces with the East German Greens, the Green-UFV alliance won only eight seats, none of which went to the feminists. While many factors contributed to this poor showing at the polls (see Ferree 1994, for a detailed discussion of the (de)mobilization of the UFV), the electoral result—especially given the large number of women involved with and sympathetic to the UFV—was very disheartening for feminist activists.

The March 1990 election also established that East and West Germany would unify, creating new obstacles and opportunities for feminists from East Germany. Suddenly, East German women were no longer in the position of trying to expand their rights under socialism; instead, they found themselves working to protect the rights they had under socialism. Recognizing the implications of West German social policy for gender relations and inequality, East German feminists clung to the policies that just a few months earlier they had hoped to change.

In spite of efforts by both East and West German feminists, unification proceeded with little regard to the interests of women. Institutional and cultural exclusionary mechanisms in the state structures of West Germany blocked women both from legislative action and from framing unification in gendered terms. The structure and control of parliamentary groups, the existing "old boys'" network in politics, and a cultural emphasis on the state as a male bond were antithetical to women's issues and representation (Young 1999). Furthermore, the male-centeredness of German unions—arguably the most powerful political interest outside of the state in Germany—prevented feminists from allying themselves with other major players to pursue their interests.

In spite of these obstacles, the UFV joined the heated debate about abortion policy, the most publicly contentious issue in the unification treaty (Funk 1993; Maleck-Lewy 1995; Maleck-Lewy and Ferree 2000). In contrast to the GDR's abortion policy, in the FRG abortion was considered criminal except in cases of documented sexual assault, medical danger, fetal deformity, or documented social hardship. Abortions performed outside of these circumstances, or with falsified documentation, were considered criminal acts, and both the woman receiving the abortion and the doctor performing the procedure could be prosecuted. The ensuing debate over abortion between East and West Germans was so heated that abortion became the only policy area that remained unresolved at the time of unification; the unification treaty signed solely by men in October 1990 gave the German parliament, the Bundestag, until December 31, 1992, to pass a new law governing abortion applicable to all Germans. Ultimately, the

Bundestag decriminalized abortion, but it mandated certified counseling that emphasizes the fetus as a life and a waiting period for any woman considering the termination of a pregnancy.[6]

The unification process, especially as represented by the abortion debate, seems to have signaled to many eastern German women that the unified German state was inhospitable to women. For eastern German women, the new abortion policy came as a major slap in the face. It indicated that eastern women were among the lowest-status of German citizens, leading some eastern German women to describe themselves as displaced, colonized, or foreign citizens in the unified Germany (Ferree Forthcoming; Wuerth 1999). For those women who attempted to work with West German feminists to preserve the GDR's abortion policy, their experiences also suggested that forty years of separation now made productive cooperation across the former border virtually impossible, thereby dimming future prospects for a unified German feminist movement.

As the debates surrounding unification unfolded, the UFV grew weaker, and national-level mobilization began to decline. Many activists were simultaneously involved in the UFV and in organizations in their local communities; complaints about burn out and exhaustion became increasingly common. Other members deepened their involvement in mainstream party politics and abandoned the UFV in favor of the major political parties, where they hoped to advance a feminist agenda. Simultaneously, the UFV faced competition in many regions from the DFB (formerly DFD). Membership dropped precipitously. In 1991, during contentious meetings in Leipzig, the UFV faced its sharpest division yet: whether to continue working as an electoral group or to reorganize as a *Verein*, or nonprofit association, which, under German law, would be prohibited from electoral activity. After much debate, members voted to incorporate the organization as a *Verein*, which opened the door for certain types of funding, but closed off the more lucrative assistance offered to political parties. While the UFV continued as an organization until 1996, it effectively disappeared from the feminist landscape by early 1993.

Localizing Feminist Social Movement Activity After 1989

Even as the UFV disintegrated, new projects were already well underway. Whereas mass mobilization targeting the national state characterized feminist social movement activity during the collapse of the GDR, the proliferation of the legacy of the UFV through local women's organizations and the development of ties between local women's organizations and the local state, especially municipal governments, defined women's mobilization after the ousting of the SED. Many of the women involved with the UFV or DFD in 1989–90 were also involved with women's organizations in their local communities, setting the stage for the transition from the national arena to the local one. Beginning in Erfurt in the winter of 1989–90, women's groups in some cities spearheaded or participated in citizen takeovers of buildings belonging to the state police, or Stasi. These takeovers not only drew public attention to women's concerns but provided women's groups with safe spaces in which they could discuss diverse issues and problems and develop responses to them. In Rostock, for example, women involved in the takeover of the Stasi barracks founded at least six women's organizations in 1989.

Focusing their efforts at the local level was not only a consequence of feeling thwarted in the national political arena. Rather, three other factors increased the appeal of localized efforts. First, the federal government introduced new programs to reduce unemployment in eastern Germany that created local opportunities for employment in emerging feminist organizations. Arbeitsbeschaffungsmaßnahmen (ABM, or Employment Creation Measures), administered through the Employment Office, allowed nonprofit organizations, as well as for-profit businesses and corporations, to utilize federal funding to pay their employees. Strukturanpassungsmaßnahmen (Structural Adjustment Measures, or SAM) also generated funding for new positions as these measures allowed the Employment Office to subsidize the salaries of people who would otherwise be unemployed to work in various types of social service, educational, and environmental positions. In the face of rapidly rising unemployment, women interested in social issues would band together, register as a nonprofit, and apply for ABM and/or SAM funding. While ABM and SAM positions were not permanently funded, they initially offered viable employment for at least one year and sometimes longer.[7] For women interested in changing careers, ABM positions also presented an opportunity to develop skills that could help in finding future employment.

The experiences of one respondent in Erfurt are quite typical of women who joined local women's projects, at least initially, as a means to stay employed. Formerly a school teacher, she was laid off immediately following unification. While at the Employment Office, she ran into an old acquaintance, the daughter of a former colleague. They fell into conversation, and the acquaintance relayed that she was working with a new women's technical center that was training women in computer usage. The technical center was looking for counselors who could work with women, evaluate their skills, advise them on possible career choices, and match them with appropriate technology courses. The job was to be funded through ABM. The respondent was eligible for ABM, so her acquaintance invited her to request this position. She subsequently spent two years in an ABM position at the technical center and then moved on to found another women's organization, where ABM funded her work again for three years. After five years of working in counseling, a third community organization—not a women's organization—recruited her in 1996, and she has worked there in a permanent, non-ABM position ever since.

While local branches of the federal Employment Office administered ABM and SAM funds, many other funding sources also became available through local government branches. Recognizing that eastern Germans would need assistance learning to navigate unfamiliar systems and institutions in the unified Germany, the federal government disbursed money to the new German states to support work by nonprofit organizations helping citizens with the transition. These funds were earmarked for areas such as job counseling and retraining, housing and welfare assistance, and educational and child-care aid. In many instances, funds were specifically made available to women's organizations, but women's organizations could also access non-gender-specific monies. Women activists suddenly had the financial resources to begin making tangible changes in their lives and the lives of others, and they seized the opportunity.

Second, in addition to the draw of employment and funding, respondents generally perceived working at the local level as having a greater potential for success than at the national level because of preexisting networks between women in the nonprofit sector and women in politics. Turning what Young (1999) calls the "old boys' network" of national politics in Germany on its head, women in eastern Germany accessed an "old girls'" network in local politics. While many of the women involved in the period of peak mobilization in 1989–90 made the transition into local-level activism through nonprofit organizations, others moved into local politics. This meant that a significant proportion of women politicians were sympathetic to the needs and demands of women's organizations.

Central figures in women's politics in many cities are the GBs. Under the German laws of municipal incorporation, GBs must be appointed in all cities with populations of ten thousand or more, although in smaller communities, these tend to be part-time, volunteer positions. In accordance with state and federal laws, the German states and the German executive body and its ministries are also required to appoint GBs. As of 2003, there were about 1,900 municipal GBs in Germany, of which roughly 450 serve in cities in eastern Germany (Bundesarbeitsgemeinschaft kommunaler Frauenbüros 2003).

GBs at the municipal level serve several functions depending on the size of the city in which they are located and, usually corresponding with city size, the budget of their office. They are accountable for ensuring that gender equity policies are carried out in the city government itself. GBs review legal and policy proposals to verify that they will not have a disparate impact on women. In some cities, as in Rostock, GBs have worked with council members to draft and pass local legislation on gender equality and mainstreaming. They are also responsible for disseminating information about gender disparities in unemployment, welfare assistance, and education in the city to mayors and council members, and work to increase the amount of attention city government pays to women's issues. In addition, the GB's office often serves as a hub for women's organizations, building and maintaining networks and coalitions between women's organizations. GBs have walk-in hours where citizens with problems can come for referrals to an appropriate agency. Municipal GBs also administer limited funds intended to support the work of women's organizations and have played an active role in providing city-owned properties to women's organizations for below-market rents.

GBs are generally appointed to the post because of their background in gender or related issues. Consequently, almost all municipal GBs appointed in 1990 were women who first became involved with gender issues through the feminist activities of the unification period. Especially in small and midsize cities, GBs were well known among feminist activists, and GBs were and are often intimately involved with feminist organizations they helped found. The GB in Erfurt, for example, was involved in the founding process of a major women's center there, while the GB in Rostock is a longtime board member of a women's organization.

Finally, interactions with western German women's groups influenced the development of localized women's organizations in eastern Germany. In both Rostock and Erfurt, several organizations received extensive support from similar organizations in the West. The women's technical center in Hamburg, for example, founded the women's technical center in Rostock, recruiting and training its first group of staff. The reach of western German feminists and feminist groups was even greater in Erfurt, where many activists received training through women's centers in western Germany. While these encounters were often not entirely positive, women's mobilization in West Germany has historically been localized, and eastern German women were influenced by this model.

Already in the establishment of localized women's organizations in eastern Germany, however, important differences emerged when compared with women's organizations in western Germany. Most notably, while the West German women's movement has historically sought to distance itself from the state, the new movement in eastern Germany has relied heavily on state assistance since 1990 (Ferree 1996). In seeking autonomy from the state, West German feminism before unification sought to create spaces for women free from male and state domination, two forms of domination that were often conflated in West German feminist thought.

Eastern German women, by contrast, were accustomed to a woman-friendly state that serves its citizens. While well aware of the inherent risks in dependence on the state for organizational survival, women's organizations in eastern Germany in general do not share the same concerns about the state as feminists in western Germany. In some sense, this type of response seems counterintuitive; the East German state was, after all, highly repressive and set an agenda for women that women involved with the UFV in 1989 actively sought to change. However, despite its repressive tendencies, women in eastern Germany generally maintain that the East German state was importantly different—and better—in its treatment of women compared with the unified Germany.

Dynamics of Institutionalization and Professionalization in Local Feminist Movements

Certainly, as will become evident in the subsequent discussions of the women's movements in Rostock and Erfurt, reliance on the state is a double-edged sword for feminist organizations in eastern Germany. On the one hand, state support often provided a relatively stable source of income and employment. In contrast to what some western thinkers have argued, reliance on the state also does not automatically translate into co-optation of feminist goals or the neutralization of feminist political energies. In fact, because most GBs had backgrounds in feminist organizing, state support could actually enhance the strength of feminist convictions rather than undermine them. Who served in these positions was often more important than the level of interdependence between GB's offices and feminist organizations.

During the 1990s, women's organizations in eastern Germany and municipal and state GBs became largely mutually dependent, although the degree of cooperation and collaboration between GBs and activists varies across specific locales. GBs already existed in West Germany before unification, but they were a new addition to eastern German state bureaucracies. The support of women's organizations helped establish the importance of GBs in the new German states, and GBs simultaneously legitimized the interests of women and women's organizations in government offices. In Rostock and Erfurt, this pattern of mutual reinforcement, especially between women's organizations and the municipal GBs, increased the institutionalization of both women's organizations and GBs.

German states also have statewide GBs.[8] Like their colleagues at the municipal level, state-level GBs ensure that state regulations governing equal opportunity are properly enforced. Usually with the help of up to a dozen staff members, state GBs work on policy proposals with members of the political parties and keep abreast of legislative and funding decisions that may affect women and women's organizations. State GBs generally include multiple departments dedicated to issues such as women in business, education, culture, politics, and justice.

Importantly, GBs at the statewide level provide substantial funding to women's organizations. GBs generally have some discretion in how to distribute funds. Also important is that while most municipal GBs are nonpartisan, statewide GBs almost always are party members and are appointed by the governor, who usually selects a GB from within the same party. While GBs often maintain their willingness and ability to work outside of the bounds of party politics, their investment in the priorities of their party can have significant implications for how various women's organizations are funded and treated.

Directly related to the development of feminist state machineries and increasing interdependence between GBs and feminist organizations, professionalism and hierarchy became more common in many women's organizations during the 1990s. As organizations that had been founded as "working groups" became more established, hierarchical structures replaced cooperative or collective structures as the dominant organizational form. These hierarchies became more formalized largely in response to the demands of state funding agencies, which favor organizations with clear structures of accountability, professional work environments, and proven efficacy.

With growing competition for funds, feminist organizations also began instituting membership requirements and incentives, and they sought the help of experts and leading activists through service as members of executive boards.

Although all such boards are democratically elected by members of an organization, boards began to include more academics, politicians, and high-status activists, many of whom serve on the board of more than one organization, thereby creating important interlocks between organizations working in overlapping fields and consolidating power. Again, this trend may be at least partially explained by state demands as state funding agencies favor those groups with high-profile board members with demonstrated expertise in relevant areas.

Simultaneously, credentials became increasingly important even within organizations that resisted the move toward hierarchies. While women who joined local feminist movements during unification were often making radical career changes, professional skills and degrees in social service, education, social work, and related fields became necessary for all but purely administrative positions in feminist organizations by the mid-1990s. Many women who had worked with organizations from their founding began taking classes to earn additional credentials, while those breaking into the field by the mid-1990s no longer found that a quick mind and a generous spirit were sufficient for a job with a women's organization. The push toward professionalization also came from the state, which increasingly required efficacy reports from organizations in order to continue their funding. Not only did data about clients, services, and outcomes factor into these reports, but funding administrators also considered who worked at a project and what kind of background and experience they could offer. In some cases, state funding guidelines specify the exact degrees that employees fulfilling certain functions at an organization must have in order for their salaries to qualify for subsidies.

Through the late 1990s and into the 2000s, smaller, localized organizations dominated feminist activity in eastern Germany, but these organizations are largely, albeit not exclusively, hierarchical, formalized, and professionalized. While there are no exact figures available, probably as many as four hundred women's organizations exist in eastern Germany today (Miethe and Ulrich-Hampele 2001). Women's centers, which offer counseling, feminist libraries, courses, and social spaces for women (and sometimes men), can be found in most eastern German cities with populations of 100,000 or more, along with shelters for battered women. Slightly larger cities often also boast technical schools for women and girls, shelters for abused girls, cooperative, feminist-organized day-care centers, feminist housing collectives, cultural centers for women, and support services for various groups of women, such as new mothers, the unemployed, or entrepreneurs.

Since 2000, organizations have continued to adapt to changing conditions, most notably the shrinking funding sources available through local state agencies and federal unemployment programs. Some organizations disappeared from the landscape altogether. In Rostock and Erfurt, women's health collectives closed in 2000 and 2001, respectively. The battered women's shelters in both cities housed fewer women in 2003 than they did in 1993. The virtual dissolution of ABM positions has been especially devastating, forcing many projects to be reduced to a skeleton staff.

As funds become increasingly limited, the new century brought with it renewed state attention to how to maximize effectiveness while minimizing cost. The emphasis on cost-effectiveness and efficacy has continued to support professionalization within state-supported organizations. Faced with higher expectations from the state, as well as with smaller funding sources from municipal and statewide GBs and greater competition for funds, some women's organizations have also begun looking beyond the local state to secure funding for their work. The EU has become an especially important source of support.

Although the EU provided a substantial proportion of funding for women's organizations in the early 2000s, especially in Rostock, women's organizations in eastern Germany operate almost exclusively at the local level and are only rarely involved in efforts targeting the national state, national electoral politics, or supranational institutions. Since the demise of the UFV, there has been little interest in mobilizing feminist interests at the national level. Although some eastern German women participate in the political party Feministische Partei DIE FRAUEN (Feminist Party THE WOMEN), a party created by western German feminists, eastern German feminists interested in electoral politics have mostly joined the larger parties, like Bündnis 90/Die Grünen (Alliance 90/The Greens, which also subsumed the former dissident group Neues Forum in most eastern German states), the PDS, and the SPD (the CDU, CSU, and FDP, with their more conservative ideologies, seem to have less appeal for feminists, although many feminists in Erfurt are aligned with the CDU). Many feminists involved in party politics also participate in the women's groups of their party.

Feminist Ideologies in Eastern Germany

Women in eastern Germany are sometimes uncomfortable describing themselves as feminists, a common trend in many countries (see, for example, Aronson 2003). This discomfort among eastern German feminists is usually grounded in multiple justifications. The SED painted feminism as a bourgeois import, and, while none of the participants in this book explicitly described feminism in this way, the SED's position does seem to have succeeded in constructing feminism as something foreign and different. Western German feminists who, in encounters with eastern German activists during and after unification often did not see eastern German women as living up to the standards expected of feminists in the West, later reinforced this underlying suspicion of feminism as something un-East German (see Miethe 2008, for a detailed discussion of the history of tensions between eastern and western German feminists). Specifically, many activists in eastern Germany defy the expectation central to the culture of the women's movement in western Germany that women advance their interests independently of men (Ferree 1996). Eastern German women spent most of their lives in a society in which class solidarity was supposed to trump all other bases of difference—at least symbolically, if not in reality. Simultaneously, the private sphere was one of few domains relatively safe from state surveillance, and women and men were often partners in preserving the private sphere. Feminists in eastern Germany typically emphasize the need for women and men to work together, a position they see as opposed to feminist doctrine.

Many participants in this book are wary of feminism because they think it is anti-men. This is the most oft-cited explanation offered by respondents for why they shun the term feminism. As one participant in Rostock responds to the question of whether she describes herself as a feminist: "I am a feminist. But I am not militant. I think that break is horrible, that border. We have to deal with men in this society, both together, equal. I do not want to live in a world of only women." Here, the respondent sees feminism as positive when used to describe broad efforts at improving the condition of women. However, she is quick to point out that she is "not militant" and is quite critical of what she sees as militant separatism.

Similarly, many respondents shun the term *Emanze*, a word derived from "emancipation," that even my trusted English-German dictionary translates simply as "women's libber" (Terrell, Schnorr, Morris et al. 2001). *Emanze* tends to fall outside of the eastern framework, but, when included, evokes a similar response as those to questions about feminist identity. One activist in Erfurt comments: "I see myself as emancipated, but not as an *Emanze*, and have determined over time that I am actually doing what women want to do. Not against men, but with men, in the spirit of equality."

In spite of their misgivings about identifying as feminists, I continue to use this term to describe participants in this book and the organizations and movements to which they belong. Scholars have debated how and where to draw the line between women's movements and feminist movements. Not all social movements that involve largely or exclusively women are feminist movements. Simultaneously, there has been a tendency in western scholarship to apply western litmus tests that ultimately lead to a view of the activism of women in the developing world as less than feminism (Ray and Korteweg 1999). For the purposes of this project, I classify as feminist those individuals, organizations, and movements who recognize that women are systematically disadvantaged relative to men due to institutionalized discrimination and exclusion and who challenge this disadvantage through the promotion of women's status and opportunities. Although some of the individuals and organizations I encountered in the course of my fieldwork appear more or less feminist than others, all satisfy this basic criteria. Treating the subjects of my research as actors within women's movements would belie the very real challenges they pose to existing ways of doing and thinking about gender. These movements advance women's interests and seek a reorganization of society to create a more gender-egalitarian world (Beckwith 2001; Ferree and Mueller 2004; Martin 1990).

Furthermore, while part of eastern German women's resistance to identification as feminist stems from discomfort with the origins of the term and its connotations, equally common were women who saw themselves as somehow unworthy of the label. I was stunned when one respondent, whom I came to know quite well and whom I would describe as an exceptionally dedicated activist, told me she was not "really" a feminist because she maintained a close relationship with a sexist male relative. In spite of her years of work building up key feminist organizations, her high visibility as an outspoken public advocate of women's issues, and her reputation as one of the major players in the local political and feminist scenes, she harbored guilt about her inability to disentangle herself from a relative with sexist attitudes and felt that her relationship with him negated her prospects of being a true feminist. Other respondents were more vague in conveying that they don't see themselves as doing enough for the feminist cause to be considered a feminist. Women invoked an ideal type of feminist to which their own efforts did not compare. Sociologists routinely ascribe categories for their subjects, and as a sociological analyst, I view the women involved in women's organizations in eastern Germany as significant actors in the feminist project, advancing the most basic premise of feminism: equality between women and men.

At the same time, eastern German feminism is far from homogenous. Three primary categories of feminism emerged from the data. Table 2.2 offers an overview of the key features of these three feminisms, which I label neosocialist, radical, and conservative. My typology clarifies some of the key differences between ideologies, reinforcing that feminism is not monolithic, but instead, like most ideologies, is rife with complexity and contradiction (Kantola 2006). I adopt Pamela E. Oliver and Hank Johnston's (2000) definition of ideology as "any system of meaning that couples assertions and theories about the nature of social life with values and norms relevant to promoting or resisting change" (37). More narrowly, feminist ideologies are idea systems that recognize an imbalance in power and resources between women and men and that prescribe remedies for this imbalance.

Of the three feminist ideologies in the two cities, neosocialist feminism is most reflective of the gender ideology of the GDR in that it stresses the importance of women's roles as workers and supports cooperation between women and men. However, neosocialist feminists in Rostock do not entirely align with the ideologies of socialism or gender as practiced in the GDR, nor with classic

Table 2.2 Varieties of feminism in Rostock and Erfurt

	Neosocialist Feminism	*Radical Feminism*	*Conservative Feminism*
Approach toward men's roles in gender issues	Men and women must work together to end gender inequality	Women must find separate spaces from men, free from patriarchy	Men and women must work together to end gender inequality
Core issues	Women's financial independence; balancing work and family for women and men	Violence against women; cultural representations of women; politics of the body and sexuality	Maintenance of the nuclear-family model; women's integration into politics to bring civility and compassion to political life
Basis for claims/ Privileged status of women	As workers and mothers, but especially as workers	As survivors	As mothers
Dominant discourse/ rhetorical emphasis	Financial independence; balancing work and family	Subordination, patriarchy, oppression	Traditional family maintenance; compassionate politics
Attitude toward the state	The state and women's organizations should cooperate as partners and allies	Cooperation with state agencies is a necessary evil; women's organizations should be autonomous	Women's organizations should be autonomous from the state, but may need initial state assistance to reach that goal

conceptualizations of socialist feminism. Western European and North American feminists and scholars who first developed socialist feminism under that label in the 1970s disagree with the Marxist assumption that gender inequality is secondary to class inequality, even as they recognize the importance of both types of inequality for capitalism (Hartmann 1997; Mitchell 1971). They center women's right to paid employment as a personal goal and approach women's roles in the family critically, asserting that the family is a site of capitalist reproduction and women's oppression. In the GDR, the family was a site of both women's uncompensated labor and of freedom from state intervention and surveillance. Neosocialist feminism reflects this complex history through its interest in supporting women's roles as workers and as mothers. In its efforts to help women balance work and family, neosocialist feminism largely strives to achieve the gender ideology that the GDR promoted but never achieved.

Like socialist feminists in the West, neosocialist feminists in Rostock stress the importance of women's economic independence, and they privilege women's status as workers. The crux of their ideology in Rostock is that women will only be fully equal with men when they achieve economic equality and full financial independence. Consequently, neosocialist feminists emphasize job creation and training, educating women in financial matters, and supporting women entrepreneurs. Unlike socialist feminism as practiced in the West, neosocialist feminists turn to the state to intervene in the economy on behalf of women and expect that the state should and will provide assistance in their efforts to minimize gender disparities in education, income, employment, and family contributions, while also protecting women from those men who pose a threat to women's physical safety. Also unlike some of their western predecessors, they do not advocate for socialism in and of itself—and in fact are often quite open to neoliberal economic models promoted by the EU—yet they do support the idea that workers must join together in mutual assistance and that the state should redress inequalities. While service provisioning and advocacy work through neosocialist feminist organizations recognizes women's statuses as workers, mothers, and as survivors of violence, neosocialist feminists emphasize balancing motherhood and paid employment, and especially stress women's identities as workers in their advocacy and service provisioning.

In contrast, radical feminists focus on women's experiences as survivors. They regard both men and the state with suspicion, asserting that the state is an inherently patriarchal institution. Radical feminists hold that women must have separate, safe spaces in which they can explore their own identities and sexualities free from the expectations and intrusions of men and the masculine, patriarchal state. While economic issues are present in their explanations of gender inequality, radical feminists tend to focus more heavily on cultural and sociohistorical reasoning. Neosocialist feminist organizations most often emphasize job training and education; by contrast, radical feminist organizations are more concerned with violence against women, cultural representations of women, sexuality, self-awareness, and feminist enlightenment. Neosocialist feminists can be understood as engaged in a type of politics of redistribution, whereas radical feminists mobilize a politics focused on recognition (Fraser 1993). Unlike many neosocialist feminists, radical feminists tend to embrace identification as feminist and, in some cases, as *Emanzen*.

In the eastern German case, this type of feminism is overwhelmingly associated with lesbians and lesbian organizations, although many nonlesbian women are also sympathetic to this position. This has also been the dominant ideology of the few autonomous feminist organizations in eastern Germany. Like their western German counterparts, eastern German radical feminists tend to be wary of the state as a source of viable solutions to their problems. However, even most women's organizations in this project that could be described as espousing a radical feminist ideology receive some funding from the state. Unlike western German women's organizations that have actively sought autonomy from the state, radical feminists in eastern Germany seem to accept that state funding is necessary in achieving their aims, and they continue to seek funding from the state and cooperate with state agencies.

Finally, conservative feminism holds that women need to be included at all levels of society because of the unique contributions they are able to make as mothers and caregivers. Conservative feminism echoes aspects of cultural, maternalist, and neofamilialist ideologies identified in various other contexts (Elshtain 1992; Lorber 2001) in that this ideology accepts essentialist notions of difference between women and men and pushes for a greater social valuation of what it deems women's attributes and strengths. Women are valued for their ability to nurture and care, and for providing a critical balance to men's tendencies toward aggression. Conservative feminists support initiatives that encourage women to focus on mothering and that bring women into politics and other positions of power where they can offer a more civil, compassionate perspective than men. In terms of state interventions in gender relations, conservative feminists tend to support a liberal state that intercedes only when necessary to protect those who cannot be protected otherwise. Interests in increasing women's status, promoting women's occupational choices, and helping women and men balance work and family obligations differentiate conservative feminism from antifeminism, which generally holds that women's entry into the workforce is detrimental to family and society.

Conservative feminists tend to avoid identification as feminists, but they commonly embrace other German terms that suggest a feminist position, such as *Frauenförderung*, or affirmative action for women. Especially as these women generally work within conservative milieus, such as in elected office for the Christian Democratic Union or in religious institutions, they see themselves as quite cutting-edge relative to their colleagues. Indeed, while their rhetoric is sometimes seemingly nonfeminist, conservative feminists maintain that they represent progressive energies within circles where more traditional attitudes toward women, work, and family are dominant. These women, and the organizations they work with, are extremely dedicated to a more gender-egalitarian model of work and family life in which men take greater responsibility in the home and women have more rights and opportunities outside of it.

Certainly, these three feminist ideologies are not entirely mutually exclusive, and some women who participated in this study accept sometimes competing ideas from more than one of these schools of thought. Still, these three varieties of feminism reflect distinct approaches to gender relations, women's welfare, and the need or desire for state involvement in redressing gender inequality. The ideologies are also grounded in the local contexts from which they emerged. The specific political, geographic, and cultural resources and constraints present in Rostock and Erfurt influenced the development of these feminisms in different ratios in Rostock and Erfurt. Simultaneously, the ideological orientation of the local feminist movements has critical explanatory power for understanding their successes and setbacks. The subsequent chapters turn to the feminist movements in Rostock and Erfurt to unravel the processes behind their ideological development and to explore the interactions between their ideologies, strategies, development, and the place characters of the cities they call home.

A World Reopened

Spending time with Carolina is one of my favorite parts of visiting Rostock. She and I met during my first visit to the Beginenhof, where she worked for more than a decade beginning in the early 1990s. After another staff member at the Beginenhof introduced us, Carolina became one of my primary contacts in Rostock, someone who helped me identify respondents and who would answer my most candid questions about the dynamics within the local feminist movement there. Carolina is warm and funny, and we share an immense curiosity about one another's lives.

Carolina zips around Rostock in a worn-down subcompact car cluttered with papers and clumps of dog fur. She smokes rigorously and drinks wine a bit too quickly to savor it. Carolina is an adventurer, always looking for new experiences. She loves to tell stories, and she has plenty to tell.

Carolina was a proud tomboy growing up in a rural village in the GDR. As a young adult, her primary identification was as a member a comedy troupe with which she traveled around the country to perform in cabarets. Shortly before the collapse of state socialism, she even performed a spoof of the life of the SED's highest-ranking leader, Erich Honecker—with Honecker in the audience. "When the routine was over, we had no idea what would happen," she remembers. "For a moment, it was completely silent. But then Honecker just leaned back in his chair and laughed and laughed."

Carolina also started a family in the GDR and had two children, now both adults. When we passed Rostock's former City Hall on our way to a pub one evening, she paused to remember that she was both married and divorced in the building. Both of her children have left Rostock.

Carolina has been active in the local feminist movement in Rostock since the autumn of 1989. She participated in the earliest meetings of the UFV, helped build Amandahaus, an apartment building for single mothers, and works for one of the city's largest and most successful feminist organizations providing job training to women across the state. She's ambivalent about the term "feminist" because it has connotations with which she is uncomfortable. She doesn't see herself as anti-men. In fact, among her favorite topics of conversation are stories of her bad luck in love with men.

Overall, Carolina finds life after the GDR both more challenging and more colorful. Having felt trapped in her career in the GDR, she is grateful for the freedom to move between jobs in the unified Germany. At the same time, she sees the painful reality that this freedom is accompanied by the loss of job security. After more than ten years working with a feminist organization, she lost her position when the funding ran out for the project on which she was working. She has most recently tried to retrain as a computer programmer.

Like most people I met in Rostock, Carolina also misses the sense of community and mutual assistance of the GDR. As she watched her daughter raise her grandson as a single mother for several years, she recognized both differences and similarities to her own experience as a single mother in the GDR. One of her biggest complaints about life in the GDR was the waiting. The most mundane tasks—grocery shopping, buying the kids clothes for school—could take hours because of shortages and rations. Her daughter's life as a single mother, she thinks, was simpler in that regard. On the downside, she could not rely on others for support the way Carolina did. Neighbors didn't share hand-me-downs or offer to help with child care. "Everyone is in it for themselves now," Carolina muses.

She identifies the freedom to travel as the single greatest advantage of unification. Carolina suffers from Wanderlust, although she can only indulge her desire to travel as much as her pocketbook will allow. One of the lessons unification has taught her is that many freedoms come at a price that not everyone can afford. Since unification, she has enjoyed ski holidays with a group of fellow feminist activists and friends. She traveled to Scandinavian destinations and even ventured to southern Africa and Southeast Asia. She remembers holidays within the Soviet bloc during the GDR, which she says made her feel closed in and trapped. She describes "a world reopened" since unification. She is amazed at all the world has to offer, and while she has ample concerns about globalization, she continues to marvel at the flow of people, goods, and ideas across borders in the postsocialist world.

One evening, Carolina and I participated in a pub crawl of sorts organized by a local business association seeking to draw attention to a rapidly gentrifying neighborhood in which trendy bars and cafés were proliferating rapidly. At our second stop, a bright-eyed young woman with a large camera dangling from her neck approached us. She introduced herself as a reporter covering the pub crawl for the local weekly paper. Carolina was delighted to offer her opinion of the event and to make known that she was attending it with her friend from America. She put her arm around me and squeezed. "That I would be sitting in Rostock in a fancy wine bar like this with an American friend—now that is something I never dreamed of," Carolina announced with a mixture of happiness and bewilderment. A picture of us, grinning like fools as we toast one another, ran in the paper the next day.

3 Place and Politics in Rostock

ORIGINALLY SETTLED BY SLAVS FOURTEEN HUNDRED YEARS AGO, Rostock was named for the Slavic word *roztoc*, or a place where water widens. Situated at the mouth of the Warnow River and curling along the river to the Baltic Sea coast, Rostock's history has centered on the sea. Under the leadership of Danish King Waldemar II, Rostock emerged as a major port by the end of the twelfth century. For nearly half a millennium from 1257 until 1699, the city was a member of the Hanseatic League, a trading union of northern European ports, and trade, shipbuilding, and fishing have long been at the heart of Rostock's economy. In 1419, the University of Rostock was founded as a Hanseatic university to educate young people from all of the member cities, attracting students and residents from what are now Germany, Denmark, Poland, Sweden, Finland, and Estonia. Low German, the lingua franca of the Hanseatic League, developed in Rostock, where two distinct dialects, Mecklenburgisch (or Mecklenborgsch), a melding of German and Danish, and Pomeranian (or Pomersch), a German and Slavic hybrid, emerged as major languages.

After the dissolution of the Hanseatic League at the end of the seventeenth century, Rostock lost much of its luster, although it remained an important port. During the Second World War, the Allies targeted the city because it housed munitions factories and shipbuilding facilities. The bombings left the city heavily damaged. The Red Army ultimately liberated Rostock, which was then zoned into the Soviet territory after the Second World War, becoming part of the German Democratic Republic, founded in 1949. The ruling party of the GDR, the SED, placed a high priority on rebuilding and redeveloping Rostock because of its strategic coastal location. By the early 1960s, Rostock was the largest port city East of the Elba River. Trading partners to the East and North once again drove Rostock's economic engine as the city claimed its place as one of the most important ports in the Soviet bloc.

German unification initially had devastating economic consequences for Rostock, as it did for many cities in the former East Germany. The economic changes accompanying German unification hit the maritime sector especially hard, resulting in significant layoffs. Rostock's wharf was too shallow and narrow to accommodate the large tankers that had come to dominate the global seafaring trade and major reconstruction increased automation and reduced the labor force in the harbor. The fishing industry could not compete in new international markets and contracted significantly after 1990. In the early 1990s, unemployment in Rostock approached 50 percent.

Economic redevelopment has focused on the shipbuilding and technology industries, as well as on a growing service sector fueled by seasonal tourism and dependent on low-wage, part-time labor. By the early 2000s, slightly less than one-fifth of residents in Rostock were unemployed. This drop in unemployment reflects new job creation, the migration of roughly sixty thousand residents to other parts of Europe, and many workers' permanent withdrawal from the labor market, including through retirement.

Downtown Rostock is positioned approximately in the middle of the city's seventy-square-mile spread, along the western bank of the Warnow River. A small pedestrian zone is home to most of the larger shops in town, many of which are western German franchises. The city's central plaza, the Universität-splatz, stands at the center of the pedestrian zone, anchored on two sides by the historic buildings of the city's university. This is the site for the liveliest expression of urban street culture in Rostock. Here, competing street musicians play on opposite corners. Children splash in the plaza's large fountain while young skinheads sit nearby puffing at cigarettes under the anxious, watchful eyes of their lockjaw dogs. Teenagers line up with sacks of food from McDonald's or the neighboring Turkish kabob stand. Yuppies and the occasional tourist sip espresso at the expensive Italian café on the corner. Seniors stroll by with their Dachshunds.

Some twenty miles away, the seaside neighborhood of Warnemünde attracts both German and foreign tourists and is a favorite weekend destination for residents from across the city. While the Baltic's cold waters appeal to only the hardiest of swimmers, the long, white sand beach offers the perfect spot for summer sunning. During the long days of August, the beach is crowded with sunbathers stretched on their rented lounge chairs. Along a nearby canal, charming Danish cottages built four hundred years ago now house guesthouses and cafés. Vendors hawk fried-fish sandwiches from tugboat restaurants, and passengers from the mammoth cruise ships docked for the day clamber aboard antique vessels for harbor tours.

Between the scenic points of downtown and Warnemünde, the view from the train reveals a more typically postsocialist landscape, framed by the graffiti scratched into the window. Vast, empty fens are abruptly interrupted by clusters of *Plattenbauten*, the cinderblock high-rises that typify East German housing. Residents of these neighborhoods, which were built to provide workers with modern dwellings in high-density communities, are disproportionately unemployed; according to city statistics, one-quarter of *Plattenbau* residents do not have work compared to an overall citywide unemployment rate of 18 percent (Hansestadt Rostock 2002). Disaffected youth with myriad facial piercings idly watch the train go by, passing around a cigarette and a bottle of beer. An elderly woman with a cane struggles up the steps to the train platform, but the conductor does not wait.

Women's organizations in Rostock operate against this backdrop of urban renewal and decay. In the southern part of the city, tucked in a neighborhood of *Plattenbauten*, an umbrella organization representing several of the city's largest and oldest women's organizations inhabits a former day-care center. Having negotiated with the city in the early 1990s to acquire the space at a reduced rent in exchange for overseeing and largely funding extensive renovations of the once dilapidated building, Rostocker Fraueninitiativen (Rostock Women's Initiatives, or RFI) named the building the Beginenhof in honor of the Beguines. The Beguines are legendary in Rostock. A quasi-monastic order of women who developed their own communities in various cities and towns in northern and central continental Europe between the twelfth and fifteenth centuries, the Beguines were residents of the city for at least three hundred years, earning their livelihood tending to the ill and infirm and engaging in craftwork.

While the Beginenhof is not a commune like the original Beguine colony, it prides itself on continuing an important tradition in the city through which women learn to sustain one another and work toward a more peaceable, egalitarian society. Like the Beguines, the Beginenhof encourages cooperation, communication, nonviolence, and self-actualization. It also stresses the importance of community, of working together, and of building solidarity between women. In many ways, the Beginenhof's ideology also reflects the gender ideology of the GDR, which focused on the importance of men and women working collectively in the socialist project. Rather than advocating autonomy from men and the state, a dominant feature of the autonomous feminist movement in western Germany (Ferree 1995; Miethe 1996), the organizations participating in the Beginenhof promote cooperation between women and men, and between women's organizations and the state, in working toward greater gender equality. With the exception of services that necessitate gender-specific space, such as support groups for sexual-assault survivors, the services at the Beginenhof are open to men and women.

The Beginenhof houses offices for the rape-crisis and advocacy project, meeting spaces for a girls' program with special services and a shelter for girls who are sexually and/or physically abused at home, a women's café, a dance and fitness studio, a cooperative day-care center, a women's technical school and job-placement program, and the office of the local UFV chapter, the last known UFV chapter in eastern Germany. The composition and the atmosphere of the Beginenhof have changed substantially over the years, reflecting the constant tension between renewal and retreat that marks so much of social life in postsocialist eastern Germany. Until 2002, when, due to financial and ideological crises, it relocated to a different building housing women's organizations in the city center, a women's cultural center, also named after the Beginen, maintained a ceramics studio, exhibition space, and offices in the Beginenhof. In the mid-1990s, a women's health project tried to grow roots here, but it was unable to take hold. The directorship of RFI changed hands three times in just five years. Yet other organizations flourish. Once filling only a few rooms, the FrauenTechnikZentrum (Women's Technical Center, or FTZ) has grown to occupy much of the second floor, its programs having expanded significantly in the early 2000s with funding from the European Union. Similarly, the offices of Frauen helfen Frauen (Women Helping Women), an organization combating violence against women, have come to dominate the first floor in a wave of renovations completed in 2004.

Although faced with many obstacles and challenges, the feminist movement in Rostock has emerged as one of the most successful local feminist movements in eastern Germany. Chronicling the development of the movement in Rostock and linking that history to the place from which it emerged reveals how the feminist movement in Rostock has benefited from specific cultural and political features of the city that have allowed the movement to position itself as a continuation of important local traditions. The city offers a particular understanding of gender relations and of the role of the state in redressing gender inequalities with which the feminist ideology of the local feminist movement is highly congruent. Convergence between the goals of the feminist movement in Rostock and the goals of the municipal government resulted in the legitimation of women's organizations and in the expanded capacity of state agencies that address gender issues. This capacity in turn feeds back to support feminist work. In this cycle, the feminist movement participates in the project of making place in Rostock after unification by contributing to the city's understanding of itself as leftist, egalitarian, and independent from the federal state.

Building the Feminist Movement in Rostock

The collapse of state socialism and the unification of East and West Germany was a period of tremendous upheaval in eastern Germany. In the state socialist system, citizens enjoyed a high level of economic security through guaranteed employment and housing, coupled with low levels of democratic freedoms, such as the freedom to associate and a free press. The introduction of democratic rule and new political and economic systems created opportunities to reinvent eastern Germany. At the same time, established community identities served as a buffer against the onslaught of changes eastern Germans experienced in 1989–90. In Rostock, feminists aligned themselves with local efforts to preserve those aspects of life in the GDR residents viewed as desirable while also integrating new issues and agendas into the city's priorities.

The first new women's organization to take shape in Rostock after the collapse of the Berlin Wall in 1989 was the local chapter of the UFV. Born out of revolutionary idealism, the UFV struggled to affect change at the national level, and the women from Rostock who were involved in the UFV became part of a core group of activists who established many of Rostock's oldest and most visible women's organizations. In the spring of 1990, women from the local UFV chapter, joined by others who were not officially part of the UFV, took up residence in a former Stasi barrack in downtown Rostock, naming the building the Beginenhaus (Beguine's House). Only informally organized, the UFV welcomed anyone with an interest in women's issues, opening its doors to a diverse range of interests and perspectives. In the old barracks, about eighty women— and a handful of men—formed working groups to address a long list of issues including employment, affordable housing, domestic violence, rape and sexual assault, day care, the environment, and women's art and culture.

During the tumult of 1990, the UFV was one of few constants for feminist activists in a rapidly evolving political, social, and economic landscape. Following the ousting of the SED from municipal governance in the late winter of 1990, the city was ruled by the Round Table government through the summer of 1990. A relatively open citizens' forum, the Round Table was comprised of activists and leaders from the Neus Forum (New Forum) organization, which led many of the protests against the SED in 1989, as well as by participants in emergent voter coalitions and eastern German members of the established West German political parties, most of which had existed in the GDR as opposition parties. The first citywide elections were held in May 1990 to elect a city council and mayor. During this election, the first "red-red" coalition emerged as the SPD and PDS together barely earned a majority.[1]

In this evolving and competitive political landscape, feminist activists sought to include women's voices and concerns in emerging political debates. Feminist activists participated in the Round Table, hoping to draw attention to women's issues in the reshaping of Rostock after the GDR. For these women, the year 1990 was an invigorating time. Comments made in a discussion with two women, Isabel and Rosamund, who joined the UFV in 1989, and who remain actively involved in feminist organizing in Rostock, reveal the level of excitement and possibility felt in 1990:

> Isabel: We had great ideas. It was wonderful, I think, to have lived through a time like that, to feel like there is a time when everything and anything is possible. You can take any idea and just take it out onto the street. And we did take our ideas out. We had no inhibitions and we just went everywhere and said, "This is what we want."

> Rosamund: We sat at the first council meetings as they dismantled the old order and then in the transitional parliament. We went to the Round Table and the votes. We were everywhere where things were happening. That was a time when we really thought anything was possible.

Here, Isabel and Rosamund express feelings of optimism and hope during unification. Suddenly free from state repression, they embraced their new ability to make demands of the state, participating in the transitional government and pushing for the inclusion of women and feminist issues in local politics. Opportunity structures opened, allowing feminists to feel like active participants in the remaking of Rostock.

In a period of significant social upheaval, the UFV headquarters in the Stasi barracks came to be a safe haven for many women, a place where they could relax and speak with friends, tapping into each other for support and encouragement as they grappled with a rapidly changing social and physical landscape marked at once by optimism and uncertainty. Many respondents described themselves as practically living in the UFV office in the barracks, enjoying the companionship of like-minded women and devising solutions for emerging problems. The women in the UFV were largely strangers to each other before unification, but strong relationships emerged from the UFV, creating important networks that women continued to draw on as they moved in different directions, founding various feminist organizations. These networks were especially critical as the initial euphoria surrounding the end of socialism eroded and women in Rostock recognized exactly what they were losing in the unified Germany.

A key relationship that developed during the tumultuous unification period of 1989–90 was that between feminist organizations and the newly appointed Gender Equity Representative for the city of Rostock. By late 1990, the first democratically elected city government in Rostock appointed a GB.[2] In Rostock, this appointee was a charismatic woman who went on to serve as an elected state representative for the SPD and as the first statewide GB.[3] Widely described as a "powerhouse" and "expert diplomat," the first GB was a key mediator between women's organizations and the city government. She immediately set about securing funding and other resources for emerging women's organizations. By late 1992, it was apparent that the old Stasi building would no longer meet the needs of the Beginen and other women's organizations operating there. Not only was the space too small to accommodate all of the feminist organizations in the city, but the old barracks were, as Alex puts it, "without a future," because ownership of the building could not be established, such that there was no prospect of a long-term lease.[4] In the spring of 1993, a group of feminist organizations banded together to form RFI, in part so that they could appoint someone who could legally sign a lease. With the help of the municipal GB, RFI began negotiating with the city to find a new home and signed a lease in May 1994.

Under the umbrella of RFI, which was managed by representatives of each of the tenant organizations in the building and a full-time director, the physical space of the Beginenhof was transformed from a run-down day-care center with hazy glass windows, failing plumbing, and a leaking roof into a clean and pleasant space. The transformation process seemed interminable; when I visited in 2000, the building was being updated, and during my visit in 2004, it was under renovation yet again.

In their new home, the member groups of RFI expanded, adding new services and occasionally off-loading existing services onto other groups. Women Helping Women, once responsible for rape-crisis counseling and the management of the battered women's shelter, began an innovative new program that offered shelter, counseling, and advocacy to girls who were sexually or physically abused at home. Other programs also emerged from Women Helping Women, including drop-in counseling for abused women and a legal advocacy project. The Women's Technical Center continued to build its staff and increase its course offerings. The Beginen refurbished an old kiln in the building, creating a drop-in ceramics studio that became a popular spot for socializing among local women. RFI also managed the new women's café, open daily for breakfast, lunch, and tea, as well as a fitness studio where dance classes and singing groups are held.

The move, and the subsequent programmatic expansion, was not without trial and tribulation. The building itself had massive structural problems, including flaws in the sewage and heating systems. The Beginenhof had signed a twenty-five–year lease on the property, but RFI was not considered creditworthy by local banks and government-based lending agencies, such that securing funds to pay for the renovations was a constant struggle. On several occasions between 1994 and 1996, RFI teetered on the edge of bankruptcy, bailed out at the last minute by donations totaling around half a million German Marks (about a quarter of a million U.S. dollars) from the local Department of Social Services, the federal Ministry of Social Issues, the city, and the municipal and statewide GBs.

Support from the city, including the GB, fueled the pattern of growth at the Beginenhof. Simultaneously, federal job-creation programs like ABM presented new opportunities for employment in women's organizations, spurring women to work full time in feminist organizations. The experiences of one member of the first group of employees of the battered women's shelter, Ute, a former school teacher, demonstrate the linkages between the UFV, the GB, ABM funding, and newly conceived feminist organizations. Between drags on her cigarette, Ute explains how she came to be one of the most senior staff members at the battered women's shelter in Rostock:

> So there was the Independent Women's Association, they were already an association here [in Rostock in 1990], and they had these initiatives, one of which was that there should be a shelter for battered women here and that we needed to incorporate a nonprofit to do this. And some of us read about this in the

newspaper. Some women just wanted a new start. And then I thought, too, "Well, just go there, see what they have to say." And so I went. And then I ended up staying there. And for the others [who founded the shelter], it was the same thing, that they wanted to start something new and, well, we didn't know each other, not really. And then so many women founded the organizations, and basically the Gleichstellungsbeauftragte made sure that we got funding through ABM. She talked to some of the founders of the shelter, and said, "Well, now we have these paid positions and you can apply." So we did. And in the beginning, there were fifteen of us who started there and built it up and worked there.

Like many feminist activists in Rostock, Ute is a somewhat accidental activist, having not initially identified with the national UFV. In seeking a career change, she found the battered women's shelter, where the GB secured funding for her position through ABM. Although the ABM funds were federal funds, the women involved with the shelter only became familiar with this resource via the GB.

The GB also provided critical assistance to other organizations by working closely with staff members in the Employment Office and other newly emerging offices and ministries whose work overlapped with that of women's organizations. Programs targeting girls and families found financial support through the Jugendamt (Youth Office), while those focusing on education and job training accessed funds from the Employment Office. The GB guided activists through these bureaucracies and came to serve as a repository of informal information about these institutions, learning from each experience how to navigate better specific institutions the next time an organization was applying for funding. She also developed contacts with bureaucrats sympathetic to women's organizations and steered activists toward, or away from, specific individuals working in state offices depending on how helpful they had been the past.

Because of her location in City Hall and her close connections with the mayor and various city council members, the GB was also able to secure funds that her office could then disburse to women's organizations. While these funds were generally quite limited, they offered seed money and emergency assistance. The GB could point to the high demand for these funds both to establish the vitality of women's organizations in the city and to legitimize demands for increased funding, not just through her office, but through other city, state, and federal departments. Just as the GB helped legitimize the work of women's organizations and the importance of addressing women's issues in local government, the continued presence and growth of the local feminist movement strengthened the GB's claims for institutional support within City Hall. The cycle of mutual reinforcement between the GB and feminist organizations contributed to both of their ability to participate in, and benefit from, local notions of place, which increasingly came to include an understanding of Rostock as a city that treats women well and works toward gender equality.

The Emergence of Neosocialist Feminism

The development of neosocialist feminist ideology as the dominant feminist ideology in Rostock reflects the place character of the city and the resonance of this ideology with the political climate of the city and region. Neosocialist feminism offered activists in Rostock an ideology that harked back to the GDR and that provided seemingly viable solutions to the problems they experienced as most immediate and pressing. Neosocialist feminism, as used in this book, refers to a feminist ideology that emphasizes the economic underpinnings of gender inequalities, views women and men as partners in the struggle to reduce such inequality, and looks to the state to regulate the economy in the interests of greater gender equality.

Focusing on women's status as workers resonates with a local culture of women's autonomy in Rostock. Beyond the continuing legacy of the gender ideology of the GDR, Rostock is a seafaring community. Shipbuilding and fishing comprised the largest segment of the city's economy for centuries and continue to be important, even though the fishing industry in particular has shrunk in Rostock since 1989. As in many seafaring communities, the social organization of family and work life in Rostock has long revolved around frequently absent husbands and consequently independent and high-status wives (Norling 1991). For centuries, women in Rostock have had to serve as the head of the family while their husbands were at sea, often working the land, tending to financial matters, engaging in trade, and making decisions for the family. This type of family economy presaged the GDR's family economy, which also centered on the labor contributions of all adults, not just of men. In some other postsocialist areas, the socialist family model was received as the state-imposed emancipation of women and emasculation of men. This was not the case in Rostock, where the GDR's model of gender relations was congruent with existing local practice and tradition. While in areas where the socialist family model encountered resistance, more traditional gender relations have again taken hold since 1989–90, the importance of women's employment and autonomy still resonates in Rostock after the collapse of the GDR.

Given the emphasis of neosocialist feminism on women's economic position in society, fledgling feminist organizations in Rostock tended to focus on women's economic independence. Feminist organizations quickly recognized that the contraction of the labor market disproportionately affected women, and in different ways than men. While men presumably also suffer emotional and psychological problems when faced with unemployment, women in the former GDR especially had to grapple with changing expectations of women's roles in family, work, and society. According to respondents in Rostock, the shift toward a male-breadwinner model in the unified Germany resulted in significant feelings of depression and worthlessness among women. Accustomed to defining themselves not just as members of families or households but also as workers and professionals, women struggled to adjust to new identities and new values.

Simultaneously, many women embraced unification because it presented new choices for occupational mobility. In the GDR, the state largely set individuals' career paths. Changing jobs, let alone careers, could be very difficult, especially for anyone with specialized training. Unification created new possibilities for exploring different areas and passions, while also limiting the real chances women had at finding any employment. In an effort to help women cope with these changing conditions, women's organizations offered opportunities for adult education and retraining, as well as spaces and events that fostered social support systems to help prevent depression and isolation among un- and underemployed women.

The shifting landscape of career choices and market constraints translated into feminist actions aimed both directly and indirectly at economic redevelopment and women's financial independence. To this end, many of the direct-service organizations in Rostock emphasize helping women achieve financial health. To support women's economic independence, women's organizations in Rostock typically focus on women's financial independence, employment, and job training, while advocating state policies that improve women's chances in the labor market and help mothers and fathers balance work and family.

Amandahaus exemplifies neosocialist feminists' emphasis on coupling women's self-reliance with interdependence and an acceptance of at least some aspects of capitalism. A small group of women in the early 1990s developed Amandahaus as an apartment building for single mothers situated in an historic neighborhood close to downtown Rostock that became one of the most desirable neighborhoods in the city after unification.[5] Realizing that they would be unable to afford renovated apartments in the central city in neighborhoods they preferred, and unwilling to continue to live in unrenovated apartments or far from the city center, these women banded together to purchase an antique building in 1994. The burned-out property was in extremely poor condition such that they had to completely gut and restore the interior. The women and their families completed all but the most technical aspects of the work themselves, working nights and weekends for almost two years and raising funds through donations and a loan from a nontraditional bank. By pooling energy and resources, these women were able to access housing that would otherwise have been out of reach. The group is incorporated as a not-for-profit and each woman and her family have an individual apartment and pay below-market rent to the organization. As one founding member and resident explains:

> We want to keep the rent as low as possible, just enough to cover the credit payments. And if there are two-income-earner families, then they can afford a higher rent than what we ask for here. So if a man and a woman—or whoever—want to live together, then they have to look somewhere else [for a place to live]. . . . We have a sort of surrogate family, and the kids, we all help watch the kids, and we have an environment here for single mothers who work and are active, and we want to make things easier for such women through small favors or help.

While not formally organized as a collective, residents of Amandahaus foster an environment of sharing and mutual assistance. During my many visits there, the doors between apartments were always open and adults and children flowed with ease through the living spaces. In providing affordable housing for single mothers and their families, Amandahaus works to promote women's financial independence while simultaneously encouraging interdependence between women.

Neosocialist feminists approach even issues women's organizations throughout eastern Germany now address, such as domestic violence and sexual abuse, by emphasizing the importance of unequal economic relations between women and men and the damaging effects of unequal gender relations on both women and men. Battering is treated as a side-effect of economic decline and unemployment and the attendant increase in alcohol and narcotic use. Perpetrators of domestic violence are also assumed to have emotional issues that they cannot otherwise express because of gendered expectations of masculinity. Counselors explain men's battering by highlighting how all men are victims of gender inequality. For example, the brochures for the battered women's shelter in Rostock feature various images of Barbie and Ken dolls; the most frequently used image is one in which Barbie is stuck inside a clear plastic water bottle with Ken standing outside of the bottle, his body arranged in what looks like a karate pose. When I asked staff members at the shelter about their interpretations of this image, they offered stories in which both Barbie and Ken are trapped in stereotypical gender roles. Rather than solely viewing the smiling Ken as responsible for Barbie's entrapment in the bottle, they argued that the bottle signifies the synthetic divide between women and men and the public and private spheres. While acknowledging that their intent in selecting this image was to convey that Ken has more power than Barbie, they were also quick to point out that just as Barbie is powerless and trapped by a man within an icon of consumerism—the Evian bottle—so Ken is "locked out of Barbie's world." This interpretation focuses on inequality as detrimental to women and men and as related to commodification and consumerism.

To help equalize gender relations, battered women who undergo counseling are subject to confidence-building work to help them regain their self-esteem with the ultimate goal of securing employment and establishing economic independence from their abusive former spouse. They learn to recognize the "Many Faces of Violence," which include psychological, physical, sexual, social, and economic violence. To counter all these forms of violence, women are taught to respect themselves and to take control of their lives. This process involves not only coming to terms with the abuse and the psychological aspects of trauma but also learning basic financial skills like budgeting, managing a bank account independent of a spouse or partner, and understanding rental agreements.

To promote the idea of economic self-sufficiency, residents of the shelter must pay €15 per day (about US$25), although the welfare office assumes this expense if the woman is a welfare recipient. One of the founders of the shelter explains, "Women must learn to be financially independent. It's like a small rent. You'd have to pay it at home, too. We don't exclude anyone because they are poor—the welfare office pays for those women—but women need to learn to take accountability for their own financial well-being. They should always contribute to the rent."

In stressing the importance of women's financial contributions to their households, shelter employees suggest a causal relationship between women's financial dependence and their physical victimization: women with economic power are less likely to be abused because of the value of their financial contributions. To further help women achieve financial independence, a coalition of local shelters and the State Women's Council of Mecklenburg-West Pomerania (Landesfrauenrat Mecklenburg-Vorpommern, or LFR-MV) pushed the state of Mecklenburg-West Pomerania to become the first and, as of late 2004, the only state in Germany to create legal provisions for evicting battering spouses, rather than battered women, from their homes.

Neosocialist feminist principles are also apparent in the job-training programs feminist organizations offer, most of which welcome women and men in Rostock. The mission statement of the Women's Educational Network exemplifies neosocialist feminist ideology:

> Through its work, the Women's Educational Network aims to foster the equality of women and men as a key part of a democratic polity. For us, women's education and a gender-sensitive adult education for men and women involves: 1. using contents and methods in line with gender equality and gender mainstreaming; 2. making visible gender-specific advantages and resources in education and employment; 3. drawing attention to all forms of deprecation, whether inflicted by ourselves or by others; 4. making women visible in language by using gender-equitable terms; 5. employing holistic methods of teaching and learning; 6. involving all participants in the process; 7. fostering accountability among participants; 8. reflecting on gender-specific patterns in communication processes; 9. learning and teaching from experience, practice, and knowledge; 10. understanding mistakes as chances to learn.

Here, the founding members of the Women's Educational Network recognize women and men as partners working to combat gender inequality. Rather than using the language of oppression or patriarchy, the mission statement invokes less confrontational and more gender-neutral concepts like gender sensitivity and gender equality. Similarly, instead of using the language of male privilege or women's oppression, the mission statement refers to "gender-specific advantages." At no point are either women or men singled out as victim or perpetrator. The mission statement also cites gender mainstreaming, a policy concept that posits that both women and men are hurt by unequal gender relations and that seeks to integrate consideration of gender and gendered effects into policymaking at all levels of governance.

By emphasizing the economic components of gender inequality, women's organizations in Rostock subtly—and sometimes not so subtly—construct gender inequality as an economic problem. In this construction, the dependent woman is seen as a victim not of men, but of an economic system that unjustly differentiates between women and men to the constant disadvantage of women in the labor market and in the home. These victims—whether unemployed women seeking to learn new computer skills or women battered by their spouses—will find emancipation and equality through their own income.

In addition to several direct-service organizations that offer individual women the tools to achieve financial independence, women's organizations pushed for economic policies that would benefit women. By late 1990, one major issue was gender discrimination in the Employment Office, which was rumored to offer equally qualified women and men different job referrals, such that men were usually directed toward higher-paying positions than women. Working in a loose coalition and with the help of the GB, women's organizations drew attention to this issue, resulting in greater awareness about gender disparities in job referrals at the Employment Office and changes in how job referrals there are handled. In a community where women's work is seen as important, neosocialist feminists' emphasis on employment issues receives high levels of public support.

As the gender composition of some professions changed, the UFV and the GB problematized women's overrepresentation among the un- and underemployed and their sudden exclusion from certain professions. The UFV and the GB also attended to how changes in local infrastructure affected women and men differently. Changes in train and streetcar schedules, for example, left many working women stranded and unable to get to work or school, especially as most eastern German couples and families had only one car, and men were most likely to have priority usage of vehicles. The UFV and GB pushed local transportation officials, the Deutsche Bahn (German rail), and unions to reintroduce canceled routes and increase service on other routes.

Women's organizations provide women with improved resources for combining paid employment and motherhood. With more than half of the city's day-care centers closed by 1993, the cost of day care rose precipitously as the availability of day care dropped, contributing to a vicious cycle: low support for parenting, coupled with economic uncertainty, led to a sharp drop in fertility in eastern Germany after 1989, which in turn reduced demand for support for parenting (Dölling, Hahn, and Scholz 2000). Women from the UFV worked with other community organizations to increase access to day-care services. The Beginen offered day-care services beginning in 1990, while Charisma, a center for women and children located in a depressed *Plattenbau* area, began offering day care, kindergarten, and after-school care in 1991. The UFV, along with two organizations of single parents, pushed the city to maintain adequate day-care spaces and especially encouraged the movement toward licensed, in-home child care, which had not existed in the GDR, and, while typically positioning women as caregivers, provides both employment for women and practical support for working mothers.

Through their emphasis on employment issues, the feminist movement in Rostock contributes to the maintenance of the city's character as a place where women's economic contributions are encouraged and valued. Rather than standing in opposition to local norms and values, the local feminist movement has positioned its goals and values as consistent with the city's history and beliefs. The neosocialist feminism practiced in Rostock reflects and reinforces the broader understanding there of women as important actors in economic and family life.

Embedding Feminism in Rostock

I first met Brigitte Thielk on a warm summer day in 2000. Tall with dark hair and olive skin, she is a striking woman. Her voice is rich, soft, and deep; though passionate, her tone remains even and her sentences thoughtful. She bemoaned her recent back problems as she offered me a seat in her compact office overlooking a quiet street corner. Around us, the building was alive with the sounds of progress; like so many buildings in Rostock, City Hall was under renovation.

Brigitte became the second GB of Rostock in 1994. Having worked in the housing office during the GDR, where she spent much of her time handling complaints about housing or trying to find growing families new homes in the face of constant housing shortages, Brigitte is a skilled civil servant, someone who specializes in soothing raw nerves and finding solutions as quickly as possible. In her role as GB, she sees herself as having three primary responsibilities: to protect and expand the rights and roles of women in the city; to support women's organizations and their goals by assisting with funding, networking, and know-how; and to strengthen the feminist movement by drawing attention to women's issues both in the city government and among the public.

Brigitte has been highly effective in achieving these goals. Since accepting the post, she has served as a bridge between women's organizations and city leaders, and she works closely both with women's organizations and with members of the various political parties in city government. Among her various initiatives is the monthly Women's Political Round Table (Frauenpolitischer-RunderTisch) during which local elected and appointed officials speak with women about their work and current issues. The Women's Political Round Table brings key policymakers into discussion with feminist activists, creating an access point for activists to government leaders and serving as a forum for activists to express their concerns and grievances. Past Round Tables have included representatives from the Ministry of Justice in Rostock speaking about policing and personal safety, state representatives discussing gender-equity legislation, and the city's mayor talking about women's issues in the city more generally. The Round Table usually begins with a thirty-minute talk by the guest—or, often, guests—and is followed by discussion and conversation that Brigitte moderates. Many of the directors of women's organizations in Rostock regularly attend, along with employees and volunteers at women's organizations and a handful of local women who are not directly involved in the women's movement. The group meets in the Beginenhof, enjoying tea and snacks from the café there as they talk. Discussion is generally lively and relaxed.

During our first conversation in 2000, Brigitte reflected on her previous five and a half years of experience as the GB in Rostock and discussed the relationship between the Women's Political Round Table and city leaders:

> Even in 1994 when I started [this job], people said, "Who are you? Who is the Women's Political Roundtable? You aren't elected like us in the City Council, so who do you represent?" We said that we may not be elected, but we see what happens in the city, and we just brought ourselves in. And I think we've accomplished a lot in the meantime, that the City Council now recognizes certain issues, and also provides financial assistance, such as the funding of the Beginenhof and for certain personnel there. The city in the meantime spent a large proportion of discretionary funding—so not money that is regulated by law, but where the Council has to set priorities, has to decide that either I want this for my city or not. And we have accomplished that the Hanseatic City of Rostock and its citizens no longer have the courage to take the red pen and say, "We don't want this women's center anymore." That would not happen here. . . . I think this is a major accomplishment that we have already achieved.

Brigitte acknowledges that even by 1994, many residents and political leaders did not recognize the work of the GB and were largely unfamiliar with the principles behind the post. Yet by 2000, in Brigitte's view, women's organizations and her own work as the GB were largely accepted as legitimate and even as important parts of the city's social life. Furthermore, women's organizations were sufficiently institutionalized so that neither the public nor elected officials would discontinue funding. While in neighboring communities, including the smaller neighboring city of Bad Doberan, many women's organizations had already closed by 2000, in Rostock they largely continued to grow through the mid- and late 1990s.

Brigitte and her staff members helped ensure the continued growth of women's organizations, and the institutionalization of both key women's organizations and the GB's office, through several strategies. In developing close relationships with key city leaders, including a mayor who reigned for almost a decade and the major players in each of the three biggest political parties (SPD, PDS, and CDU), Brigitte followed in her predecessor's footsteps by ensuring that women's interests were represented in new initiatives. Using the language of expertise, Brigitte consistently maintained that women's organizations in Rostock provided important services and knowledge and therefore needed to be included in decision making. Over time, she herself came to be viewed as an expert, such that by the late 1990s, city policymakers would routinely seek her assistance in drafting and reviewing new initiatives and agendas.

Importantly, the political climate of the city also offered opportunities for positioning women's issues as important for the welfare of the city and to its sense of place. Since unification, the specific place character of Rostock has supported the work of women's organizations. This place character involves several interrelated trends in the political and cultural climates of the city. Taken together, these dimensions of place in Rostock have presented feminist activists and organizations with opportunities to develop women's organizations, build an effective feminist policy machinery within the municipal government, and position themselves symbolically and discursively as part of the place of the city.

While the CDU remains an important opposition party in city governance, the PDS is a legitimate political actor and has partnered with the SPD in a coalition governing the city. Whereas many eastern German cities and states sought to distance themselves from the postsocialist reincarnation of the SED, particularly in the early 1990s when the dominant national discourse focused on the repressive nature of the SED, Rostock's political culture has never turned its back on the PDS. In fact, support for the PDS increased between 1990 and 2004 (Hansestadt Rostock 2002, 2004). The legitimacy of the PDS and the dominance of the PDS-SPD coalition in city politics is important for feminist organizing not because these parties necessarily started out as interested in women's issues, but because their overall ideology of supporting state interventions in inequality rendered them more amenable to feminist influences. Feminist activists in Rostock widely acknowledge that none of the major German political parties truly satisfy their desire for a platform that explicitly includes women's issues at the national level. Still, they largely view the PDS and SPD as more hospitable to women's concerns—and to issues of inequality broadly—than the more conservative CDU.

In addition, political discourse in Rostock focuses on those aspects of the city that make it unique and often shuns the agenda of the national government. The city has a long history of asserting its autonomy from larger governing bodies. Already as early as 1323, Rostock earned monetary sovereignty from the ruling local princes. Through the collapse of the Hanseatic League in 1699, Rostock maintained its ability to be self-determining. More recently, beginning with the GDR's 1952 land reform and lasting through the creation of Mecklenburg-West Pomerania as a state (*Land*) in 1990, Rostock was its own *Bezirk*, or district, the major subunit of governance in the GDR. Reflecting the power of the city in overseas trade and the economy of the GDR, the Rostock district included the entire Baltic Sea coast of East Germany. The municipal government, the tourism office, and local residents often highlight this history of power, self-sufficiency, and self-determination in representing the city to themselves and to outsiders.

Since unification, the city has persevered in seeking alternatives to policy messages and ideas advanced by the federal state. The unified German government fell out of local favor almost immediately after unification. Many respondents point to the federal decision to make Schwerin, a city less than half the size of Rostock, the state capital of Mecklenburg-West Pomerania after unification as a key source of local distrust for the unified German state. A state official in Rostock, who has also been active in women's organizations, expressed her dismay at this decision, which led her to question national agendas for the city: "For us, it was such a blow when the state capital [of Mecklenburg-West Pomerania] was moved to Schwerin [after unification]. The new government did this just as symbol—we could not be the state capital in the GDR and then in the 'new' Germany. They have tried to destroy all that is tradition here, all that is meaningful to us. But the people will not let that happen. We cannot just stand by and watch while our city is sanitized by the West."

This comment reflects the anguish of losing status as the state capitol and the anger that some residents of Rostock harbor for the unified federal state. Virtually all respondents echoed this sentiment, reflecting the perception that their city is at odds with the national government by highlighting the importance of resistance to the national government's plans for Rostock and Mecklenburg-West Pomerania. While extremely grateful for their democratic freedoms, and for the financial resources of western Germany, activists and community leaders also appreciate that Germany is a federal state, which creates opportunities for local states to develop their own agendas. Respondents consistently represented the national political field as hostile to both women and easterners, while describing the local government as "a bastion of sanity in a crazy world," "a safe haven for women," "responsive and responsible," and "the only level of government that accomplishes anything."

Local animosity toward the federal government was perhaps most pronounced during the chancellorship of CDU leader Helmut Kohl, which ended with his defeat by the SPD's Gerhard Schröder in 1998. While widely championed as the mastermind behind German unification, Kohl's promise of the rapid modernization and integration of eastern Germany did not hold in Rostock or in Mecklenburg-West Pomerania, which continues to take first place as the state with the highest levels of poverty and unemployment in Germany. Disappointment in the unification process and a growing sense of deprivation relative to the old German states, or the states that constituted the former Federal Republic of Germany, and even relative to some of the other new German states, contributed to a local attitude of self-reliance in which municipal and state decision-makers freely shunned federal agendas. So far as many leaders in Rostock were concerned, the federal government was failing to make good on its promises, and it was therefore preferable to focus on local ideas and initiatives.

How outsiders perceive a place also influences its identity. In western Germany, Rostock is often viewed as an underdeveloped backwater. A violent neo-Nazi riot targeting Vietnamese and Mozambican asylum seekers propelled Rostock into the international media limelight in 1992, and, although neo-Nazis from Hamburg (in western Germany) organized that riot, Rostock became an early symbol for the alleged rise in neo-Nazism in eastern Germany.[6] When I told western German family and friends that I would spend months living in Rostock, they consistently responded with a mixture of bewilderment, disapproval, and fear.

Not surprisingly, such negative views from the outside feed into an oppositional identity in Rostock. While recognizing that neo-Nazism is a concern in the city that requires public attention, locals reject accusations that the city harbors large numbers of far-right extremists and present a counternarrative of the city as welcoming to outsiders. Building on the city's status as a port and trading hub, the city prides itself on an outward orientation. Many respondents commented on this aspect of the city's character, noting that the city has a history of openness to new ideas and new people because of its coastal geography and trading activities.

Through the branding of local places, tourism discourses in particular present interesting opportunities for examining narratives of place. Tourist materials in Rostock emphasize the city's eight-hundred-year history, while also noting that it is "still a young city," thanks in large part to the presence of the university. Various tourism campaigns highlighting the Hanseatic history of the city make claims about the city's beautiful coastline and impressive harbors, openness, and internationalism. Visitors from abroad are identified as simply belonging to the makeup of the city. The presence of an active feminist movement reinforces the city's sense of place by contributing to the self-image of openness and commitment to innovation.

Both support for leftist political parties and feelings of animosity toward the federal state reflect a widespread ambivalence toward the city's socialist past. Virtually everyone I spoke with expressed mixed feelings about the benefits and drawbacks of the unified Germany in comparison to the GDR. Most felt that in many core respects, Rostock as a city was better off in the GDR. The city consistently received high levels of support from the SED, which prized Rostock for its economically and strategically critical port, and residents felt valued and respected in the GDR, rather than ignored or maligned, as in the unified Germany.

Respondents reported that the SED seemed less repressive in Rostock than in other cities. This perception may be explained by the fact that respondents also believed that dissident activity in Rostock was quite low. Indeed, northern eastern Germany is often described as having been slow to wake up to the calls for reform in the GDR (Schröder 2003). Although dissident activity was present in Rostock and developed quite strongly toward the end of 1989, Rostock was consistently among the last, or the last, of cities of its size to join specific nationwide protests. When such protests did occur, they were also smaller than in many other cities.

That residents of Rostock were slow to react to the reform movement of 1989 reflects the city's geographic isolation from the rest of the GDR. Large swaths of rural, lightly populated areas surround the city that inhibited effective communication. Religious institutions, which became the primary shelters for dissidents in East Germany, were less powerful in the rural northern regions of the GDR. It would be an overstatement to assert that residents of Rostock were happy in the old GDR; people I met in Rostock, as elsewhere in the new German states, openly criticized aspects of the GDR. Nevertheless, *organized* social movement activity against the SED does seem to have been lower here than in other cities of comparable size, which consequently resulted in less of a need for the SED to engage in surveillance and repression. For the most part, residents of Rostock felt that the SED treated them well and respected the city's contributions to the East German economy and its cultural life.

Feelings of being shunned, ignored, or deprived by the unified German state heighten ambivalent responses to the socialist past. While respondents were unilaterally grateful for increased personal freedoms and an improving standard of living since unification, most also expressed great regret about what they felt had been lost: a sense of community, a feeling of security, and a belief in the importance of the city for its nation. As a whole, these attitudes increased local support for programs and services reminiscent of the GDR, including those women's organizations offer that at once work to maintain a gender ideology more like that of the GDR than of the unified Germany, and to build a sense of community and solidarity among women.

Reinventing Rostock After 1990

Among the federal agendas that municipal officials rebuffed were those promoting welfare-state retrenchment and the introduction of traditional gender roles. Municipal government and the public have supported programs aimed at reducing poverty and inequality. The community maintains a commitment to the public sphere as the appropriate site for redressing inequalities. Faced with unemployment that soared as high as 50 percent in 1991, the city government has long been aware that unemployment is a problem for both women and men, but has not privileged men as primary breadwinners. Instead, the city has sought to support economic redevelopment that would create jobs for both women and men and to improve options for both women and men in balancing paid work and family life.

Of particular concern to city leaders in Rostock—as in other shrinking cities in eastern Germany—is the emigration of young people. Between 1990 and 2000, the population of Rostock dropped by some fifty thousand people, or 20 percent of the city's total population at the time of unification (Hansestadt Rostock 2002). City officials estimate that as many as thirty thousand women between the ages of eighteen and thirty have been among those who have moved to western Germany, Sweden, Norway, the Netherlands, and Denmark in search of employment. This trend is evident in the family dynamics of feminist activists, too: slightly more than a dozen respondents in this sample have adult children, but only two had any children still living in eastern Germany when I first met them in 2000. The outmigration of young people has resulted in a rapidly dropping fertility rate, lost taxes, and an age distribution heavily skewed toward older people. With a growing number of senior citizens, and fewer and fewer younger people to take care of them, the city faces impending demographic and fiscal crises. One respondent lamented that Rostock's best hope for economic revitalization is in nursing homes, where older residents could live and younger people could find jobs. Yet even she conceded that there may not be enough young people to fill those jobs.

Job creation has naturally been at the top of the local agenda. One aspect of this has been developing Rostock as a tourist destination. Each year, more than two million passengers ride the high-speed ferries that depart daily from Rostock's harbor for Denmark, Sweden, Finland, and Estonia. Many major cruise lines, including Crystal Cruises, Norwegian Cruise Lines, Holland America, Celebrity Cruises, and Cunard Cruise Lines, regularly include a stop in Warnemünde, the city's quaint seaside district, on their itineraries. Unfortunately, cruise lines tend to bill this stop as Berlin; cruise-ship passengers disembark in Warnemünde where they board an express train for the three-plus-hour ride to Berlin, bypassing Rostock altogether. Similarly, ferry passengers usually drive to Rostock for the sole purpose of boarding the ferry.

A major goal then has been to entice travelers not just to pass through Rostock, but to spend one or more days there. To this end, the city has spent a great deal of money and energy on renovating the historic inner city and the community of Warnemünde. The city encouraged the renovations of larger hotels both downtown and in Warnemünde and has created tourist-friendly programs and tourism infrastructure. Since 1990, the city has also hosted the annual Hansesail (Hanseatic Sail), a three-day sailing regatta held each August which by the late 1990s was attracting upwards of 150 antique sailing vessels and more than a million visitors each year.

While building the tourism industry in Rostock, city leaders have also long been aware that tourism generally produces low-wage, part-time, and seasonal work—what Germans call "one Euro" jobs because employers may pay only one Euro per hour in the absence of minimum wage laws—that is often completed by women. Consequently, city planners have not focused solely on tourism, but have also attempted to attract other businesses to the city and its environs and to keep existing businesses in the city. The city has played an active role in fostering the development of the maritime industries and has especially focused on expanding the city's harbor and shipbuilding and repair facilities. This included city subsidies for a new, deeper dry dock, the addition of a new pier, and a wider canal to feed large tankers up to the dry docks. The city has also worked to bring western German businesses to Rostock with mixed success.

Creating jobs, however, is not enough to keep women in the workforce. Thus, the city government has also taken steps to maintain day care. After the initial closing of dozens of day-care centers in the early 1990s, mainly because of the loss of federal funding to keep these centers open and because many were located on the grounds of factories that also became defunct, the city turned toward improving day-care availability and quality in 1994. A city initiative provided training for individuals starting day-care centers, either in their homes or in local business districts, and offered financial incentives to individuals who started in-home, flexible, neighborhood day care. While the cost of day care is still widely viewed as problematic, the shortage of day-care spaces eased substantially between 1994 and 2000 with the growth of in-home care.

Although unemployment remains a stubborn social problem in Rostock for women and men, with about one-fifth of the city's adult residents unemployed each year since 1995, respondents overwhelmingly approved of the municipal government's efforts at economic revitalization. Most respondents recognized the complexity of the local economic situation and felt that the city government was performing well in its effort to balance human interests and business interests. Several respondents specifically commented on the city's efforts at making sure that women would benefit from economic revitalization, pointing especially to city support for adult education programs that train women in technology necessary for obtaining positions in many of the smaller technology-driven businesses in the city. Irma, who founded an organization that helps women start their own small businesses, notes:

> I think the city leaders in Rostock have done well trying to make our economy strong again, and it seems we have done much better here than in many other places in the new [German] states. It's especially difficult here because it is such a rural state, and the city is so isolated. But in some ways, perhaps this helps because we can make our own way, and not do what everyone else is doing. In my opinion, Rostock has been especially cognizant of women's concerns in this

regard. They realize that big events only bring short-term jobs, and that cruise ships only create work for trash collectors and waitresses. It's a difficult balance, but our leaders respond to us because we all share the same goal of having jobs available to anyone who wants them, male or female. It helps that we think alike in this way; all of us still believe that in regards to work and women, the GDR had it right, not the West.

Here, Irma acknowledges the complexity of postsocialist economics, but she also asserts that Rostock has done a better job than most cities in taking proactive steps to combat un- and underemployment, especially among women. Her comment highlights how, in her view, the neosocialist feminist ideology of the local women's movement resonates with the broader political climate, providing the feminist movement with greater legitimacy and stronger ties with the local state.

Making a Feminist Future from the Socialist Past

The 1990s began as a tumultuous time in Rostock with so many new opportunities and constraints resulting from the collapse of socialism and the unification of East and West Germany. Initially organized through the local UFV chapter, the young feminist movement in Rostock started out with tremendous energy and optimism, expanding quickly to develop multiple organizations, many of which are formally linked together through RFI and the Beginenhof. Some visions—like a stable, healthy economy and employment market—have yet to be realized, but activists and community leaders overwhelmingly share the feeling that the city and the local feminist movement are heading in the right direction. Together, they are working to construct Rostock as a city that values equality and that protects all of its citizens from the market.

Thanks to a political climate sympathetic to women's issues, and in which the neosocialist feminist ideology of the movement resonates and largely converges with the goals of the local government, women's organizations in Rostock have been able to work effectively with the city government to secure funding for programs aimed at helping women navigate the transformation from socialism to capitalism. In allying itself with state actors, apparatuses, and institutions at the municipal level, the feminist movement in Rostock succeeded in securing stable funding for many of its most central organizations and established the legitimacy of women's organizations that provide social services. Women's organizations and municipal agencies addressing gender issues became increasingly interconnected and interdependent, thereby expanding the capacity and legitimacy of both women's organizations and core state agencies and the femocrats, or feminist state officials, that head them. The pattern of cooperation between women's organizations and the municipal and statewide GBs in particular, which began in the early 1990s, was deeply entrenched by the close of the decade.

Four interrelated aspects of the city's political culture have been especially supportive of feminists' efforts to align themselves as a legitimate and important part of the place of the city. First, the PDS has consistently remained a legitimate political player and the overall political orientation of the city leans to the left. Second, the city sees itself as unique from the rest of Germany because of its political leanings and its geographic isolation. Third, socialism was never thoroughly rejected in public discourse or political life here, and aspects of life in the GDR retain strong public appeal. Finally, support for state interventions in (gender) inequality is high. Coupled with the city's history both as a seafaring community and as home to a large colony of Beguines, feminists in Rostock found themselves in an environment where they could draw on a legacy of women's autonomy and assert their relevance for place with virtually no resistance.

Under these conditions, many of the feminist organizations in Rostock became a solid part of the city's social life. Yet toward the end of the 1990s, funds from the federal government to the new eastern German states became ever scarcer, such that women's organizations reliant on state funding found themselves facing smaller budgets. The city of Rostock could no longer make significant outlays in support of the work of women's organizations. Fortunately, the feminist movement in Rostock also built relationships across scales of social action. The subsequent chapter examines issues of scale and the webs of interaction between the feminist movement in Rostock and other levels of activity, such as the local state of Mecklenburg-West Pomerania, Baltic neighbors, and the European Union.

Fishing for Happiness

My bad luck has struck again. I have seriously injured my foot a few weeks after starting another round of fieldwork in Rostock. My foot and lower leg are in a cast, and I am hopping about gracelessly on crutches that I find impossible to use. My apartment is a third-floor walk-up, and I can barely make it in and out with the crutches. I return to the doctor for my first follow-up appointment ashamed that I have cracked the cast completely.

Although it's an expense I really cannot justify, I start taking cabs to most of my appointments. The three blocks of hopping from my apartment building to the tram stop is more than I can bear when already contending with the stairs. I end up being driven repeatedly by the same talkative driver. He is a tall, solidly built, bearded man, and although the cultural reference is off, he reminds me of a burly lumberjack.

In fact, he is a former fisherman. On our drives around town, he tells me about the problem of overfishing on the Baltic Sea. He rails against a local fish franchise that he thinks offers substandard fish at high prices. He laments his newer status as a landlubber, but tells me with pride about the small skiff he and his wife still sail on their days off. In the GDR, she worked in a fish-processing plant. Now she works as a fish buyer for local restaurants and is the family's primary breadwinner. He boasts about her position, noting his wife's skills in identifying the healthiest, freshest, most flavorful fish. She also knows how to drive a hard bargain.

He seems satisfied with how things have gone for him and his family since unification. Although not delighted with his new occupation, he suspects commercial fishing would have become rough on his body. He's also heard from friends that the practices and organization of the fishing industry have changed, and he's not sure he would still thrive in that workplace.

He thinks the city itself is more beautiful than ever. Sometimes, he says, when the sun is shining just so, he can't believe how colorful and warm Rostock has become. "It was a diamond in the rough," he muses, "and only now is it really starting to shine." I ask him if Rostock could have evolved this way in the GDR, and I am surprised when he answers "yes" without skipping a beat. He insists it might have been even better, if only the SED could have managed the economy better. "Then we could have had all of the beauty outside and been happy as a people. No skinheads, no gamblers, no drunks."

I ask him to tell me what he likes most about Rostock. Not surprisingly, he tells me about the sea, about the smell of sea salt and fish, about the quiet inlets where you can catch eels in the Warnow estuary. He tells me about the view of rustic sailboats, glossy yachts, and rusting steamers crowded along the docks. He tells me about his favorite pub and what seafood dish to order there. He tells me about his old friends, mostly fishermen, with whom he and his wife meet up on weekends to drink beer and grill fish on portable barbeques on their skiffs. He tells me about the feeling of morning fog rubbing against his skin and kissing him with wetness, and about the magic of the seemingly endless sunlight of summer nights. For the duration of the ride, I forget about my throbbing foot.

4 Making Claims Across Scale and Space in Rostock

Looking to Sweden and the EU

RATHER THAN OPERATING IN ISOLATION, places are nested within complex networks that cut across scales. The boundaries between different places and scales are not permanent social facts, but rather evolve over time as the outcomes of social and political processes. Rostock, for example, was formerly part of the German Democratic Republic and the Soviet bloc. Since 1990, it is part of the state of Mecklenburg-West Pomerania, the nation of Germany, and the supranational European Union. Rostock also occupies a particular geopolitical space and interacts with other spaces, most notably within the Baltic region.

In trying to participate in making place, social movements engage in defining the boundaries and relationships between places and across spaces. Social movements also can jump across scales of activity and spaces of differentiation to further their goals. One level of the state or other arena of social action, for example, may offer a different set of opportunities and constraints than another, and social movements can manipulate these differences strategically. Jumping scales can help movements across scales; sometimes gaining legitimacy at one level of action will support expansion to another level, or will reinforce a movement's demands to participate in making place at a different level.

The feminist movement in Rostock participates in, and manipulates, spatial resources to maximize its participation in the place of the city. I focus on three specific relationships, namely those between the feminist movement in Rostock and the state of Mecklenburg-West Pomerania, the Scandinavian nations—especially Sweden—and the European Union. Understandings of the space between each of these scales of activity and the city of Rostock, and how those spaces have changed over time, have been critical to the success of the feminist movement in Rostock.

Feminist Mobilizing at the State Level: Securing a Future for Feminist Organizations

The state of Mecklenburg-West Pomerania is home to 1.85 million people spread over just under nine thousand square miles. The state stretches from east of Hamburg all the way to the Polish border. Two provinces before the Second World War, Mecklenburg and West Pomerania were briefly joined in the postwar period before the GDR split them into separate administrative zones to be rejoined again after German unification in 1990. Mecklenburg-West Pomerania is the least densely populated of the German states and Rostock, a small city with slightly fewer than two hundred thousand residents, is twice as large as any other city in the region. Northern Mecklenburg-West Pomerania runs along the Baltic Sea, while in the far South, the state encompasses the Mecklenburg lake plateau that gives the area the moniker Land of a Thousand Lakes. Most of the state is rural and agricultural; more than two-thirds of the surface area of the state is used for farming. Outside of Rostock and a few small cities, idyllic villages dot the bucolic landscape of gently rolling hills.

Map 4.1 Map of Mecklenburg-West Pomerania

West Pomerania, sometimes called Hither Pomerania in English, is a fragment of the Polish Pomeranian region and runs along the Polish border. The most remarkable pieces of contemporary German Pomerania are the islands of Rügen and Usedom where the gray Baltic crashes onto chalk cliffs and long, sandy beaches. The islands' natural beauty has attracted visitors for centuries. Today, Rügen and Usedom are popular with outdoor enthusiasts and sun-seeking tourists. Poverty and unemployment along the Polish border are the highest anywhere in Germany; in some small border towns, as many as half of adults of working age are involuntarily unemployed. Since unification, these rural areas have benefited from farming subsidies and improvements in farming technology, but have seen little else by way of economic development.

Denmark and Sweden have both ruled over parts of Mecklenburg-West Pomerania at different times, but the region's primary allegiances have been to Germany in the western portion of the state and to Poland in the eastern part of the state. The coastal northern region also has a strong Baltic identity that celebrates trade and fishing on the Baltic Sea. The GDR embraced and maintained this identity, which served its strategic interests economically and militarily. Between 1958 and 1975, coastal cities and towns in Mecklenburg-West Pomerania hosted the Ostseewoche, or Baltic Sea Week, an event intended to promote the GDR's standing in the Baltic region and to pressure the FRG to recognize the GDR (the event was discontinued when the GDR joined the United Nations and signed a treaty with the FRG). Participants included dignitaries from the Baltic nations, Iceland, and Norway, and the event also attracted everyday citizens from these countries. Through such interactions, many people I met in Rostock felt that the Baltic nations had always remained friendly to Mecklenburg-West Pomerania, even during the GDR when other countries, particularly West Germany and other western European nations, were seen as hostile.

Organized dissident activity in the region during the GDR was generally low. This may be explained by four features of the region that echo characteristics of Rostock, as well. First, rural areas typically do not lend themselves to the creation of dissident networks because of the challenges of communication and the absence of the industrial workplaces that facilitated dissident activity in southern East Germany (Probst 1993). Second, the area had relatively weak religious institutions, the primary conduits of dissident activity in East Germany. At the time of unification, only 25 percent of residents of Mecklenburg-West Pomerania and 16 percent of residents of Rostock were practicing Lutherans, compared to a national average of 40 percent (Heinecke 2002; Mazur-Stommen 2003). Third, as an area that was consistently underdeveloped relative to the rest of Germany, many of the subsidization policies of the GDR appealed to struggling farmers, thus inhibiting dissent. Finally, the SED seems to have treated the region reasonably well, taking important symbolic steps to rebuild damaged landmarks after the Second World War and to honor important local traditions, including Baltic identity and the harbor industries, again reducing dissatisfaction.

Mecklenburg-West Pomerania maintained its centuries-old split economic base after unification. Fishing and harbor industries, including shipbuilding, are the economic engine of the coastal region. As in the city of Rostock, the particular family structures associated with seafaring have contributed to widespread acceptance of women's independence and economic activity. Agriculture dominates inland areas, where women have also been vital to family economies, but where more traditional gender norms are more common than along the coasts. Tourism is a rapidly growing economic sector, as well, although the region primarily attracts regional tourists from northern Germany, Denmark, and Sweden, with far fewer visitors from farther away. These specific tourist flows reinforce the region's Baltic identity.

Since the introduction of democracy in 1990, the region's political culture has developed as politically heterogeneous with a leftist twist. Like in the city of Rostock, support for the postsocialist reincarnation of the ruling party of the GDR was higher statewide in the 1990s than in most other eastern German states. The PDS and SPD governed the state in a red-red coalition from 1990 until 2006. Still, the CDU has retained considerable popularity, typically netting between 25 and 30 percent of the vote statewide in elections for the state parliament.

The state parliament sits in Schwerin in the far western portion of the state, but most of the state's major feminist organizations are headquartered some fifty miles eastward in Rostock. In the mid- to late 1990s, the nature of relations between the feminist movement in Rostock and the state government of Mecklenburg-West Pomerania was very similar to that between the movement and the municipal government of Rostock. The government of Mecklenburg-West Pomerania is generally sympathetic to concerns about gender inequality. Political leaders from the PDS, and, to a somewhat lesser degree from the SPD, tend to prioritize reducing social inequality, including gender inequality, and support maintaining or expanding the responsibilities of the state to do so. Also like the municipal government in Rostock, state leaders tend to assert the state's autonomy from the federal government.

The state of Mecklenburg-West Pomerania was frequently a pioneer in passing legislation on women's rights and presented fertile ground for the growth of a powerful feminist policy machinery. The statewide GB remains the most relevant and influential political actor for the feminist movement in Rostock. However, it was the left-leaning orientation of the state parliament and its governors that created opportunities for the GB and women's organizations to advance legislative changes that benefit women and women's organizations.

The most important formal linkage between the feminist movement in Rostock and the government of Mecklenburg-West Pomerania is the Landesfrauenrat Mecklenburg-Vorpommern (LFR-MV, or State Women's Council of Mecklenburg-West Pomerania). During the first three years after unification, the demands made by the women's movement in Rostock focused almost exclusively on the municipal level. Although participants in the UFV continued to fire off letters to the national government, the vast majority of activism took place at, and was concerned with, the city of Rostock. Not until 1993 did women's organizations in the state of Mecklenburg-West Pomerania form a statewide coalition to formally advance their interests. The LFR-MV, first convened in Schwerin, operates out of Rostock, where the overwhelming majority of its member organizations are concentrated. Any organization addressing women's issues in the state may participate by signing a statement of agreement and paying dues in accordance with the financial means of the organization.

According to the original mission statement of the LFR-MV:

> Our goals are (1) the equality and equal treatment of women and men in state politics; (2) women's political participation at various levels of politics; and (3) the strengthening of women's solidarity. The working areas are: (1) consolidating women's interests and overcoming the isolation of women's groups; (2) the mutual exchange of information; and (3) the representation of women's interests in the public, in business, and in politics. The most urgent issues are: (1) the implementation of woman-friendly developments in business and government; (2) the struggle against long-term unemployment among women; (3) the support of child care; (4) the end of financial crisis for single mothers; (5) awareness of gender differences in health care and research for women; and (6) employment opportunities for young women.

In addressing not just women's inclusion in political life but also women's employment and ability to balance work and family, the LFR-MV adopted a neosocialist feminist ideology. Here, women's economic positions and their positions within the family are inextricably linked to their positions in the state.

According to the founders of the LFR-MV, only by advocating for policy changes could women be fully included in economic life.

To achieve their goals of women's increased political participation and economic independence, the LFR-MV attempted to make inroads with state officials. As one founding member, Barbara, relayed:

> From the founding moment on, it was crucial to us that we really put expert political work in the forefront and not just assume a role in which we make demands and participate in polemical discussions. We certainly didn't want to be endless moaners. And we didn't want to be treated as disadvantaged or as some kind of fringe group, which we were at first, but rather as confident women who were capable of having good ideas, drawn from our own life experiences, and as working effectively with others.

Here, Barbara distinguishes between politics and polemics. She notes that it was important to the founders of the LFR-MV that their organization not be perceived as a group of whining women or as some kind of "fringe group." To avoid such interpretations of their work, leaders and members focused on developing their political skills, building a broad coalition headed by articulate women, assuming a more professional presentation, and strengthening the LFR-MV by working closely with state leaders.

Initial efforts were only partially successful. For example, an early attempt at creating a working group comprised of the parliamentarians who were appointed as their party's speakers for women's issues fell apart when, as Barbara recalls, "It became apparent that party solidarity among elected women was stronger than women's solidarity." Yet while unable to organize elected women officials across party lines, the effort paid off in building relationships with individual state representatives, many of whom became important allies as the LFR-MV sought to influence legislation and policy.

Furthermore, activists benefited from the appointment of a statewide GB in 1993. This became the most important office for the LFR-MV. Especially lucky for women's organizations in Rostock was that the first woman appointed to this position was none other than the first municipal GB of Rostock. Already deeply familiar with women's organizations in Rostock and their concerns and demands, she became a key ally for the local women's movement at the state level. She also developed a system to allow the LFR-MV to review and comment on proposed legislation.

The LFR-MV and GB shared many legislative victories in the 1990s, including language in the new state constitution regarding gender equality, legislation specifying the state's obligation to fund shelters for battered women, funding for violence prevention and victim-advocacy programs, resources and state-financed credit for women entrepreneurs, and one of the first gender-equity laws in the new eastern German states.

Women's organizations exerted increasing influence on statewide politics through their cooperation and collaboration with the statewide GB and rapidly earned legitimacy in the eyes of state policymakers and the public. For example, an employee in the state office of the GB recalls how in 2000 and again in 2002 the CDU proposed combining the Office of the Gender Equity Representative with the Ministry of Family Issues, an office more concerned with supporting families than with supporting women. She remembers the response of one key elected leader to this proposal: "'What is this idiocy?' he asked. 'I'll never get this past the people, even if it becomes state law. . . .' Politicians realize that they cannot afford to do away with these positions. The people won't have it, not here."

Indeed, while successful in other eastern German states, the CDU's efforts failed on both occasions in Mecklenburg-West Pomerania and only seemed to rally the feminist movement, sympathetic parliamentarians, and public opinion against CDU politics. In specifying that the public will not tolerate such a move in Mecklenburg-West Pomerania, this state official invokes geographic specificity and the belief that the place of Mecklenburg-West Pomerania has uniquely high levels of support for feminist issues. Even in the face of financial shortfalls in the state's coffers, women's issues were not to be subsumed under the rubric of family. Instead, the office of the GB was firmly entrenched as an important state institution with an agenda for women independent from concerns about family.

Regina, a leader within the LFR-MV, is in a constant hurry, and even among the fast-talking Rostocker, as residents of Rostock are called, the number of words she can slip into one minute in extraordinary. Under her leadership, the LFR-MV has continued to expand its reach with a membership of almost forty women's organizations in 2004, of which thirteen are based in Rostock (including RFI, which itself represents half a dozen organizations) and of which an additional seven have chapters or offices in Rostock. The LFR-MV coordinates five major working groups, including groups dedicated to women's health, women and poverty, violence against women, and equality in business and politics. The working groups frequently report their findings and concerns both to other members of the organization and to state actors, including the statewide GB and relevant ministries, such as those for health, family, culture, rural development, business, and employment.

In spite of close ties to the statewide GB, the organization remains relatively autonomous with no state intervention in its daily operation. A staff member at one member organization reflects a common feeling when she asserts that the goals of the LFR-MV would be the same regardless of whether the statewide GB happened to have the same goals. This is difficult to assess; through 2004, the LFR-MV and the statewide GB's office had never encountered a major difference of opinion. The actors involved maintain that if a conflict were to emerge, the LFR-MV would be as likely to unduly influence the GB as the GB would be to unduly influence the LFR-MV. While the GB holds the purse strings, the LFR-MV can harness the force of an extensive, statewide web of politically experienced women that seems to result in a balance of power between the two offices rendering the LFR-MV and the GB mutually interdependent.

When asked which organization she thinks is the most successful and far-reaching in the state, Kathrin, a senior staff member in the statewide GB's office who is also a lifelong resident of Rostock, points to the LFR-MV without hesitation. She says that her work, and that of her office, would have been nearly impossible without the lobby of the LFR: "Without this work [on the part of the LFR-MV], at least half would fall apart." This is due in part to Regina's strong leadership. Kathrin posits that "honestly, no one gets past [Regina] anymore." The LFR-MV is, in Kathrin's estimation, an entrenched institution that contributes to the identity of the state and a force with which policymakers and politicians must reckon.

Even within this supportive environment, constantly shifting economic conditions continue to create funding problems for many women's organizations. State coffers steadily shrunk each year after 2000. Battered women's shelters, for example, saw a 3 percent annual reduction in their state funding during each of these years. While these cuts are still among the smallest anywhere in Germany, women's organizations in Rostock are well aware that they must diversify their sources of income and reduce outlays in order to survive. Jumping scales has proven fruitful for reaffirming the right to participate in place at the level of the municipality and the state and for securing resources for feminist organizations.

Becoming European:
The EU's Agenda for Gender Mainstreaming in Rostock

The offices of GM Consult are housed in a quaint brick building in the shadow of Rostock's largest church. The building was renovated after unification and has become a second hub for women's organizations in the city, housing the offices of half a dozen women's organizations, including those of the LFR-MV and the Women's Educational Network. On an unusually warm morning in late September, I climb the two flights of stairs leading to the offices of GM Consult, where I am scheduled to meet one of its founders, an elfin woman named Uschi. I am welcomed at the top of the stairs by Uschi's assistant, who invites me to sit me down and immediately begins a friendly interrogation about my life in the United States.

When Uschi appears a few minutes later, she welcomes me into her office with a hearty handshake. Her office is spacious with sleek furnishings and a smattering of potted plants; several windows and skylights fill the room with bright light. We seat ourselves in a lounge area away from her desk. She perches on the edge of a chair and arranges a pile of papers and brochures she has apparently collected for me. Her features are small and sharp, but her eyes are warm and open; she promptly suggests that we use the informal *Du* instead of the formal *Sie*.

With a doctorate in the social sciences, Uschi lost her job during the massive educational restructuring that followed unification. Shortly thereafter, she obtained a position as the director of a community organization. In 1993, after a difficult pregnancy, she requested that the board of directors of the community organization allow her to continue her position as a part-time employee since her child, who had medical issues, needed her at home. The board of directors, which was comprised entirely of men, rejected her request, and she was ultimately forced to resign in order to care for her child.

Frustrated by this experience, Uschi sought out the young feminist movement in Rostock, joining the UFV and participating in events hosted by other women's organizations, such as the LFR-MV. Yet she felt uncomfortable with some of the attitudes she encountered among women working with these organizations. Uschi was concerned about what she saw as an overemphasis on women's needs in the local feminist movement, even among other neosocialist feminists. While laughingly acknowledging that she quickly became "the woman who always talked about men," she was genuinely interested in improving the situation of both women *and* men. Ultimately, she found what she was looking for in gender mainstreaming, learning about it in late 1995, just as the concept began to enter the European arena. She reflects, "For me, equality was always two-sided [involving both women and men]. I rediscovered this in the EU, specifically in gender mainstreaming, and said to myself, 'This is totally silly! I need to *do* something, and not just sit around and think.'"

Do something indeed she did. In 1996, with the assistance of GB Brigitte Thielk and other activists, Uschi submitted a successful proposal for EU funding through the EU's Fourth Action Program for Equal Opportunity for Women and Men. She received four years of funding for a gender mainstreaming project within the Women's Educational Network.

Through this new project, Uschi began to learn and to educate others about gender mainstreaming. She traveled to various seminars on gender mainstreaming and soon began teaching such seminars herself. When the initial grant money expired, she successfully applied for a renewed grant from the EU, this time with the assistance of both the GB of Rostock and the statewide GB. She and a colleague, a professor at a nearby university, published a handbook that is widely used by gender mainstreaming advocates throughout Germany and that has become standard issue during training sessions on the topic. In that same year, Rostock became the first city in Germany to pass a gender mainstreaming resolution.

Since its formal introduction into the European Commission in 1996, gender mainstreaming has been the source of considerable confusion and consternation among EU policymakers and the EU public alike. According to the Group of Specialists of the Council of Europe, gender mainstreaming is "the (re)organization, improvement, development and evaluation of policy processes, so that a gender-equality perspective is incorporated in all policies, at all levels and at all stages, by the actors normally involved in policymaking" (Group of Specialists on Mainstreaming 1998). Alternately described in EU documents and by gender mainstreaming advocates as a theory, method, tool, strategy, concept, approach, program, framework, or mechanism (Booth and Bennett 2002), gender mainstreaming seeks to provide new approaches for gender-sensitive policymaking by drawing attention to how policies at various levels of governance may differentially affect women and men and by redressing differences when they are discovered. Recognizing that even policies that appear gender neutral can have a differential impact, the gender mainstreaming approach calls for examination of the potentially gendered effects of policies, ideally before they are implemented (Squires 2007).

A core assumption underlying gender mainstreaming is that gender is socially created and embedded in organizations, including the state. Rather than denying the state's complicity in gender inequality, the gender mainstreaming framework recognizes that states (re)produce gender relations and inequalities and therefore must be activated if gender equality is to be achieved (Schmidt 2005). Specifically, gender mainstreaming accepts the feminist contention that many state policies and practices that appear to be gender neutral are, in fact, based on men's interests and an expectation of men citizens. Gender mainstreaming also calls for an interrogation of state policies to identify if and how gender is embedded. Gender mainstreaming pushes for incorporation of gender issues into all aspects of governance and public policy and moves against the treatment of women's issues as a distinct policy problem (Mazey 2001).

The gender mainstreaming approach also holds that gender inequalities harm both men and women. The goal, then, is to alter social structures so that gender inequalities are neutralized. Gender mainstreaming is thus different from equal treatment and positive action, which typically target only women in their efforts at placing women on equal footing with men, and represents a "third path" toward gender equality (Rees 1998). Gender mainstreaming also implies a vision of a future in which women and men share equal responsibilities in work, family, and politics.

To date, scholarship on the implementation of gender mainstreaming has largely focused either on implementation within the EU itself (for example, Pollack and Hafner-Burton 2000; Shaw 2002) or on differences in implementation between the member states (for example, Beveridge, Nott, and Stephen 2000a; Beveridge, Nott, and Stephen 2000b; Liebert 2002). However, the autonomy of local states allows smaller-scale levels of government to deviate from expectations set forth by the national state apparatus (Greer 1986; Martin and Miller 2003). In embracing gender mainstreaming, the city government in Rostock and the state government of Mecklenburg-West Pomerania established themselves as a pioneers within Germany on gender issues (Guenther 2008). Although the federal government has begrudgingly adopted the minimum requirements for gender mainstreaming set by the EU and is widely viewed as a laggard state on this issue, the early and enthusiastic response to gender mainstreaming in Rostock and Mecklenburg-West Pomerania again suggests that this region is, indeed, importantly differentiated from the German federal state. This differentiation characterizes Rostock and is an important part of the city's sense of place.

Resisting the West, Embracing the North: The Spatial Alliance with Sweden

A key part of embracing the EU and its agenda for gender mainstreaming involves identification with Scandinavian, and especially Swedish, models of politics and social life. The political culture in Rostock embraces local autonomy from the national state. Although only about 115 miles from the western

German city of Hamburg, Rostock, as the largest city in the most rural state in Germany, is an isolated city that is not well connected to western Germany. The *Autobahn*, Germany's famed highway system, only reached Rostock a decade after unification, and the city has neither a major airport nor access via the German high-speed railway system.

While relatively isolated from other parts of Germany, Rostock has high-speed ferry access to several Scandinavian nations, and in many respects, participants in this study from Rostock identify more with their Scandinavian neighbors than with the unified Germany. Rostock sits directly across the Baltic Sea from Sweden and, even in the GDR, maintained close ties to its northern neighbor. Some respondents explained their initial openness to Sweden as the consequence of historic connections between Rostock and Sweden, pointing out that even during the GDR, Sweden, a neutral country, maintained ties with East Germany. While West Germany treated the GDR as an enemy, Scandinavian states offered friendship and cooperation.

Map 4.2 Map of the Baltic Sea Region

These feelings of goodwill continued in Rostock after unification. Daily ferry service between Rostock and various Scandinavian nations ensures a regular flow of people across borders. Rostock's annual Hansesail is a perennial favorite among Swedes, Danes, and Finns, who are also frequent vacationers in the city's beach district. Swedes constitute approximately 10 percent of the home audience for the games of the FC Hansa soccer team based in Rostock. Workers in the hospitality industry in Rostock routinely learn to speak basic Swedish and Danish, and Scandinavian nations are common destinations for outmigrating young people and vacationers from Rostock. Fully half of respondents mentioned such travel (Swedish and Norwegian fjord tours and Danish beach vacations seem especially popular), and at least four respondents in Rostock have adult children who moved to Sweden, Norway, or Denmark.

Given the history of cooperation between Rostock and Sweden, and the political climate in the city overall, it comes as no surprise that the introduction of gender mainstreaming, a policy paradigm already entrenched in Sweden, is generally well received in Rostock. Crucial to this reception is the creation of a spatial alliance between Rostock and Sweden. Beyond simply framing the issue of gender mainstreaming as Swedish, a spatial alliance allows inhabitants of Rostock to claim membership in a geographically and geopolitically bounded area to which they do not ostensibly belong, namely Sweden or, more broadly, Scandinavia. Both feminist activists and state leaders who look to Scandinavia, rather than to the federal German state, for models of social policy, quality of life, and ideology created and maintain this spatial alliance. The cultural emphasis in the city lies on Rostock's history as a Hanseatic city, as is reflected in its hosting of the annual Hansesail and participation in the annual Balticsail, as well as through political rhetoric that often describes Rostock not as a German city, but as "Baltic" or "northern European." The tourism office pitches Rostock as a "gateway to the North," and "the first step to Scandinavia" and promises visitors an "un-German experience." Taken together, the historic connection with Scandinavia, the current desire to maintain autonomy from the national state, and the local rhetoric emphasizing Rostock's traditions as a Hanseatic city contribute to the legitimacy of the spatial alliance with Sweden.

The spatial alliance had important practical implications for the diffusion of gender mainstreaming and other gender-equity practices to the feminist movement in Rostock. Given how closely tied Rostock is to Sweden, many government officials and feminist activists made the sea voyage to Sweden to study its system of governance and the effects of its social policies, especially with regard to gender relations and inequality. Between 1996 and 2000, the Women's Educational Network and other women's organizations in the city, including the LFR-MV, sponsored more than a dozen educational trips to Sweden. Participants included feminist activists and several key political leaders in city and state offices. Through these exchanges, activists and politicians learned about both the benefits of social democratic policies for women, as well as about the problems experienced by women in Sweden and other Scandinavian states.

Uschi recounts the importance of the Swedish influence in her own work, while also addressing the importance of interorganizational networks:

> We tried quite hard to build this project out of the Swedish experience. In Sweden, people just take gender mainstreaming for granted; it's just seen as something normal, as something that simply belongs in society, and as something that benefits everyone, women and men. And somehow it's fun and just a part of their quality of life, and so we said, "Good, we'll go check this thing out, to see what it's all about," and then we organized many educational trips to Sweden. We also took many politicians with us so that they could just see what the situation there was like and truly experience the spirit of it, and we did a lot of publicizing about Swedish equality politics and gender mainstreaming. And Rosamund organized a whole series of events about it, and really worked to build up a network. . . . And it became ever clearer to me that gender mainstreaming was practical, and that we really needed to bring it into our politics here, and also into the regional politics of Mecklenburg-West Pomerania. And with the help of the LFR-MV, we did just that.

Clearly impressed by the level to which gender mainstreaming is integrated into daily life in Sweden, Uschi, along with colleagues at other women's organizations, including the Women's Educational Network and the LFR-MV, made it a priority to encourage direct experiences with gender mainstreaming by bringing activists and politicians to Sweden.

These trips were popular; in fact, the majority of participants in this project had direct contact with Swedish feminists and policymakers, either through educational trips to Sweden, or through visits to Rostock by Swedish feminists and policymakers. Many work regularly in a transnational and regional advocacy network (or TANs: see Keck and Sikkink 1998; Zippel 2004) with feminist leaders and policymakers in Sweden, sharing ideas, information, and strategies during in-person meetings and via the Internet. As a staff member in the GB's office in Rostock told me:

> We were in Sweden often—well, not me personally—I have only been there once—but many women from Mecklenburg-West Pomerania were there through women's organizations, which sponsored these educational trips to Sweden and really helped us build very close relationships there. Rostock also has a sister city in Sweden, Göteburg, and back in 1999 . . . we also had an International Women's Day event and really invited people from our sister cities . . . and many came from our sister city there, even the [female] mayor of Göteburg. We heard a lot about Sweden and how gender politics there work. Sweden is really the world leader in that regard, in my opinion.

Activists and political leaders in Rostock repeatedly invoked their efforts at following the Swedish model of high levels of state support for working parents and for gender mainstreaming, implicitly or explicitly critiquing the German federal state's approach to gender relations and inequality. Although most respondents recognized that even Sweden continues to experience significant gender disparities in employment, as well as other evidence of persistent gender inequalities, activists in Rostock generally felt they had more in common with Sweden than with Germany in terms of gender politics and feminist goals. A politician with the PDS, for example, notes that Swedish social policies "simply make more sense" in Rostock than those set forth by the federal German government, a sentiment other respondents widely echoed. This construction of the place of the city as tied not only to Germany but also to Scandinavia reinforces a sense of autonomy from the national state and a local understanding of Rostock and Mecklenburg-West Pomerania as highly progressive in their adoption of Swedish models of social and political life.

The spatial alliance between Rostock and Sweden, and the almost complete absence of such an alliance between Rostock and western Germany, provides support for gender mainstreaming and for the broader goals of the local feminist movement. While not entirely uncontested, the concept of gender mainstreaming largely resonates with feminists, policymakers, and the public and certainly appears to be more appealing in Rostock than western German feminism. In presenting gender mainstreaming as Swedish in origin, feminist activists have been able to establish the congruence between gender mainstreaming and Rostock's image of itself as aligned with its more gender-egalitarian northern neighbor.

Nowhere is the city's support for gender mainstreaming more evident than in the passage of a gender mainstreaming ordinance in 2001. With this innovation, Rostock became the first city in Germany to formalize its commitment to gender mainstreaming, and, as of 2005, it remained the only city in Germany to have introduced or passed a gender mainstreaming resolution.[1] The implementation of gender mainstreaming at the municipal level was possible due to the overall support for gender mainstreaming in the city, the close working relationships between gender mainstreaming advocates in women's organizations and the city GB, the capacity of the GB's office, and the GB's connections with city council members who were willing and able to introduce and support the initiative.

The city's GB, Brigitte Thielk, played a central role in the introduction and adoption of the gender mainstreaming resolution. As Brigitte told me, she discussed the possibility of introducing gender mainstreaming into the city government with several members of city council. A city council member from Bündnis 90 (Alliance 90), a center-left party, was especially interested in introducing an ordinance about gender mainstreaming and asked Brigitte to help her in drafting the resolution. With the assistance of various staff members and Uschi, they developed a preliminary draft in 2000.

The language of the measure provided important symbolic support for gender mainstreaming and also has concrete expectations for assessing and addressing gender disparities in Rostock. The primary provisions of the resolution were that all measures, resolutions, and laws established by the city council and the mayor's office must be examined and tested for gendered effects. Furthermore, the Office of Statistics and Elections, along with various other departments, would need to track gender disparities among employees of the city, including those working for subcontractors and directly for the city, and in programs and organizations that receive city funding. For example, the new law would require that the city develop an annual report on the gender composition of its workforce with analyses of gender disparities in salary. Similarly, the Office of Cultural Affairs would have to track the gender composition of both guests and the included artists at art exhibitions it sponsors. Depending on the findings, corrective measures would be required.

Brigitte reported that the bulk of resistance she encountered to the resolution on the part of other city officials was based not on ideological differences, but on concerns about the changing responsibilities of different offices. The Office of Statistics and Elections balked at the idea of keeping track of extensive new data on gender inequality, and Brigitte herself was alarmed when it was suggested that her office be responsible for collecting and disseminating statistical data. When the resolution came before the council, it received almost unanimous support. The resolution was an undisputed victory for Brigitte and the resolution's cosponsors.

Brigitte and her collaborators within City Hall utilized various tools and re-sources to garner support for the resolution. First, Brigitte mobilized her existing networks with feminist activists to acquire their endorsements of the proposed resolution. Even activists with some reservations about gender mainstreaming supported the effort to pass the resolution because they thought it was likely to draw renewed attention to issues of gender inequality. Second, Brigitte and her collaborators had access to expert knowledge, largely through GM Consult and the Women's Educational Network. Harnessing the brain power and technocratic knowledge of women who had attended Swedish and EU seminars and confer-ences on gender mainstreaming, and who were responsible for developing various educational materials about gender mainstreaming for the courses they taught on the topic, Brigitte provided council members with detailed information about gender mainstreaming. She was also able to point city council members to addi-tional resources available in their community. GM Consult's success in securing EU and statewide funding in 2000 to develop a statewide gender mainstreaming coalition also established the legitimacy of gender mainstreaming in that this funding influx clearly suggested that the EU and the state of Mecklenburg-West Pomerania regarded gender mainstreaming as important and worthwhile. Fi-nally, Brigitte and her collaborators drew on the spatial alliance between Rostock and Sweden, the growing local interest in tapping into EU resources, and the city council's reservations about the German federal state by highlighting that gender mainstreaming was initially developed by Swedes, propagated by the EU, and largely ignored by the federal German state. Both the origin of the concept and its actual content, which reflects neosocialist feminist principles in spite of its own neoliberal origins, resonated with members of the city council.

The resolution evidences the influence of Swedish ideas and neosocialist feminism. The preamble to the resolution on gender mainstreaming in Rostock begins:

> In Sweden, equality between women and men is viewed as a critical precondition for the positive development of society and is therefore understood as a central issue for women and men. The goal of gender-equity politics is the achievement of an equitable society that reaches all classes of people and offers the same

rights, responsibilities, and opportunities to women and men in all realms of life. The following goals were established by the [Swedish] government: (1) the equal distribution of power between women and men; (2) the same opportunities for economic independence for women and men; (3) the same conditions and opportunities for women and men with regard to entrepreneurship, work, promotion, and other work-related situations including possibilities for development and advancement in employment; (4) the same educational access for girls and boys, women and men, and the same opportunities for developing their personal ambitions, interests, and talents; (5) the same responsibility for men and women for work in the household and with children; and (6) freedom from sexual (and gender-specific) violence.

The preamble thus specifically invokes the Swedish example and offers an interpretive review of the Swedish approach. Given its emphasis on women *and* men, its attention to economic issues, and its emphasis on gender sameness, this review echoed neosocialist feminist ideas and broader leftist discourses about equality already dominant in Rostock.

In making reference to the creation of "an equitable society that reaches all classes of people," the review also echoes the Marxist-Leninist rhetoric of the GDR, thereby linking gender mainstreaming to the socialist past. Gender mainstreaming is reminiscent of the gender ideology of the GDR, but it should not be understood as identical, in part because the GDR often espoused ideas it failed to enact in any meaningful way.[2] Furthermore, gender mainstreaming advocates problematize gender inequality in ways that the GDR and its ruling party, the SED, did not. Although the SED encouraged a view of men and women as equal partners in the socialist project, activists from Rostock assert that the GDR discouraged critical dialogue about gender inequality, adopting a strategy that silenced any claims that it was not equitable.

My conversation with Alice, the director of an organization dedicated to women's employment issues and an advocate of gender mainstreaming, demonstrates her ideas on the differences between feminism, gender mainstreaming, and the gender ideology of the GDR:

Katja: So in principle, gender mainstreaming is more like the politics of the GDR than like feminism?

Alice: You have to be careful with feminism. Feminists have never paid attention to men. I don't honestly think I understand that. We don't need to fight against men. And that's what always bothers me about it.

Katja: Right, that's what I meant. That maybe this is more like the GDR's ideology—

Alice: Yes! . . . Men were also—well, they had no problem with equal rights [in the GDR]. But it was also the case that we [women] were too stuck in the women's sphere. Just think about the Household Day in the GDR—only women could take this day off.

In this exchange, Alice maintains that feminism wrongly pits women and men against each other. However, she also asserts that the GDR's promise of gender equality was rarely realized. Like many critics of the GDR's "mommy politics," she observes that family-friendly policies often placed women at a disadvantage relative to men. As an example, she points to the Household Day (more often referred to as *Muttitag*, or Mother's Day), which allowed workers one day off each month to attend to household errands, like doctor's visits, shopping, and so forth. However, until the mid-1980s, only women and single men with children were permitted to use the Household Day, such that the policy shifted responsibility for family life away from men and onto women.

Monika, who sits on the board of directors of a women's organization addressing employment issues, explains why gender mainstreaming resonates especially well in Rostock in spite of its clear linkage to the EU's focus on markets. In a portrait of women's experiences in the GDR that is rosier than Alice's, she comments on gender mainstreaming:

You will conclude that there is a difference between East German and West German women in that respect [in terms of their level of support for gender mainstreaming]. For East German women, it's an idea that they carry with them, that they understand, that they think is good, and where they also think that it's a solution to real problems. For West German women, it's more about fear because this whole time, they really had to fight to get these spaces and this recognition. So they are afraid that gender mainstreaming will result in them losing the ground they worked so hard for and fought so much for. That's just not the case among East German women because they never had to fight for anything [in the GDR]. They were simply told that the state valued them and that they would be taken care of, whether they wanted to be or not. They never worked or fought for anything. And through that experience also came this knowledge that you *can* work with men, you *can* do things with men.

In Monika's account, the GDR introduced and reinforced the idea of men and women working together, which is also a core component of gender mainstreaming. In comparing the reception of gender mainstreaming in eastern and western Germany, Monika recognizes that western German feminists experienced tremendous hardship in gaining recognition and legitimacy, whereas in East Germany, women were largely handed state protections and rights without ever asking for them. Consequently, women in eastern Germany experienced men and the state as allies rather than as enemies. This history, coupled with the support of the spatial alliance with Sweden, renders gender mainstreaming highly resonant in Rostock, and it enables feminist activists in Rostock to overlook the EU's interest in gender mainstreaming as a tool for labor market activation in a free-market system. Thus, local lenses in Rostock refilter the supranational agenda of the EU to align with local needs and frames.

Skipping Scales:
Rostock's Feminist Movement, the Federal State, and the EU

Jumping scales has proven overwhelmingly beneficial to the feminist movement in Rostock. Activists in Rostock embrace the local governments at the municipal and state level, as well as the EU, but strategically skip engaging with the federal German government or a national public. They agree that the local state and the EU are far more concerned with, and active about, women's and gender issues than the federal German state. Few activists I spoke with could find anything redeeming about the national state, although they continue to emphasize that they are, on the whole, grateful for unification. However, their gratitude is rarely expressed in terms of political support for the national state apparatus; instead, most respondents point to increased career choices and travel opportunities as the best changes since unification. They appreciate no longer living under a repressive form of socialism, but they do not embrace the policies and practices of the unified federal state.

The women I met in Rostock were sharply critical of the national state apparatus, which they typically described as representing men, businesses, and western Germans. Most viewed the national state as impenetrable and as closed off to them and their interests. While these women continue to vote in national elections, suggesting that they think who serves in national elected office does matter at least a little, they view organizing to target the national state as futile. Many women pointed to national leaders' disregard for the UFV in 1989–90 as evidence that feminists would not be listened to in the capitol.

Feminist activists reported feeling thwarted, ignored, and shut out by the national state as women, feminists, and eastern Germans.

In contrast to the city of Rostock and the state government of Mecklenburg-West Pomerania, the federal state is indeed closed to feminist interests. The feminist policy machinery within federal institutions is notoriously weak, and the West German feminist movement also had not established inroads prior to unification. That the local became the most important arena of activity for feminists reflects several interrelated dynamics. Women across cultures and political systems are most likely to organize at the local level. In Germany, the institutions and agencies most relevant for feminist organizing—such as GBs— are strongest at the local level and weaker at the federal level. As a federal state, most policy decisions about gender issues in Germany occur at subnational levels of governance. There has never been a strong national feminist movement in Germany, and the chances of such a movement emerging after unification and overcoming the East-West divide seem low. These structural conditions have contributed to the localization of feminist activity throughout Germany.

Since the late 1990s, the EU has become almost a substitute for the federal state in the minds of many activists and policymakers in Rostock, who see their interests as more aligned with the EU than with the federal German state, and who view the EU as granting greater autonomy and self-direction than the federal state. This is not to say that feminists in Rostock don't criticize the EU sometimes, too. Most respondents in Rostock were critical of the EU for promoting a neoliberal economic agenda that stresses privatization. Many also view EU bureaucrats as disconnected from local issues and thus misguided in some of their efforts at economic redevelopment. One of the most frequently lambasted programs I heard about from respondents was an EU initiative to retrain women agricultural scientists as florists, a laughable deskilling. More commonly, however, activists view the EU as an engine of positive change, particularly insofar as the EU has brought public attention to issues of human rights and social inequalities across the member states, and many describe the EU as a source for cutting-edge ideas in terms of social issues.

Women's organizations in Rostock have profited from the new attention to gender mainstreaming and the increasing influence of the EU. For some organizations, like GM Consult, the EU is primarily responsible for their existence. In other cases, EU funding provided much-needed, albeit nonessential, funding. The Women's Technical Center is such a case. Because it offers educational programs to unemployed women and men, it receives payment from the Employment Office on a per-pupil basis. This funding, however, was insufficient for maintaining employee salaries and covering overhead costs. Although the center might have survived on payments from the Employment Office, occasional donations, and smaller grants through the city and statewide GBs, its exponential growth in the late 1990s and early 2000s was made possible by the EU's EQUAL initiatives, part of the EU's program for employment and social inclusion. EQUAL funded the center's largest program, Feminet, and its successor, Feminet XXL. Feminet offered computer-training programs to un- and underemployed women living in the rural areas of Mecklenburg-West Pomerania; Feminet XXL trained graduates of Feminet in computer instruction in the hopes of propagating the program.

The shifting orientation among women's organizations toward the EU reflects ideological identification with the EU's gender mainstreaming agenda, capitalization on a strategic alliance that increases the legitimacy of the feminist movement at home, and the more pragmatic issue of shifting funding sources. In the late 1990s, women's organizations in Rostock witnessed the scaling back of many city and statewide funding pools due to the softening economy and the shrinking tax base in Rostock and Mecklenburg-West Pomerania. However, during this same time period, the EU increasingly introduced funding programs that required matching funds from local agencies, or that were entirely funded by the EU's structural funds. Many women's organizations tapped into these new money sources, capitalizing on the EU's interest in women's issues, or what the EU typically terms social inclusion without respect to gender, especially as they pertain to employment, economic development, and violence against women. Consequently, those organizations that were able to access EU funding experienced significant growth in the late 1990s and especially the early 2000s. Simultaneously, those organizations that in the late 1990s began utilizing funds not specifically earmarked for women's organizations—for example, the Women's Educational Network, which drew on funding for state-accredited adult education programs—also flourished.[3]

The feminist movement in Rostock makes use of EU policy paradigms and funding programs, but it does not specifically attempt to engage in any type of dialogue with the EU or EU institutions. While the relationship between the feminist movement in Rostock and the city and local state governments center on an open feedback loop, the relationship between the feminist movement and the EU is a one-way street in spite of the presence of mechanisms that make mutual engagement feasible. Although there are occasional complaints about

EU policies and practices, no feminist organizations in Rostock acknowledged or knew of any effort to challenge EU policies or programs. Instead, the EU is seen as a benevolent benefactor with its own unalterable direction and logic.

Becoming Baltic and European

The feminist movement in Rostock primarily targets the city government and the local public in its efforts to effect change. However, the city does not operate in a vacuum, but rather is nested within multiple layers of place. It is part of the local state of Mecklenburg-West Pomerania and the nation of Germany. It is also a subunit within the European Union. These formations are quite recent compared to the city's historic identity as a Baltic Sea port, which links it to the Baltic region and especially to Sweden, Poland, and Denmark.

Spatial forces played important and interrelated roles in shaping the feminist movement in Rostock. The state of Mecklenburg-West Pomerania offered feminists a political environment similar to that within the city of Rostock. The strength of the political left and ambivalence about unification across the state provided traction for feminist claims to state interventions and public attention to issues of inequality. Feminists have been able to work successfully within the state government, especially through the State Women's Council.

Given the state's long-standing ties northward—ties that predated unification by centuries—and admiration for the social democratic principles of Sweden, Rostock and the state of Mecklenburg-West Pomerania built a spatial alliance with Sweden. This spatial alliance reinforces the city's image of itself as innovative and un-German, while also strengthening the appeal of the basic tenets of neosocialist feminism. These factors all contributed to the feminist movement's ability to establish its legitimacy with policymakers at the municipal and statewide level, and to co-opt and expand the capacity of key state offices at both of these levels.

Mobilizing the spatial alliance between Rostock and Sweden, activists in Rostock championed the EU's gender mainstreaming agenda as a new and innovative method for tackling gender inequality. While reminiscent of the gender ideology of the GDR, activists presented gender mainstreaming as an exciting new possibility for reducing gender inequality. Gender mainstreaming, and especially its implementation in Sweden, its propagation by the EU, and its resonance with the gender ideology of the GDR and neosocialist feminism, appealed to city and statewide leaders' desire to ally themselves with the Baltic North and the EU rather than with the federal German state.

In gender mainstreaming, activists and policymakers found a new tool for challenging the federal state's agenda for gender relations. Rather than accepting the unified Germany's vision of women and men as operating in separate spheres, activists and leaders in Rostock continued to assert the potential for *sameness* between women and men through neosocialist feminism and its incarnation in gender mainstreaming. Local state support for gender mainstreaming, coupled with an effective feminist policy machinery, translated into new laws and programs in both the city of Rostock and the state of Mecklenburg-West Pomerania to institutionalize gender mainstreaming. In promoting gender mainstreaming and tying itself to Swedish models of gender, the feminist movement was able to participate in the city and region's important spatial alliance with Sweden, thereby increasing the movement's legitimacy and capacity at home. The local feminist movement in Rostock has organized at multiple scales, choosing arenas of engagement that not only hold the most promise for successful outcomes but that also feed back to support the movement's claims to be part of the place of Rostock.

Who Needs Feminism?

Sandy and I meet through a housing Web site on the Internet. I will be subletting her apartment in Erfurt through the end of a lease she can no longer keep. She holds a master's degree in engineering and spent five years working with a firm in Erfurt. They can no longer afford to keep her, and she has accepted job in Paderborn, in western Germany, where she hopes her luck will be better.

I arrive on her doorstep with my few bags from Rostock just before dinner. Sandy is small and what Germans call pfiffig, or clever and cute. She welcomes me in, shows me what little there is to see of the flat, and invites me to dinner as an opportunity to show me around town, after which she will leave me the keys and head back to her new life in Paderborn.

We tromp into the city center. It is early autumn, and there is a slight chill and the scent of burning wood in the air. I have never been to Erfurt before, and Sandy identifies various points of interest for me. Her landmarks are largely practical: the post office, the bank, the supermarket. When we pass historic landmarks, she walks on in silence.

Sandy takes me to a slick urban pizzeria. The music is throbbing, but we are the only patrons. I ask her if it is always so quiet. Sandy advises me that even though Erfurt has a university, there is a dearth of young people in the city. She conjectures that things pick up closer to eight o'clock, but that the bar and restaurant scene is quiet. One of the things she loves about being in western Germany now is the crowds.

I ask Sandy about herself. She was born in a small town on the border of Thuringia and Sachsen-Anhalt. Her parents were both skilled factory workers in the GDR. They had high expectations of their two daughters, encouraging their interests in science and technology. Sandy is of the generation that spent their childhood in the GDR, but entered adulthood in the unified Germany. She has studied and worked hard to succeed economically in the new Germany, and I am impressed by her obvious commitment to upward mobility.

When I ask her about what it's like to be a woman working in a male-dominated field, she is quick to share horror stories about her male colleagues and their sexist attitudes. She finds the situation far worse at her new firm in Paderborn than it was in Erfurt. Sandy has heard countless remarks about her appearance, insinuations that she got her position because of her good looks, and queries about a husband and children she does not have. During her interview, her prospective boss asked her point blank how she planned to balance her job with child care. Sandy finds these comments disheartening on several fronts. Not only do male coworkers seem to assume that all women employees have children, but their questions drive home just how difficult she knows it will be to balance her career with the children she does hope to have some day. "Things are supposed to get better from one generation to the next," she muses, "but in this domain of work-family, it is just getting worse. I wish I could have access to the kinds of supports my mother—and my father—had when they were raising a family."

We pause for a moment over our pizzas, contemplating the challenges Sandy faces as a highly educated woman in a technical field in the unified Germany. Sandy sighs, turns her smile back on, and asks me to remind her again what I am studying in Erfurt. "I am looking at the development of local feminist movements in eastern Germany since unification, and I am here to speak with women involved in feminist organizations in Erfurt," I tell her.

Sandy's brow furrows. "Oh," she replies. "That's interesting." She pauses, then regards me earnestly, "But who really needs feminism anymore?"

5 How Conservatism, Religion, and Enthusiasm for Unification Shut Feminists Out of Erfurt

ON THE EVENING OF DECEMBER 3, 1989, a group of East German dissidents met in Berlin to discuss a disturbing new development. Not even a month had passed since the collapse of the Berlin Wall, and the future of the GDR remained uncertain. Hundreds of thousands of East Germans had applied for newly available visas to visit the West, but outside of Berlin, the borders to West Germany remained largely closed, containing an anxious and restless population. Peaceful protests had spread across the country, starting with the famous Monday-night vigils in Leipzig and quickly moving on to other cities. The SED had not taken violent action against its subjects, but rumors swirled that the secret police, the Stasi, were arming themselves to protect their facilities while their officers hurriedly destroyed millions of pages of classified data about the citizenry.

That night, members of the dissident group Neues Forum (New Forum) learned that Stasi commanders in Berlin had sent lists with the names of dissidents whose files were to be purged to each of their regional offices. The Stasi were reportedly destroying thousands of files and loading others onto aircraft bound for Romania, in an effort to erase their history of surveillance. New Forum and other dissident groups were deeply committed to saving these records because they would demonstrate the breadth of Stasi surveillance, provide dissidents with important information about their past experiences and persecution, and reveal the identities of Stasi informers. Without the files, the full extent of Stasi power would never be understood and could therefore never be reconciled.

The dissidents in Berlin sent messages to colleagues in cities throughout Germany. One of these messages reached Dr. Kerstin Schön, a thirty-two-year-old physician in Erfurt.[1] Active in the nuclear-disarmament movement, in September 1989 Dr. Schön had cofounded an organization in Erfurt called Frauen für Veränderung, or Women for Change. A small group of women who mostly knew each other through their employment or involvement with antinuclear or environmental groups, Women for Change was started with the hope of harnessing women's interests in peace and government reform.

While not a religious group, Women for Change, like many other political groups in the GDR, found a safe haven in the Evangelical Lutheran Church.[2] Houses of worship—both Catholic and Lutheran, the two major religions in East Germany—often hosted dissident groups in the GDR because the church was one of few arenas where the state did not assert its control. In the repressive GDR, convening in extra-familial groups was illegal, with the exception of religious meetings. Policies intended to protect religious worship and learning shielded dissidents, who often met within churches under the auspices of Bible study or other church-related business. Although the state police's informant networks also permeated churches—by 1989, it is estimated that as many as one in three East Germans informed for the secret police, or Stasi, and many members of the clergy were implicated as Stasi informers in the early 1990s—churches were one place where the risk of direct state interference was relatively limited. In Erfurt, an abundance of churches and strong central religious institutions such as the Evangelical Lutheran synod provided political groups with opportunities to convene.

Aware of the destruction and deportation of Stasi files, Dr. Schön was alarmed to awaken on December 4 to find black smoke rising from the chimneys of the Stasi's headquarters in Erfurt, the so-called Stasiburg, or Stasi castle. Dr. Schön called a close friend, and they quickly summoned their colleagues from Women for Change, setting out for Erfurt's City Hall to demand that the city government, which was still under SED control, order the Stasi to stop destroying files. The city government was unprepared to take action on the issue. Dr. Schön and her colleagues notified members of other dissident groups in Erfurt that they intended to go to the Stasi headquarters and demand an audience with the commanding officer. Word of the protest quickly spread, and within hours, at least several hundred, and perhaps as many as a thousand, protestors stood outside of the gates of the Stasi compound. By early afternoon, the officer in command agreed to meet with ten representatives from among the hundreds of protestors. While he was meeting with these representatives, members of Women for Change discovered a poorly guarded rear entrance, entered the main building, and opened the front gates to the protestors. At least two hundred protestors stormed the Stasi headquarters.

The storming of the Stasiburg in Erfurt set off a domino effect across East Germany. Within hours, similar citizen occupations of Stasi buildings followed in other cities in East Germany and continued to spread over the next several days. While records would later reveal that the Stasi had prepared for this onslaught with an influx of new guns, batons, and tear gas, the Stasi made no effort to use force to stop the occupations.

These peaceful protests were the final symbolic defeat of the SED in Erfurt and elsewhere. December 5 marked the founding of the Erfurt Citizen's Committee, which stood in opposition to the SED's local leadership and became the controlling group in Erfurt, overseeing the dissolution of the state security apparatus in Erfurt. A few days later, the SED mayor of Erfurt resigned. While the certainty of unification was still months in the future, the reinvention of Erfurt was already underway.

The collapse of the GDR and the unification of East and West Germany was cause for great celebration in Erfurt. The SED actively sought to secularize the GDR, a strategy that was poorly received in this religiously oriented swath of East Germany. Religious institutions insisted on autonomy from the state and refused to endorse or legitimize the SED's authority. This conflict in turn contributed to the public's distrust of the SED and the apparently high levels of dissident activity in Erfurt. Erfurt is also close to the East-West border, and while information never flowed easily over the border, it did flow both through West German television and radio signals and through personal networks, fomenting dissatisfaction with socialism and feeding into oppositional activity that involved dissidents with a range of political stripes. While the dissident movement in East Germany did not initially demand or anticipate unification, the collapse of the GDR and the unification of East and West Germany was an especially joyous occasion in those places like in Erfurt where dissident activity and resistance to the SED had been high. Since German unification, Erfurt has eagerly sought to put its socialist history to rest and to embrace democracy and open markets.

The chaos and jubilation of the unification period of 1989–90 presented feminists with a short window of opportunity to integrate their interests into the new politics of the city. In the days, weeks, months, and even years after the occupation of the Stasi barracks, the public hailed Dr. Schön and Women for Change for catalyzing significant changes in Erfurt and across the GDR, and for setting a precedent that Stasi files warranted protection. As the official organizer of the protest, Women for Change was also given the right to use the Stasi headquarters, and in June 1990 Women for Change formally reappropriated the building as the city's first women's center.

During the autumn of 1989 when the nonviolent citizens' movement pushed the SED from power, Women for Change attracted women from diverse backgrounds, urging them to become politically active and ultimately promoting their gender consciousness, or awareness of structured inequalities between women and men. Rosa, a high-school teacher in the GDR who joined the protests of 1989 and ultimately became a state legislator, remembers how she became drawn into women's mobilizations in Erfurt:

> I participated in the first demonstrations at the Cathedral Plaza, where there were thousands of people. And there was a woman there who fascinated us, who had just started an organization called Women for Change. She was a gynecologist named Dr. Kerstin Schön. She also spoke there [at the demonstration] and really tried to involve us, and promoted a meeting for women from all of the [political] parties to meet at the former Stasi headquarters. There we were supposed to discuss what we were facing, and that was the core reason behind the meeting. And really all associations, unions, parties showed up. And Dr. Schön, she had been working in these movements already—Doctors Against the Atom Bomb, against nuclear war, and so forth, and so she already knew a little about the West German system and she offered us some thoughts and some warnings. We just had this rosy picture [of the future] in front of us, you know? And it was clear to all of us that we all needed to work and *had* to work. . . . In contrast, what we heard from the West was that only 50 percent of women worked. It was unimaginable [that so few women should work]! And she [Dr. Schön] already warned us that we, too, could be victims of unemployment like that. [She said,] "We must do something. We must talk to women and get them to run for elected office in the city council, for example, or in the state legislature, or in the national parliament." So the call to all women was: get organized, get involved. . . . It was all totally inconceivable. Because we were so wide-eyed and naïve. But in actuality, everything she predicted came true.

At first, Rosa, like other women I met, was flabbergasted by some of Dr. Schön's stories about the experiences of women in West Germany and by her predictions for the future of women in the East. Remembering herself as idealistic and naïve, Rosa concludes that, in the end, Dr. Schön was right in foreseeing women's expulsion from the labor market in the East. Even the vocal participation of Women for Change in the Round Table government, and the subsequent political successes of individual women, like Rosa herself, could not slow the massive waves of change that tried to push women in Erfurt—as elsewhere in eastern Germany—out of the paid labor force and back into the home.

Yet Rosa's narrative also omits part of the story. While Women for Change did initially attract participants from across the ideological and religious spectrum, the organization was fraught with ideological tension almost from its inception. In fact, a few weeks after Women for Change's public victory in storming the Stasi barracks, it splintered. By January 1990, just a few months after its founding, Women for Change was losing members and rife with conflict and in-fighting. Members parted ways with the organization for many reasons. Some decided to pursue careers in elected office, or to work with other organizations that sprung up in the city. Others found Women for Change ideologically alienating. By June 1990, Women for Change no longer existed, although it left important legacies through new organizations and through the fractiousness that came to characterize the feminist movement in Erfurt. After a bright beginning in the national spotlight, the local feminist movement wavered under the pressures of competing beliefs, contradictory goals, and conflicting personalities. Pressures external to the emerging feminist movement exacerbated tensions within the movement. In a politically conservative and traditionally minded city, feminists found few footholds and struggled to establish their legitimacy.

After a short window of opportunity during the tumult of 1989–90, feminists and feminist organizations found it difficult to embed themselves in the place of Erfurt. The city's culture, political climate, and history offered few political or discursive opportunities for feminists. Two dominant feminist ideologies developed as almost opposite responses to this conservative place. Radical feminism emerged as reactionary to the traditionalism that characterizes Erfurt, whereas conservative feminism evolved as more complementary to the local context. A political and cultural climate hostile to feminism in Erfurt worked to create and maintain this ideological division and inhibited the creation of a centralized, cohesive social movement community. In turn, ideological heterogeneity within the local feminist movement crippled feminist efforts to participate in making the place of Erfurt.

Early Organizing, Early Conflicts

Christened *Erphesphurt* by missionary bishop Saint Boniface in 742, Erfurt celebrates its status as a center of religious history, and religious participation has long been a significant component of social life in the city. Situated at the intersection of the Via Regia, which connected Paris, France, with Novgorod, Russia, and a second route connecting the Baltic lands to Rome, Erfurt emerged as an important center for trade in the Middle Ages and attracted the interest of numerous leaders from the Roman Catholic Church during its expansion northward. Saint Boniface began his missionary work in eighth-century Germany here. The twin spires of the Cathedral of the Holy Mary and the St. Severus Church, both mostly built in the twelfth and thirteenth centuries, tower above the city's shallow skyline.[3] Erfurt was the birthplace and home of the thirteenth-century Christian mystic Meister Eckhart (1260–1327/8). Martin Luther (1483–1546), the Reformation leader who lived in Erfurt as a monk for five years, coined the description of the city as "spired Erfurt," because of the many spires of its fifty churches, chapels, convents, and monasteries.

Religious traditions and institutions were important in shaping Erfurt's experience in the GDR. Religious identification in Thuringia has historically been higher than in other eastern German states and, bordering Bavaria, long West Germany's most conservative and religious state to the South and a stronghold for Christian parties, Thuringia shares the Bavarian sensibility that church and family should be at the center of community life. Religious leaders were generally at odds with the SED leadership. In a socialist state, the state was supposed to be at the center of the lives of its citizens. Communist governments in much of the Soviet bloc viewed religion as irrational, a tool of capitalism, and threatening to the sovereignty and centrality of the state. To this end, the SED attempted to assert its primacy in the lives of its citizens. The SED co-opted many church rituals, for example by requiring children to undergo a socialist naming ceremony and later, around the traditional early adolescent age of confirmation, a *Jugendweihe*, a political confirmation of sorts through which young people completed political education culminating in the public taking of an oath of loyalty to the GDR. Church leaders often butted heads with SED leaders about the role of the church in socialist society and about the autonomy of churches from state interference.

Protestantism was the dominant religion in East Germany, and most Protestants were Lutherans. In Erfurt and the state of Thuringia, however, the Catholic and Evangelical Lutheran churches were both key actors. Although Catholic and Protestant church leaders struggled with many of the same issues with the SED, the churches dissented in different ways (Heinecke 2002). Lutheran synods were more political and vocal. In the 1970s, some Lutheran clergy adopted what was called a "critical solidarity" approach, working to align themselves positively with state socialism while also encouraging critical evaluation of the SED and its policies. The nuclear accident in Chernobyl in the Ukraine, then part of the Soviet Union, in 1986 especially galvanized resistance to nuclear power in East Germany, and leadership around this tragedy came largely out of Protestant churches. By the 1980s, Lutheran leaders and churches were actively cultivating the peace, antinuclear, and environmental movements, thereby also building civil society in East Germany.

Marginalized both in the face of the GDR's atheism and the dominance of Protestantism (the ratio of Protestants to Catholics in the GDR was an estimated 7 to 1), the Catholic Church was more vulnerable and adopted a dissenting strategy of isolation and disengagement. Church leaders refused to recognize the division of the two Germanies and maintained bishoprics that crossed the East-West border, and churches in the East maintained ideological opposition to the GDR. Simultaneously, Catholic leaders and churches took an accommodationist stance toward the GDR, avoiding conflict and remaining under the radar as much as possible.

Churches, especially Lutheran and other Protestant denominations, created structures conducive to social movement activity because they were relatively free from state interference.[4] Before and during unification, churches facilitated dissident activities and the emergence of women's self-help groups. Already by 1988, at least half a dozen groups of women had begun informal women's organizations in Erfurt (Kenawi 1995). These included a group of Evangelical Lutheran women committed to nuclear disarmament, a mutual-help group for new mothers, a group of women artists, and a social group for lesbian and bisexual women. The groups were not always explicitly political, although some participants engaged in dissident activity and were active in environmental and antinuclear weapons work.

Helbing, who went on to become a major figure in the women's movement in Erfurt, describes her initial involvement with a church-based women's group in the late 1980s:

> I was of the tender age of twenty-three then. I'm an *Erfurterin*; I was born and raised here. And this was in the late 80s, or maybe '88 or '89. That's when the

citizens' desire for change really started getting stronger. And at that time, many different women's groups were founded—self-help groups—to address the problems of single parents, or with partners, or raising children. And a friend of mine took me to one of these women's groups that had just been founded. And there the focus was on women's health, but also more broadly on the general position of women in the East. . . . For example, we read the book *Our Bodies, Ourselves*, which was making the rounds then. We had so few models, if any, at that time. But then as a group, we read that book and discussed it and women and questions of women's health. And then it became political very quickly. It was obvious that this was tied to societal issues. That was how I joined the women's group and entered the women's movement. I simply started to look at things from women's viewpoint, to recognize certain things about society. What is a patriarchy anyway? Where does the word come from and what does it mean?

Like most political and self-help groups in Erfurt before unification, the group Helbing joined met under the auspices of the Protestant Church. Through her involvement with the group, Helbing was exposed to West German and western feminist thought, including feminist theology. The Boston Women's Health Book Collective's *Our Bodies, Ourselves* (1979) and writings by West German feminist author and cultural critic Alice Schwarzer (1975, 1984, 1985) provided the fuel for discussions about patriarchy, gender inequality, oppression, women's health, violence against women, sexuality, and women's work, and these works helped Helbing to start looking at the world from what she calls a "woman's viewpoint." This group functioned to promote feminist consciousness among members like Helbing who were exposed to reading and thinking about gender inequalities for the first time.

Initially brought into a women's group through a friend, Helbing soon took on a major—and high-risk—role through her photographic duplication and dissemination of feminist writings from the West. Distribution of materials not approved by the state was illegal in the GDR. Printed information promoting any number of causes ranging from environmentalism to nuclear disarmament to feminism to state reform was banned. Through her employment as a portrait and events photographer, Helbing had access to photographic supplies and a darkroom, which she could use to reproduce materials for the women's group. As she recalls, "At that time, I was a photographer. . . . I photographed books for the women, page by page, and duplicated the books in that way. That was very important, because there weren't any photocopiers [in the GDR], except maybe in the churches. And you weren't allowed to copy things, not even a little scrap of paper. So it was very important for the dissemination of this diverse literature, already the works of [West German feminist] Alice Shwarzer and about feminist theology." Helbing's experience demonstrates the challenges feminists and other dissidents faced in the GDR, as well as the high level of commitment required of members of these types of groups. Helbing's participation with this group before and during the collapse of the GDR laid the foundation for her future political action, as it did for many women like her.

Instability in the GDR increased in 1988 and 1989, during which time many church-based groups, including those not specifically involving women, became more publicly political. With protests spreading across the GDR in the autumn of 1989, women who had already been involved with dissident, environmental, or antinuclear groups based in churches began to focus on the gendered implications of the collapse of the GDR. In September 1989, Women for Change drafted an open letter to SED leader Erich Honecker in which they asserted the need for open discussions about reform and for a free press. The document made no demands specific to women, but rather appealed to broader discourses of human rights and personal freedoms. Women for Change asserted women's moral authority and their right to be heard in the political realm, but did not primarily focus on gender-specific issues.

In October 1989, the new organization completed its mission statement, which addressed seven areas representing the broad interests of women in Erfurt: democratic rights, socialist reform, child rearing and educational systems, ecology and the economy, health and social life, art and culture, and demilitarization. The authors asserted the importance of realizing true gender equality under a democratically reformed socialist system, calling for affirmative action for women, the equalization of household responsibilities between women and men, and an end to patriarchal expectations of gender relations. Although occasionally utilizing the language of radical feminism through references to patriarchy, the founding document of Women for Change focused most heavily on social issues of concern not only to women at that time but also to many East Germans. Women for Change appealed to broad, gender-neutral discussions about issues such as freedom of association, press, and expression, all core issues of the growing citizens' movement calling for a reformed socialism in East Germany.

Through the processes of developing their own mission statement, ideological tensions between women active in Women for Change came to the fore. For some women, the goals and demands of Women for Change were too main-stream. For example, Helbing, at the time a young artist coming to terms with her own lesbian identity, was concerned that Women for Change did not suf-ficiently emphasize women's oppression, was becoming too hierarchical, and ex-pected an unrealistic degree of cooperation from men. Along with a small group of women, including recent arrivals from West Germany, members of Women for Change from Erfurt, and other women, she broke from Women for Change and founded the Autonome Brennessel, or the Autonomous Brennessel (here-inafter, Brennessel). The organization was named for stinging nettles, which are common throughout Germany. Stinging nettles possess medicinal properties when dried and used as tea leaves or as part of herbal creams and pills, and they are associated with the German tradition of herbal medicine. The name thus invokes pain, aggression, and healing.

The brief first statement of mission and goals produced by the women of Brennessel in 1990 reveals its departure from the rhetorical strategies and goals of Women for Change: "There will be no societal change without increasing consciousness about the dynamics of power between men and women. We want women to make their own demands for the future society. This way, we free men from the double burden of having to think and speak for women. As feminists, we work creatively, with an emphasis on consensus, and without hierarchies. Therefore, the DFD and Women for Change do not represent us."

Here, the members of this new organization directly call attention to the power dynamics between women and men. The mission statement sarcastically invokes the concept of the double burden—usually reserved for discussions of women's dual roles as workers and homemakers—to argue that men no lon-ger need to assume the double burden of thinking and speaking for women. Because of their desire to engage critically with women's oppression, and to operate nonhierarchically, the two most visible women's organizations in Erfurt and Thuringia at that time, Women for Change and the DFD, did not repre-sent women from Brennessel who, unlike most members of these other groups, publicly and vocally identified themselves as feminists.

Recollections of the split between Women for Change and the women of Brennessel vary; some of the women in Erfurt remember it as a volatile dispute, while others shrug it off as a minor event. The immediate consequence was that Erfurt became home to two separate women's centers. Furthermore, while Brennessel also received the bulk of its early funding from city coffers, the city of Erfurt owned and operated the women's center established by members of

Women for Change, the Kommunales Frauenzentrum, or the Municipal Women's Center, ultimately resulting in significant disparities in financial and political support for the two organizations that lasted for almost twenty years.

The push for the Municipal Women's Center came from Women for Change. In the spring of 1990, the Round Table interim government, which counted activists from Women for Change among its members, announced that several city-owned properties would be made available to new social service organizations. One of these buildings was the former Stasi headquarters, the takeover of which Women for Change had organized. Through June 1990, several organizations had been using the building for meetings and administrative offices, and Women for Change had already claimed the bulk of the space. The city officially considered thirty-two proposals and accepted that submitted by a group from Women for Change. They proposed that the building become a women's center aimed at aiding women through the unification process with funding and management through the city government. With the formal approval of the city arriving in late June 1990, just months before the official unification of the two Germanies, the Municipal Women's Center in Erfurt claimed its place as the first officially incorporated municipal women's center in the GDR.

Activists at the center were optimistic that the city government and the public were recognizing women's issues as important to the future of the city and the well-being of its people, and that Erfurt's postsocialist development would remake the city as a place committed to gender equity and the promotion of women's status. Unfortunately, in spite of an auspicious start in the limelight for the local feminist movement in Erfurt, feminists there soon found themselves shut out of the politics of place. Facing a municipal government increasingly hostile to feminist concerns, a public committed to traditional Christian understandings of family, ideological divisiveness within the feminist movement, and the inability of any of the core feminist organizations to rally public support, the feminist movement in Erfurt saw its fortunes change dramatically by the mid-1990s.

Emerging Relationships Between Feminists and the Municipal Government

In 1989–90, feminists capitalized on openings within the political opportunity structure in Erfurt, but, in part due to rifts among feminists, not all feminist organizations benefited equally from this brief period of positive relations between the city and the feminist movement. During the months of relative anomie in the winter and spring of 1989–90, some advocates for women effectively asserted their interests through the Round Table government, which included representatives from a number of political parties and voter coalitions. Advocates for women were able to appeal to a group of leaders with diverse political sensibilities. Many of these leaders agreed with the assertion that some women's issues that had not been addressed in the GDR—such as violence against women—required attention through reform, while others supported claims that women would face unique challenges as a consequence of unification and therefore deserved additional or specialized services.

In the interest of creating an office that reflected the diversity of both the Round Table government and of the women's movement, the Round Table government selected three women to head a new Women's Office (as in many German cities, Gender Equity Representatives were originally Women's Representatives). Each of the three was responsible for a set of specific domains, such as women's employment opportunities or violence against women. They also shared many duties and worked closely together. All were familiar with Women for Change and supported that group's bid to permanently take over the Stasi building.

Birgit Adamek, one of the original staff members in the Women's Office, has been the city's sole GB since a reorganization of the Women's Office in 1993.[5] Her office is located in the beautiful post-and-beam annex of City Hall, where she and I met in her crowded office. Her involvement with social movements during unification began in Berlin, where she was completing an advanced degree in school administration in the months leading up to the fall of the Wall. Birgit returned to Thuringia during the late autumn of 1989. She recalls:

> When I came back here to Erfurt, an amazing change had taken place. I was completing an internship at a school and at night I walked from one meeting to the next. I was a member of [the dissident group] Democratic Change; I checked out the women's groups, who were already starting the women's center and organizing things. We took over the Stasi headquarters where they were throwing out the files. And during this time, I considered whether I wanted to find a new path, and then there was this application process as part of the 8th of March [International Women's Day]. And since I had already started in this school, but everything was so uncertain—and the job was in [the town of] Hochheim, but I lived somewhere else, so that was not the solution—I applied for one of these jobs to help establish the new Women's Office in Erfurt.

Not active in dissident activity or women's groups until the very end of 1989, Birgit is an example of the many women who were pulled into activism through the broader social movement activity that contributed to the collapse of the GDR. As it became apparent to her that her training as a teacher and school administrator might not protect her from unemployment, and as her commute was less than ideal, she decided to apply for a position in the new Women's Office. Here, she became a major player within the feminist movement, helping to secure spaces and funds for women's organizations. She was a central actor in the founding of the Municipal Women's Center and helped the women spearheading the center secure city funding for specific projects and federal employment subsidies through ABM.

Officially opening its doors in the summer of 1990, the Municipal Women's Center employed a dozen women, all of whom were funded through ABM with matching funds from the city. The city also assumed the costs for overhead expenses such as utilities and equipment and officially signed over the use of the Stasi building to the center. The center offered counseling and assistance in a wide range of areas with an emphasis on employment, education, and, through late 1991, when a separate battered women's shelter opened, domestic violence.

Silke, one of the first employees at the Municipal Women's Center, remembers the establishment of the center as a time of great optimism and hope: "When the city accepted our proposal [for a women's center in the Stasiburg], it was a tremendous validation for us. We felt that our concerns as women were being taken seriously, and that we would have a role in the future of the city. The timing was critical; if this had happened later, after unification, the city would never have funded us."

Silke's account reveals how important the city's support was for women involved with the new women's center. In adopting women's issues as part of the responsibility of the city government, the Round Table offered validation and legitimation. Importantly, as Silke notes, the timing of the founding of the Municipal Women's Center was also crucial. In May 1990, the city held its first local, democratic election, choosing a CDU mayor and making the CDU the largest party in the city government with slightly less than 37 percent of the vote (Amt für Statistik und Wahlen der Stadt Erfurt 1990). Combined, the SPD (22 percent) and the PDS (15 percent) earned two more seats on the city council than the CDU, but these two parties were not working as a coalition and did not have control over the mayor's office (Amt für Statistik und Wahlen der Stadt Erfurt 1990). The CDU is typically less supportive of feminist goals and less interested in women's issues than either of the more leftist political parties. The party's platform regarding gender is typically described as "Women and the Three K's: *Kinder* (children), *Küche* (kitchen), *Kirche* (church)." Had this city leadership already taken office, the Municipal Women's Center may not have been so successful in securing support from the city government.

The women involved with the founding of the Municipal Women's Center were largely radical feminists who recognize the existence of structural inequalities grounded in gender and view society as patriarchal and as oppressive to women. Radical feminists in Erfurt seek to help individual women find empowerment in their own lives while also challenging social structures that maintain women's subordinate status. In other contexts, radical feminists typically eschew state funding on the grounds that it renders feminist organizations dependent on patriarchal institutions. This tendency is less pronounced in eastern Germany than in many western contexts, however, because women in eastern Germany experienced the state as benevolent. Their feelings about being funded and controlled by the city are quite ambivalent.

Although activists involved with the Women's Center were pleased to have secured municipal support, direct municipal sponsorship was a mixed blessing. Silke's former colleague, Anja, echoes sentiments Silke also shared in acknowledging that the center's status as managed by the city inhibited the organization's original aspirations for political action and change:

> I was also aware that a city-run women's center is different from an autonomous organization. Naturally, we weren't funded to be politically active. Many were uncertain—even our directors were uncertain—on the one hand, they wanted to be political, but on the other hand, they didn't know how to activate us politically as public employees. . . . We were public employees there. And we knew that on the 15th of the month, our salaries would be there. At the autonomous organizations, it was different. Our situation was much more secure. But an attachment to a structure like that [of the city government] also hampered us in many ways.

From Anja's point of view, the positioning of the Municipal Women's Center's as part of the city increased employee security and provided assurance that funds would consistently be available. However, the city hardly encouraged the women at the center to engage in political action; as Anja notes, the city's funds weren't intended to support political work. Consequently, the directors of the center were uncertain about if and how to reconcile their political interests with their status as public employees.

Ultimately, politics never became a major part of the life of the center. Instead, as Anja suggests, the center remained politically hobbled by its dependence on the city and its status as a municipal facility. Especially as the city government moved away from supporting women's advocacy organizations over the course of the 1990s, the staff at the Women's Center felt increasingly afraid of making demands of the city. Rather than working to mobilize women for social change, the Municipal Women's Center focused on service provisioning and, over time, moved away from explicitly feminist approaches to counseling and teaching and toward more generic, mainstream counseling strategies. The neutral language of equal opportunity came to replace the more critical language of oppression, patriarchy, and empowerment (Guenther 2009).

By attaching the center to the city, the Round Table government—seemingly inadvertently—co-opted this organization and its political impulses, thereby transforming what had originally been a group of highly visible, actively and critically political women into service-oriented civil servants. Simultaneously, by keeping the Municipal Women's Center at arm's length and distanced from the political machinations of the city, the Women's Center could not attain an insider status. Physically separated from city offices and without a formal position within the city government, staff at the Municipal Women's Center had no effective mechanism for influencing city policies and practices other than through their close relationship with the city's GB. They also felt that they could not engage in noninstitutional tactics involving a broader public to press a more political agenda without jeopardizing their livelihoods and the future of the Women's Center. The failure of the Municipal Women's Center to use either institutional or noninstitutional tactics to establish its centrality to, and necessity in, the city in its early years would cost the center dearly in the early 2000s.

That most other feminist organizations in Erfurt were completely shut out of the city's funding programs by the early 1990s augmented the sense of threat at the Women's Center. The radical feminist organization Brennessel in particular faced dire budgetary conditions. Even though the GB attempted to help this organization, the political will to support radical feminist organizations in the city was lacking. One self-identified feminist and city policymaker I spoke with, Ursula, exemplifies a common attitude among municipal leaders toward feminist organizations: only those organizations that have broad appeal should receive public funds. In many respects, Ursula is a CDU hardliner. She believes that a fetus is its own person from the point of conception. She believes in the sanctity of the traditional two-parent, heterosexual family, and disapproves of both no-fault divorce and marriage rights for same-sex couples. In the late 1990s, she supported statewide legislation guaranteeing child care for all children aged two and a half or older, but soundly objects to guaranteed child care for younger children, insisting that young children need at least one full-time parent. While Ursula doesn't believe that being a "C" (Christian) is a requirement for participation in the CDU, she places great weight on the CDU's moral leanings, as well on its faith in free-market principles.

Not someone sympathetic to radical feminism or socialist politics, Ursula defended multiple decisions made during her tenure as a city council member in the 1990s to deny Brennessel city funding:

> It wasn't acceptable that city funds—public, taxpayer monies—benefit someplace where really only a specific group of women go. . . . I mean, if I go to the mayor or to the committees and say, "We need a women's center," already the first thing the men say is, "Why do you need a women's center?" I can respond, "You've always had your associations before where women couldn't join. Now it's our turn." But still, those are public funds. And therefore I have to attend to the fact that everyone can go in, and here [at the Municipal Women's Center] everyone can. From the right to the left and not just from one side. And we were under the impression at that time—I don't know what they told you—I don't have anything against the women from Brennessel, absolutely nothing, but it just isn't acceptable that they be the dominating group here [in Erfurt] because then no one else from the city participates who isn't already on that side. We want a women's center for everyone, irrespective of their political stripes or denomination or whatever. In this space, one should just be a woman and discuss the problems women have. Each with a different perspective, sure, but not, as I said, one-sided. . . . That's my take on the situation because I was in the middle of it. And the mayor said point-blank, "If it's one-sided, I will block the money." And I can understand that, and I supported that [decision]. It's not acceptable. A city space must be open to everyone.

In Ursula's mind, Brennessel offered a limited view of women's issues and appealed only to a certain group of women; while she doesn't say so explicitly, the reference here is both to radical feminists and to lesbian women. Given the political beliefs and believed sexual orientations of the women involved with Brennessel, both Ursula and the city's CDU mayor deemed the organization too "one-sided" to receive city funding. Such attitudes not only blocked Brennessel and similar organizations from receiving municipal funds but also made the staff at the Municipal Women's Center fearful that if their actions, programmatic offerings, and/or demands seemed too radical, they, too, could lose the municipal support on which they were completely reliant. Consequently, the Municipal Women's Center never worked to build a political presence in the city because it could not reconcile political advocacy with state support. As such, the Municipal Women's Center could not establish its right to participate in governance or its centrality to place in Erfurt.

Ideological Conflict Among Radical Feminists

Accounts of the differences between the Municipal Women's Center and Brennessel I heard from women not affiliated with either organization tended to position the organizations as opposites, even as enemies. Yet feminists at the Municipal Women's Center and at Brennessel actually shared much in common. Both organizations emphasized women's empowerment and focused on helping women challenge gender-based inequalities in their own lives. Both groups stemmed from Women for Change, and activists at the two organizations shared similar narratives of being drawn into women's groups sheltered in churches during the GDR. The radical feminist ideology dominant at both organizations rejected the gender ideology of the GDR insofar as it rebuffs the primacy of class-based social solidarity over the acknowledgment of gender inequality. Activists within these groups challenge the GDR's claims to be building an egalitarian society. While recognizing many of the policy strengths of the GDR vis-à-vis women's employment especially, feminists who founded Brennessel and the Municipal Women's Center maintained that gender inequality was a problem in the GDR that required redress. These radical feminists also react against the conservative place of Erfurt. They reject the traditional family model of a stay-at-home mother and breadwinning father popular in political and public rhetoric in the city, particularly within the CDU.

In spite of these many core similarities, ideological conflict between radical feminists has been a continuing problem for the feminist movement since 1990. Radical feminists faced disagreement and strife within their ranks. Given the apolitical nature of the Municipal Women's Center, it is not surprising that women with a strong commitment to feminist political action couldn't find a comfortable foothold there. Many activists regret the split within the radical feminist camp in Erfurt. Silke, a founding member of the Municipal Women's Center, remembered the opening of the center with pride and happiness, but she also feels the accomplishment was tainted by strife:

"We [founders of the Municipal Women's Center] also were bothered by the conflicts between our group and other women's groups. It would have been better if we could have all come together. I think in the long run, it hurt us all that we couldn't find a way to share, to come together." Well aware of the differing ideologies within the feminist movement in Erfurt, Silke laments the absence of cohesiveness and solidarity. Conflict between the women of Brennessel and those at the Municipal Women's Center generally centered on several interrelated issues: men's access to women's centers, the expression and politicization of nonheterosexuality, the structure of organizations, and the degree of feminist autonomy from the state. Both the Municipal Women's Center, in its early years, and Brennessel initially excluded men, asserting that women deserved spaces safe from male influence and violence. When the center opened its doors to men by 1992 in response to city pressure to be more inclusive and a resource for all members of the community, activists at Brennessel did not approve.

Activists at Brennesel also maintained that the Municipal Women's Center was not open to all women and specifically sought to discourage participation and involvement by publicly political and lesbian and bisexual women. A heated conversation with two cofounders of Brennessel, Ulrike and Margot, reveals the differences they perceived between Brennessel and the Municipal Women's Center:

> Ulrike: The two women who took over the Municipal Women's Center, they were both lesbians. But they weren't radical lesbians, or at least not especially radically feminist . . .
>
> Margot: Yes, those were in quotations, "just lesbians." And of course that is radical, that openness, to be somewhat out. That was already a bit radical. But they didn't—first and foremost, they didn't tie that to any structural content, or to how they organized themselves—
>
> Ulrike: First and foremost, it wasn't critical of society. I mean, they didn't examine the whole situation to emphasize how women are doing—all women living in a patriarchal society, irrespective of whether they are lesbian. And what needs to change here. Instead, they very quickly built up the Women's Center as a patriarchal hierarchy. And it was just the same terrible patriarchal system, only with women instead of with men. And in that way, that claim, or maybe that transmission of the radical lesbian idea, changed very quickly.

As Ulrike and Margot note, core leaders at the Women's Center in the early 1990s openly identified as lesbians, but their sexuality did not translate into what Ulrike and Margot describe as a more radical understanding of gender inequality and the oppressive powers of patriarchy. In Ulrike and Margot's view, these women didn't draw on their experiences as "out" lesbians to question broader, societal structures of patriarchy. Rather than working to create a new workplace in which women could be freed from inherently patriarchal power relations, they established the Women's Center as a hierarchy, thereby losing sight of feminist goals and ideals. The issue then is not that the Municipal Women's Center didn't include lesbians, but that it didn't translate this inclusion into what Ulrike and Margot view as a truly radically feminist approach to social life.

Further discussion with Ulrike and Margot, as well as with other women at Brennessel and at other women's organizations in Erfurt, also reveals a broader dispute about what constitutes political action. For women involved with Brennessel, political action necessarily occurs outside of, and against, the state, and organizations should be as autonomous from the state as possible. Activists at Brennessel were wary of what they describe as state-sponsored feminism within the Municipal Women's Center. Although Brennessel also receives funds through city and state coffers and through the federal ABM program, activists here argued that the distinction between receiving state funds and being managed by the state was important. While the staff at Brennessel could make their own decisions about staffing and programming, such decisions were made through the city at the Municipal Women's Center.

By many measures, the Municipal Women's Center *did* engage in political activity: it participated in educational campaigns on several core women's issues, thereby transforming formerly invisible problems such as women's un- and underemployment and domestic violence into publicly accepted social problems; it offered meeting spaces to various political groups, including the women's groups of the major political parties; and, on a more individual level, its initial counseling programs offered women feminist ways of thinking about their lives in relation to men, employers, and society. For the women of Brennessel, however, political action must include action aimed at the state and which occurs outside of state-sponsored forums. Public protests, guerilla tactics like confrontational street theater and "kiss-ins," and the creation and maintenance of social spaces for women free from male and state influence define meaningful political activity for these women. While voting, attending meetings with relevant state leaders, and lobbying also constitute political action, such activities alone are not sufficient to define an organization or individual as political.

As Anja's comments about the Municipal Women's Center suggest, some of the women involved with the center agreed with the assessment that the center was not political enough, or was not politically active in a meaningful way that created change within the city. While a few of the women who had been active in the founding of the center defended their role as relatively apolitical service providers, arguing that they do what is necessary to help women effectively, their accounts often contained notable contradictions through which they conveyed their own ambivalence about what constitutes feminism and feminist political action. Silke, for example, maintained that it was important for there to be a continuum of political approaches represented among the various women's organizations in Erfurt so that all women could find an environment in which they felt comfortable. She also argued against the radical feminist perspective that men should not be included. Yet simultaneously, she expressed concerns that the Municipal Women's Center was "bought out" by the city and could have "offered women in Erfurt more if we had only been more autonomous." She went on to praise Brennessel for offering a "truly political version of feminism."

Women active with the Municipal Women's Center were also well aware that their status could be enviable because they were assured financial resources and office space. Brennessel received far more limited municipal funds and in the early 1990s struggled to secure telephones, office supplies, and other basic necessities. Meanwhile, the center's position as part of the city ensured that it received office space, furniture, and equipment, as well as a budget for programming and services. Women at Brennessel recognized, of course, that full funding from the city came with strings attached, but they nevertheless expressed remorse that the city didn't do more to distribute resources rather than to expend all of its financial efforts on one organization at the expense of all other organizations. Jealousy about funding doesn't seem to have created the underlying tension between the women of Brennessel and those of the Municipal Women's Center, a tension largely rooted in ideological differences, but envy certainly helped to maintain it.

Carving a Feminist Niche in Conservative Politics

One irony in the dispute between women involved with Brennessel and those involved with the Municipal Women's Center is that some women active with the feminist politics of religious institutions and the CDU assert that the even the Municipal Women's Center was too radical, too political, and too oriented toward lesbians to be deemed appropriate for municipal involvement, at least in the 1990s. Ilse is the coordinator of a local support group called the Convent Group, a support and social-networking group for women. As we sat and talked in the modest living room of her apartment in the parsonage of one of the city's Lutheran churches, Ilse explained why and how she decided to devote her retirement to strengthening resources for women in Erfurt. She noted that she founded the Convent Group as an alternative to the support groups at the Municipal Women's Center, which she felt appealed only to radicalized women. Wanting to provide a forum in which un- and underemployed women could discuss their experiences, and where women could build social networks and maintain some part of the social cohesion common in the GDR, she and two friends placed an advertisement in the local newspaper announcing their first meeting in June 1991. Ilse was overwhelmed by the response, and for more than a decade, the Convent Group continued to attract close to thirty regular attendees at its weekly meetings. While participants frequently discuss and debate political issues, the group is not a political one; in their fourteen-year history, they have yet to engage in any type of protest or direct political activity as a group.

While the Convent Group is nondenominational—its name derives simply from the fact that the group meets in a convent—the vast majority of its participants are women who are, or who, through the group, have become, involved in religious life. Ilse herself is heavily involved in the Evangelical Lutheran Church. She focused her career in the GDR on coordinating youth programs for Lutheran girls. Group members seem to embrace her religious leaning. The group frequently discusses religious issues and the role of women in religious life, and local religious leaders regularly attend as invited guest speakers. Ilse notes that the initiative to bring religious themes into the group came not from her, but from the group. She views their discussions about religion as important and notes that many women only felt free to explore organized religion, and especially the city's larger churches, after the collapse of the GDR. One of the group's first outings after its founding was to the famous cathedral in Erfurt; as Ilse explains, many women in the group were afraid to enter the cathedral in the GDR as it was well known that the Stasi monitored who entered and left the church because of its reputation as a shelter for dissident activity.

Ilse's experiences with state repression have left her suspicious of state institutions and ideology. Born in 1932 in a rural village at the outskirts of the Erfurt, she was raised on a farm with her parents, siblings, and her grandmother, who was a nun. During the Third Reich, her grandmother organized local fund-raisers to help Jews, Catholics, and political "undesirables" flee to the United Kingdom or Mexico. The GDR was formed while Ilse was in high school. She still recalls the day when all students at her school were asked to sign a pledge of allegiance to the SED. She told the SED officials who had come to supervise the signing that she could not sign something she did not believe because to do so would violate her relationship of trust with God. She believes that she was thereafter subject to surveillance.

Much later, after she had completed an advanced degree in pedagogy, she opened a specialized day-care facility in Erfurt for children with speech impediments. While running the special-education center, parents of children without language problems sought out her services because they wanted to avoid the ideological indoctrination of state-operated day-care facilities. Reflecting on the current push, especially within the feminist movement, to re-open state-funded day-care facilities in eastern Germany, Ilse muses that this is perhaps not such a good idea as state-funded child care, in her view, is laden with ideological messages determined by the state. Her anxiety about surveillance and state interference is so great that, although she was exceptionally warm and open with me during our multiple meetings, she asked me not to tape record our conversations out of concerns about surveillance, insisting that "recording devices are the stuff of nightmares."[6]

Ilse's, and the Convent Group's, overall orientation toward mutual support and religious learning align the Convent Group with conservative feminism. Conservative feminism seeks to improve women's status by stressing women's unique contributions as mothers and caregivers. While pushing for more egalitarian family models than currently dominant in Germany, conservative feminists support the general structure of the traditional two-parent family and work to make the combination of mothering and paid employment more accessible for women.

The earliest inception of organized, overtly political conservative feminism in Erfurt was through the Women's Union of the Christian Democratic Union (CDU-FrauenUnion, or CDU-FU). The CDU, the leading right-leaning political party in West Germany since the Second World War, made inroads in the GDR well before unification. The CDU maintained a foothold as an opposition party during the GDR and quickly grew to be the strongest party in Thuringia after unification, fomenting resistance against the SED and contributing to Erfurt's pro-unification attitude. Since the first elections in 1990, the

CDU has been the dominant party in both the city council of Erfurt and the state parliament of Thuringia, and it has also controlled the governor's office.

In contrast to radical feminism, conservative feminism is more congruous with the political goals of the city and state, as well as with the broader character of the city. Still, even efforts by conservative feminists at embedding themselves in political institutions and in the place of the city have not been particularly successful. Conservative feminists sit at the edge of public and political life in Erfurt. The local feminist policy machineries, which primarily involve conservative feminists, are notably weak. Feminist goals and agendas have not been integrated into the city or state's identity and, in fact, are often resisted.

Maria's experiences illuminate some of the challenges and possibilities for conservative feminists in Erfurt. An elected state representative for the CDU, Maria grew up in a border town near Erfurt where the barbed wire and watchtowers between East and West, stretches of which have been preserved as a local monument, were simply part of the daily landscape. Her parents were active in the CDU, a legal, albeit disfavored, minority party in the GDR. Already in high school, Maria served as a leader in the local CDU youth group. For her, the CDU held the promise of a free market and a free society with an emphasis on the importance of religious values. After unification, she was elected as the mayor of her town, and she worked her way up to assume several leadership positions within the party, ultimately becoming an elected state representative in 1994.

Although Maria feels uncomfortable with the term "feminist," she sees herself as deeply committed to equal opportunity for women. As an eastern German member of the CDU she is more focused on women's employment opportunities than her party compatriots from the former West Germany. In asserting that women can work outside of the home and still be good mothers, she brings an eastern German sensibility to CDU politics.

For her, the issue of balancing work and family is also intensely personal. In the face of criticism from her mother, other family members, and the broader community of her small hometown, she has continued to pursue her political career. As a single mother (her husband asked for a divorce shortly after the birth of their last child in 1991, just as her political career was taking flight), Maria is sensitive to the needs of working women and doesn't approve of the CDU's emphasis on women's roles as wives and mothers. In fact, she argues that it is often women's skills as nurturers and household leaders that make them such valuable elected officials. She argues that women are especially strong as the mayors of small towns and as local council members, noting that the leap from managing a household with several children to managing a town with a few hundred residents is not especially large.

Maria's accounts of the proper place of women in society are also rife with contradictions. On the one hand, she is herself a working mother (at the time I first met her, her youngest child was twelve) who has been quite successful in working her way up the political hierarchy. On the other hand, she is a firm believer in the importance of traditional Christian religious institutions and teachings in guiding human behavior. She feels that the nuclear family model is the ideal model, and that while women who need to work should be able to do so, women should also be able to take advantage of what Maria sees as their natural talents as caregivers whenever possible. Maria's comments about the role of women in the CDU reveals some of the conflicts with which she routinely grapples:

> Men in my party gladly see women if it's Hiking Day and they make us some coffee and have a booth set up in the woods with some baked goods all ready for us, so the CDU can have a nice Hiking Day. That's important, but there are also local party branches where women have real political influence, not just as coffee-makers or to distribute roses on Mother's Day—which is important, too—organizing a Christmas party at the retirement home, that's important, too. And I am opposed to just randomly recruiting women, pulling them out of their element. Instead, I say, if you want charity work to be the emphasis in your local party branch, so be it. Each to their own. I'm not going to mow someone over and tell them what to do. But I also know there are some women who are politically really smart and who have a lot of influence.

While bothered by the attitudes toward women she sometimes encounters among her male colleagues, who seem to appreciate women most when they are serving men in traditional care-giving roles, Maria is herself conflicted about how to balance women's roles as nurturers and their potential as leaders. Maria sees women "in their element" when they are baking, making coffee, and engaged in charity work. Rather than asserting that all women should be more politically active, she suggests that only a select group of women are predisposed to politics. Later in her interview, she went on to describe herself as a sort of martyr, arguing that women need some representation in government, and she has obviously been "chosen" to do that, even though she believes it led to the disintegration of her own marriage, leaving her to rely on her elderly mother to care for her children while she spends long hours at work in the state parliament. Yet in her view, most women's key contributions are in the home and to the family, and only women with an unusual predisposition toward politics should be called on to represent women in the government.

Maria points to Angela Merkel as the kind of woman uniquely predisposed to politics. Chancellor Merkel, a member of the CDU, is Germany's first female chancellor and the highest-ranking female government official in German history (Ferree 2006).[7] She is eastern German and childless. She has become a top celebrity among women in Erfurt involved with the CDU-FU, and she is the person everyone in the CDU and CDU-FU pointed to as evidence of the CDU's support for women in its ranks.

The CDU-FU, which was founded in West Germany in 1949, grew rapidly in Thuringia in the wake of unification, paralleling the rapid growth of the CDU there. The CDU-FU has 155,000 members nationwide, and with more than 30,000 in Thuringia, it is the largest women's organization in the state. Its appeal is in part thanks to its grassroots approach of recruitment through local churches and extant social networks, and in its ability to combine politics with domestic life through events like knitting circles, charity work at hospitals and nursing homes, and religious discussion groups. As I quickly discovered in speaking with members of the CDU-FU in Erfurt, participation in CDU-FU events is often an extension of church-based activities, especially in the more heavily Catholic areas of rural Thuringia.

Women I spoke with in Erfurt who participate in the CDU-FU share Maria's view that women overall should be more involved in political life, but this does not necessarily require elected office. While part of the CDU-FU's stated mission is to increase the percentage of women within the CDU—including among elected CDU members—many of the women active in the CDU-FU in Erfurt rely on the organization to keep abreast of political developments and to lobby around specific issues. The CDU-FU regularly offers workshops on how to start a political career, adopting a bottom-up approach by urging women in small towns to run for mayor (usually unpaid, part-time positions more reminiscent of charity work than organized politics) in the hopes that women will gradually feed up the political pipeline. To date, there is little evidence to suggest that the CDU-FU in Erfurt or in Thuringia has succeeded in increasing the number of CDU women in elected public office. In spite of women in key leadership positions both in Thuringia and nationwide, the CDU lags well behind the PDS and SPD in the percentage of women elected.

The CDU-FU more effectively serves as a social and lobbying organization. In Thuringia, the CDU-FU has worked to elect and reelect CDU members, to push for gender equity legislation, and to draw attention to women's disadvantages in income, education, and family life. During my tenure in Erfurt, the CDU-FU held its annual national convention in nearby Weimar; at Maria's invitation, I attended the event, which included speeches by Angela Merkel and the president of the State Parliament of Thuringia, Christine Lieberknecht, who I also interviewed several weeks later. The theme of the convention was "Women and Globalization." Upon my arrival, I was handed a canvas shopping bag with a black, white, and pink theme (pink is the official color of the CDU-FU). The optimistic slogan "We're taking part, too!" topped a grainy photographic image of a slender pair of women's legs taking long strides in high heels. Inside, I found the customary notepad, pen, and convention schedule, along with several CDU-FU publications on women and globalization, women's use of technology, and the then-proposed Hartz IV legislation, which in 2004 resulted in significant changes to Germany's antipoverty and state-pension programs. The bag also contained a little something for attendees' feminine sides: an official CDU-FU lip gloss (which, admittedly, I loved) and several Calvin Klein fragrances. The swag bag captured the essence of the modern CDU-FU: smart, polished, and feminine.

Christine Lieberknecht epitomizes this image of the CDU-FU. When we met, she cheerfully gave me an edited volume, *Kinder, Kirche, und Karriere* (Children, church, career; a play on the "3 Ks" of the CDU: *Kinder, Küche, Kirche*, or children, kitchen, church) to which she contributed an essay (Althausen, Berlis, Busch et al. 2000). She is an ordained minister and mother of three. When I met her in her glass-walled office overlooking the state capitol, she was serving as the president of the State Parliament of Thuringia, making her the highest-ranked woman official in the state. Like Maria, she advocates the maintenance of nuclear families, but she believes women can be better mothers if they work outside of the home. She objects to glass ceilings and sexual harassment, but she also thinks children need full-time mothering until they are at least three years of age and that extramarital sex is, at a minimum, unwise because it so often creates single-parent families. Also like Maria, she entered politics almost immediately after unification, working her way up through a series of elected and appointed offices. Unlike Maria, she is relatively uncritical of the CDU for failing to take a more active role in promoting women's political involvement. In her experience, the party has been tremendously supportive, and she mobilizes her current office as evidence. When I confront her with the CDU's rather dismal record on gender issues and on increasing women's political representation, she diplomatically acknowledges that the party could "do more to recognize and encourage political talent among women."

Conservative feminists experience competing loyalties and their narratives correspondingly reflect contradictions. The ideology of gender that most women involved with CDU and church-based women's groups hold clearly contrasts with the gender ideologies of more radical feminists. The two ideological camps have nonetheless been able to cooperate around a few issues, most notably in efforts to introduce and pass legislation that improved services and resources for survivors of domestic violence. Although their interpretation of this issue varies—radical feminists see domestic violence as a tool of patriarchal domination while conservative feminists view it as a by-product of social instability, a morally suspect mass media, and an increasingly violent society—the two groups together worked to educate the public about domestic violence and coordinated lobbying efforts. More often, radical and conservative feminists simply keep a distance from one another, avoiding open conflict by staying out of each other's way. This strategy inhibits coalition work and entrenches differences rather than seeks to discuss how those differences might be addressed and overcome to foster a more cohesive and effective local feminist movement.

Navigating the Ideological Spectrum in Erfurt

While the women of Brennessel mark the most radical end of the feminist spectrum in Erfurt, and those involved with the CDU the most conservative end, a few organizations occupy the middle-ground. The FrauenTechnikZentrum (Women's Technical Center, or FTZ) is the lone organization in Erfurt not affiliated with a political party that adopts a more neosocialist feminist perspective through its almost singular emphasis on women's employment and economic independence. Founded in April 1991, the FTZ initially relied heavily on ABM positions to fund its work, along with grants from the local state for adult education and technology training. At the FTZ, un- and underemployed women can participate in training in computer technology, as well as in traditionally male trades like house painting, electrical work, carpentry, and mechanics. Tuition is covered by the Unemployment Office for eligible students. Women's employment and income lie at the core of the FTZ's mission.

The early 1990s also witnessed the founding of several other organizations that are largely apolitical insofar as they do engage in political or other advocacy work. Erfurt's two battered women's shelters openly avoided political involvement and remained largely removed from the ideological strife within the feminist movement. Both organizations are based in religious institutions, are nonpartisan and nondenominational, and work relatively closely with the women of Brennessel, who provide extensive counseling to battered women and who often refer clients to the two shelters in Erfurt.

The first shelter for battered women in Erfurt was founded by a group of women who had been active in a group called Frauen helfen Frauen (Women Helping Women), which was founded in 1983 within the Lutheran Church. Part of the underground women's movement in the GDR, this group sought to assist women in battering situations in Erfurt during the GDR by arranging crisis shelter through a network of volunteers who were willing to harbor battered women in their homes. In the fall of 1989, members of this group joined Women for Change and created an informal shelter system for battered women, arranging for hotel rooms for women in crisis situations. The group then opened a shelter after unification. For the first two years after unification, when municipal support for women's issues was high, the city funded and managed this facility in the same way as the Municipal Women's Center. However, the city then relinquished responsibility for the shelter to the Evangelical City Mission. In accordance with state law, a large proportion of the shelter's financial obligations are covered by the state, and the Evangelical City Mission provides the remaining funds.[8]

The second shelter for battered women in Erfurt, which also opened in 1991, was founded by the Order of the Good Shepherd, a group of nuns who came to Erfurt from Munich (in western Germany). The Catholic archdiocese and the Order of the Good Shepherd help finance this shelter. This shelter has a more traditional emphasis aligned with conservative feminism, but it is not involved in advocacy or political work.

These two organizations are important because they demonstrate the entrance of church-based groups into the field of social service provisioning after unification and the possibility of competition between church-based and feminist services. As the social services opened as a major market niche, strong religious institutions in Erfurt were well positioned to become service providers or to expand services offered in the GDR. Feminist groups have had to vie with these organizations for resources. Several respondents also noted that church-based service providers established norms of hierarchy and bureaucratization that other service providers are now compelled to follow, especially if they hope to remain competitive in the social service market. While respondents agreed that the two shelters offer quality services, many also expressed a sense of disappointment and loss that feminists do not operate a shelter in the city.

Ultimately, the only true bridge at the municipal level between women from various ideological viewpoints has been the GB's office. Although primarily aligned with the Municipal Women's Center and the municipal battered women's shelter, the office coordinates interorganizational events, publishes a quarterly calendar of events at women's organizations, and maintains a resource and referral guide that is widely distributed to women's organizations so they can keep abreast of one another's services and activities. The city's GB generally has worked amicably with all groups and is widely respected. However, even with a relatively neutral leader in one of the most central positions in the feminist movement in Erfurt, ideological conflicts continued to hamper the movement through the second half of the 1990s.

A Closed Place: Excluding Feminism from Erfurt

The Women's Center is situated in a quiet side street not far from the Domplatz, or Cathedral Plaza, cast in the shadow of the Cathedral of the Holy Mary and the neighboring St. Severus Church. From the street, the building is innocuous: a row of small windows interrupts a wall of stucco, edged on one side by a large gate. Passing through the gate, however, leads me into a modern marvel. After crossing a beautiful cobblestone courtyard, I find myself in a sparkling new building with shining hardwood floors, a bar sophisticated enough for a Berlin nightclub, and a fusion of Zen and modern design elements which together create a calming, stylish interior.

As I stand in the foyer wondering if it's possible that I have walked into the wrong building, I am met by Helga, an upper-level staff member at the Women's Center. She is relatively new on the job, having started working here only about six months before we met. This building and the organization that houses it are, in fact, both new to the city. In January 2002, the city council and mayor of Erfurt resolved that the city needed to stop all "nonessential" funding due to the city's fiscal crisis. The Municipal Women's Center was costing the city at least €50,000 each year during the late 1990s, excluding the costs of the renovation of this building.[9] The city announced that it would no longer fund the Municipal Women's Center and instead intended to hand it over to a "free carrier" (*freier Träger*), or an autonomous organization. The city invited registered nonprofits to submit proposals describing how they would restructure the center, what programs and services they would offer, and how they would fund the center. In conjunction with the city council, a special committee then reviewed the proposals and se-lected which organization would take over the Municipal Women's Center.

Three organizations submitted proposals. The first was ProFamilia, the Ger-man equivalent of Planned Parenthood. A national organization, ProFamilia specializes in reproductive health care and in 2002 operated two clinics in Erfurt, as well as four others elsewhere in Thuringia. Services at these clinics include sexual education, provisioning of birth control, gynecological and pre- and postnatal care, counseling for pregnant women and couples on pregnancy and family planning, and treatment of menopausal symptoms and support for menopausal women. In accordance with German laws governing abortion, Pro-Familia clinics are also accredited to provide the required counseling and cer-tification of counseling for the termination of pregnancy, and most ProFamilia clinics, including one of the two in Erfurt, offer abortion services.

ProFamilia's bid to take over the Municipal Women's Center in Erfurt rep-resented the entering of new terrain for this group. ProFamilia submitted a proposal that envisioned the center as a hub for women in the city offering classes and workshops on a number of topics, including, but not necessarily emphasizing, women's health. In their vision, the center would offer support groups, as well as individual short-term counseling, for women facing various health and personal issues. The center would also host events for women and children, provide educational and personal enrichment programs, and have drop-in hours for referrals to other agencies.

The second organization to make a bid for the Municipal Women's Center was Brennessel, Erfurt's oldest organization of radical feminists. Brennessel es-sentially proposed combining their programs, which included counseling for victims of sexual assault, self-help groups for lesbian and bisexual women, and their active calendar of social events, with the offerings of the existing Municipal Women's Center, which included self-help groups for under- and unemployed women, as well as counseling services on employment and relationships, and a range of educational and "personal improvement" courses. The new center would continue to offer programs for women and girls, drawing on the skills and talents of women working at Brennessel and at the Municipal Women's Center.

The third proposal came from the Center for Women and Families in Er-furt, which already operated a center in downtown Erfurt with the primary goal of strengthening families, especially those considered at risk. Services at their downtown location include crisis counseling, child care, addiction counsel-ing, debt counseling and consolidation advocacy, and family-oriented activities aimed at building the bond between parents—mostly mothers—and children. The Center for Women and Families is not a feminist-identified organization and does not engage in political organizing or advocacy work. The proposal submitted by this organization asserted that it was important that the center remain in local hands and appeal to as many women as possible. To that end, the Center for Women and Families presented a vision of the center as one with an array of workshops and classes that would draw in women from different backgrounds, including seniors, young women, and mothers. Ideas included aerobics classes for the elderly, support groups for new mothers, and regular social events.

The city's decision to cease funding the center was heartbreaking for the women involved with the Municipal Women's Center, especially as many of them had worked there since its inception. While the women I spoke with who had worked at the center retrospectively acknowledged that the management shift forced them to reassess their lives, in many cases pushing them to pursue new interests they have found very fulfilling, they equated losing the center to losing a child. Birgit Adamek, the GB of Erfurt and the executive director of the Municipal Women's Center for more than ten years who also counted the employees at the center among her close friends, found the city's decision to cut formal ties with the center devastating:

> If you've already spoken with Helga, then you know that in principle what I was passing on there [to her] was a piece of my heart. There is still one municipal women's center in Thuringia, the one on Gotha. The second one was always the one in Erfurt. All the other ones were autonomous organizations; they have to beg for every penny, they have to write these proposals, like at Brennessel and the Women's Technical Center, which have no [financial] security. It was different at the Municipal Women's Center. I was the director and could invite who I wanted to invite, so the conditions were really optimal. . . . When I stop and think about it, that I managed to secure €1.8 million in support of a building for a *women's center*, then I realize it was a major accomplishment that I sometimes have to remind myself of—that I really achieved something. Because I really experienced the handing over of the Center to an outside organization . . . as a personal failure. For me personally, I interpreted this as, "You must not have done this well enough, or else they wouldn't have taken the Center from you."

Birgit reveals the depth of her connection to the center when she describes the center as "a piece of her heart" and her own sense of personal failure after learning of the city's decision. She also asserts that the center's relatively unique status as part of the city created "optimal conditions," guaranteeing funding for the center while also giving her the freedom to run the center as she saw fit. Unlike other women's organizations in Erfurt, which had to "beg for every penny," the Municipal Women's Center had a steady cash flow, and Birgit thought it was protected from the whims of financial restructuring.

Initially, Birgit tried to push the mayor and city council to reconsider, but the decision was final. Unable to lobby public or political support for keeping the center within the public domain and slowly coming to a degree of personal resolution about the issue, Birgit turned her attention to the future of the center and to the proposals submitted by organizations interested in assuming control of it. The women who already worked at the Municipal Women's Center mostly rooted for ProFamilia. They felt that this organization would continue to run the center as a middle-of-the-road facility where women from diverse backgrounds would feel comfortable. Because of ProFamilia's national reputation and strong financial position, Birgit and the employees at the Municipal Women's Center also felt that ProFamilia would be the most capable steward of the center's financial future, ensuring its long-term survival. So strong was the desire for ProFamilia to win the bid that several employees at the center told the GB and the city council that they would only continue to work at the center if ProFamilia was chosen to lead the center. Some also thought Brennessel was an acceptable choice.

But the city council had other ideas and selected what existing staff members considered the worst choice: the Center for Women and Families. The official explanation for this choice focused on wanting to select a group that was locally based, as opposed to ProFamilia with its national scope, and accessible to all women, as opposed to Brennessel, which key city leaders consistently view as exclusionary. Women from the first generation of the Women's Center, however, largely interpreted the choice of the Center for Women and Families as an effort at eliminating any feminist impulses from the Women's Center.

The transfer took place in March 2003, at which time the existing employees of the Municipal Women's Center left and began working elsewhere. A new cohort of staff members took over, and while some programs were maintained, the renamed Women's Center radically departed from the programmatic offerings of the Municipal Women's Center. Programs targeting battered women, survivors of assault, and immigrant women were dismantled or curtailed. In their stead came classes in yoga and aerobics, courses on flower arranging, home décor, and women's health, and support groups for new mothers and senior women. The beautiful new café and bar offers an informal meeting place for women to meet and socialize, although during five of my six visits to the center when the café was open, it was empty.

That the city released the Municipal Women's Center from city control, and that the Center for Women and Families was chosen to take over the center, exemplifies the general trend in Erfurt and Thuringia toward reducing direct state involvement in women's issues, curbing state outlays for social services, being most supportive of centrist or conservative women's organizations. Funding shortages were due to the conclusion of various federal programs aimed at redeveloping eastern Germany and to declining tax bases. Erfurt, like other cities in eastern Germany, experienced substantial depopulation in the 1990s, shrinking from a city of 240,000 in 1989 to barely 190,000 in 1998. With employment hovering around 18 percent in the years between 1996 and 2001 (Landeshauptstadt Erfurt Stadtverwaltung 2002), economic growth has been slow.

Erfurt's primary industry before unification was agriculture, and the city was widely known as the City of Flowers as seed development and flower growing dominated the local economy. Unification resulted in an end to state protectionism of the floral industry, and that industry has largely collapsed in the face of international competition since 1990. Today, swaths of the city's growing fields, as well as the fairgrounds for its annual flower show in the GDR, lie dormant.

Since 1990, the city has focused on developing tourism as a major industry, as well as high technology, most especially microelectronics. Corporations in the West also purchased a handful of agricultural facilities that continue to develop plants and pesticides there. As elsewhere in eastern Germany, the construction boom of the 1990s improved the job market, primarily for men, as dilapidated buildings were renovated. Also critical for the local economy is that Erfurt is the state capitol of Thuringia, and the municipality benefits from the income, spending, and taxes of a large pool of civil servants living in the city. Redevelopment of the city has been patchy: while downtown and the residential neighborhoods closest to the capitol buildings are quite lovely, lively, and easy to access via public transportation, outlying neighborhoods continue to suffer from bleak, run-down buildings and empty streets.

To cope with shrinking coffers, the city government reduced its outlays for social services and the promotion of civil society. It also began outsourcing and offloading its fiscal responsibilities onto private organizations. Across the range of women's organizations, contributions from the city and from the state of Thuringia shrank precipitously, beginning with the severing of the municipal shelter for battered women in 1993 from city control and continuing for more than a decade.

While feminists in Erfurt find the city's lack of financial commitment to women's and feminist organizations distressing, they have not had opportunities for recourse. The ease with which the city was able to offload obligations like those to the Municipal Women's Center reflects the lack of entrenchment of feminist goals into local policymaking or public priorities. Feminists in Erfurt never built an effective feminist policy machinery and have no lobbying power. In the early winter of 1989, the emergent feminist movement in Erfurt appeared to be one of the most promising in East Germany, but the movement weakened politically over time. Ideological divisions between camps of feminists developed even before the opening of the Municipal Women's Center in the summer of 1990. These rifts created animosity between both radical and conservative feminists and between radical feminists working at different organizations.

The two primary ideologies in Erfurt have different relationships with the place of the city: radical feminism reacts against the conservatism and traditionalism of the city, while conservative feminism is more congruous with these aspects of the city. Both feminist ideologies are born out of the conservative, traditional character of the place of the city, but they are largely unable to feed back into it. A brief window of political opportunity in 1990 closed quickly, and the rapid ascent of the conservative CDU shut out feminist interests within the local government. Because of their small number and fringe position within the CDU, even conservative feminists are ineffectual at securing attention and resources for women's and gender issues. Ideological divisiveness inhibited the creation of a unified feminist movement or local lobbying network. Feminist interests could not align with the dominance of traditional approaches to gender and family in both the culture and politics of the city.

The strength of religious institutions initially helped women's organizations, providing them with space and resources to develop and network before and during the unification process. Women's organizations formed in churches before German unification, even though many had little direct interest in religion. During the unification process, women from these groups, as well as women who joined the women's movement through the protest movement against the SED, founded a myriad of organizations, creating a vibrant field of women's organizations. After unification, however, the religiosity of the city, especially as it related to conservative political and gender ideologies, hampered effective mobilization. Churches as institutions have not generally attempted to thwart feminist agendas, but the more traditional views of the city and region that stem from these institutions proved problematic for feminist goals. Feminist organizations struggled to assert their legitimacy in a political and cultural climate with no particular stake in gender inequality. Perhaps because Women for Change itself ceased to exist, and because its legacy organizations splintered, its accomplishments did not provide longer-term leverage for public or policy attention. Feminists failed to capitalize on Women for Change's auspicious start by cementing its contributions in the collective memory of the city. Instead, collective forgetting made it easy for policymakers and the public at large to ignore feminist demands.

Certainly, the city government's co-optation of Women for Change in 1990, which later became the Municipal Women's Center, provided important legitimization for this group. Unfortunately, this support came at the expense of reducing, if not obliterating, this organization's political leanings. By centralizing its resources, the city also supported one feminist organization at the expense of others, thus escalating tensions between groups. With most of its monies tied up in the Municipal Women's Center, and later the municipal shelter for battered women, by 1991 the city had only limited funds remaining for other organizations. Eventually the costs of the municipal organizations became the public reason for passing both the battered women's shelter and the Municipal Women's Center on to nonprofit organizations with questionably feminist positions. Structural, institutional, and symbolic doors closed for the feminist movement in Erfurt. Rather than finding a way to integrate feminist interests into the place of the city, feminist organizations were shut out of the project of making place after the end of socialism.

Rethinking Sisterhood

When I set out to study feminist organizations in eastern Germany since the collapse of state socialism there, I didn't expect to be interviewing nuns. Yet in Erfurt, I find myself in the company of Sister Benedicta, the eighty-year-old leader of the local chapter of the Order of the Sisters of the Good Shepherd. The Order is organized around the idea that those in crisis and need sometimes need a good shepherd to guide them. With five thousand members working in seventy countries around the world, the Order seeks to minister to those who are marginalized and vulnerable, with a particular focus on women and children in crisis situations.

After German unification, the Order decided to expand into eastern Germany. Sister Benedicta, who had previously worked with the Order in Munich, took the lead in organizing a move eastward. She and her colleagues arrived in Erfurt in late 1990 where they opened a shelter for battered women and their children in 1993. The Order has since expanded their services in Erfurt to include counseling for pregnant women and advocacy for trafficked women. They also help staff an interfaith crisis line, and participate in various initiatives through the Catholic diocese.

The nuns live and work in the shelter along with their clients. The shelter occupies an older building that was renovated after unification. The large windows let in blocks of light that brighten the wooden floors and moldings. There are no locks on any interior doors, and the children staying at the shelter pass freely from one room to the next, visiting with their mothers, other women and children, and the sisters.

Sister Benedicta is both energetic and calming. Her bright eyes peer out at me from behind thick glasses. A giant silver cross swings from her neck and a habit covers her white hair. She speaks about her work with great enthusiasm and is happy to share with me stories of former guests at the shelter who have gone on to find fulfilling careers and relationships. As is typical of battered women's shelters, the location of the shelter is not released to the public to protect the privacy and safety of its inhabitants. However, unlike many other shelter programs, counseling with both partners can be arranged. Sister Benedicta feels that domestic violence is in part a symptom of broader social strain. "Yes, there was domestic violence in the GDR," she says, "but with the unemployment and economic strain so high since unification, it increased. More and more women are affected in Erfurt." To help couples cope with the stress, the sisters offer couples counseling and work toward an end goal of peaceful family reunification, especially in cases where children are involved. Of course, they recognize that this is not always possible, but they do not automatically assume that men who have injured or threatened their partners cannot be rehabilitated. This perspective is growing in popularity in eastern Germany where there are more and more rehabilitative support services for battering men.

Sister Benedicta is especially proud of the art-therapy program for children at the shelter. She sees violence as cyclical and transmitted intergenerationally. It is therefore a top priority for her to reach children while they are still impressionable to break the cycle of violence. Prior to joining the Order in her late thirties, Sister Benedicta was a social worker, and she keeps up on advances in that field to assure that the shelter offers innovative and high-quality services to women and children.

Sister Benedicta had lived in Erfurt for thirteen years when we first met, and she considers the city her home. The welcome she has received there has been warm, she notes, even though at first, some leaders she encountered, both in local government and in the Catholic diocese, were unclear if a shelter for battered women was really needed. Given that both shelters in Erfurt (the Evangelical Lutheran synod also operates a shelter) are continuously at capacity evidences the continued demand for this service. Sister Benedicta notes that the goals of the Order of the Sisters of the Good Shepherd have been especially well supported in Erfurt because the diocese there has substantial resources. The diocese owns the building in which the shelter is located, and the diocese renovated it for the sisters.

"When we decided to move eastward," Sister Benedicta recalls, "we needed to be strategic about it, to go someplace where we thought we would be supported and where a group of nuns setting up shop would not be unwelcome. Erfurt was the perfect place."

6 Making Claims Across Scale and Space in Erfurt

Wanting to Be Western

BOTH THE FEMINIST MOVEMENT IN ERFURT and the city of Erfurt are connected to other places and scales of activity. Place is "an intermingling of the effects of multiple geographic locations in the practices of everyday life" (Agnew 2002: 60). This intermingling changes over time. While historically grounded, neither places themselves nor the relationships between them remain unchanged. In the aftermath of unification, ties to western Germany that predated unification emerged as especially salient for the city of Erfurt and the feminist movement there. Compounding Erfurt's eagerness to lay the socialist past to rest, connections westward facilitated the development of a "catching up" mentality through which policymakers and the public emphasized emulating western Germany and asserted the city's place as "truly" German. Extensive contact between western Germans and residents of Erfurt heightened historical ambitions for westernization, and brought West German ideas and ideologies—including feminist ideologies and practices—to Erfurt.

As the state capital of Thuringia, Erfurt is considered a major German city and is easily accessed via highways and railways. Many larger West German cities, including Frankfurt am Main, Hannover, Kassel, and Göttingen, are about two to three hours drive from Erfurt. Literally the geographic center of Germany, the tourism office welcomes visitors to the heart of Germany.[1] Some fifty miles from the former East-West border, Erfurt is situated in a relatively populous part of the country, is en route to other larger cities in eastern Germany, and draws tourists visiting nearby Weimar, Eisenach, and the famous Thüringerwald (Thuringian Forest), such that travel and contacts across the former border are frequent.

Thuringia is home to 2.38 million people and occupies slightly more than six thousand square miles in southeastern Germany. The state is bordered by the Saxon regions, Hesse, and Bavaria. More than half of the former border between East and West Germany runs along Thuringia's western and southern edges. Although Thuringia has several urban areas, including Erfurt, Gera, and Jena, roughly half of the state's population lives in towns and villages with populations of fewer than ten thousand. During the GDR era, central industries included agriculture in the rural areas and manufacturing, especially of textiles and electronics, in more densely populated areas. Since unification, the region has sought to maintain both of these sectors, but it experienced significant contractions in the labor market. Roughly half a million people left Thuringia between 1990 and 2000, presumably in search of better economic opportunities elsewhere.

In part because of Women for Change's high-profile action in storming the Stasi headquarters, western German feminist organizations quickly latched on to Erfurt as a promising site for feminist activity during and immediately after unification (Guenther Forthcoming). Western German women's organizations typically take a radical feminist stance, especially within the autonomous feminist movement. These organizations sent representatives to Erfurt to help fledgling organizations there. Other women from western Germany, like one of the cofounders of Brennessel, came more as individuals than as organizational representatives, but were also drawn to Erfurt by the media reports about Women for Change. In addition, many western German organizations invited women from Erfurt to come to the West to build coalitions and to exchange information and ideas. Women active in young women's organizations in Erfurt were exposed to West German feminist theory and praxis. In some cases, this exposure even predated unification as West German feminist materials passed through dissident networks.

At Brennessel, Erfurt's premier radical feminist organization, women who met radical feminists from western Germany described these experiences as positive. Western German organizations donated books for the feminist library at Brennessel, shared their experiences working with survivors of domestic violence and sexual assault to prepare the new counselors at Brennessel for their work, and were generally enamored with the high level of political engagement among the women at Brennessel. Rather than feeling belittled or exoticized by western German feminists as the few activists in Rostock who came into contact with western German feminists did, radical feminists in

Map 6.1 Map of Thuringia

Erfurt felt appreciated and revered by their western German counterparts. As one respondent noted, "Without them, we would not have known what to do" to build up a feminist organization.

Conservative women's groups, most notably the CDU-FU, also enlisted new members in Erfurt and Thuringia. The CDU had already made important inroads into Erfurt and Thuringia before unification, and the CDU-FU followed this path. These encounters were occasionally problematic for women in Erfurt. Maria, for example, was shocked by how few of the women from the CDU-FU in the West worked outside of the home or had large families:

> In the beginning, when I joined the Women's Union (CDU-FU) and went to our first meeting together at the national level and saw the ladies from the old German states—those were still very well-situated ladies who I met then, often housewives with one kid and politics as a hobby. With us, it was still different. At that age, you'd have at least two kids, or more. Women of my age [in the GDR] had more than just one child! Here it's just a given that you have multiple children and are still involved. Mrs. Rita Süssmuth, she also said something— she was the nationwide president [of the CDU-FU] for years. We had an event that dealt with the theme of employment, political engagement, and family. And Mrs. Süssmuth says there, "Well, fine, if you have two kids, maybe you can still do this, but with three kids, it's just not possible [to be a political leader]. It just can't be done." To which I said, "Frau Süssmuth, if that's the case, then I have to stand up now and get my bag and drive home again because I am all alone as a single mother and have three children and yet *here I am*."

Maria identifies differences in attitudes toward family and work life as the primary difference between women from East and West Germany involved with the CDU-FU.[2] While those from the East generally had several children and long careers working outside of the home, women from the West more often had only one child, or no children, or had not worked outside of the home or only on a part-time basis, and considered politics a recreational activity. Mrs. Süssmuth's comments came as an affront to Maria, who was building a successful political career *and* acting as a single mother to three children.

Instead of responding to such incidents and attitudes by shunning women from the West, however, Maria, and others who had similar experiences, tried to integrate their life histories as working parents into the CDU-FU. Their presence among elected officials opened the eyes of western German feminists to the possibility of combining elected office and parenthood, and eastern

German members also urged the CDU-FU to become friendlier toward mothering women by making free or low-cost child care available at major events, and by better integrating work-family issues into the organization's platform. Seeing no way to avoid working with these women other than defecting from the party to which they had been dedicated for so long, Maria and her peers in the CDU-FU pushed western German members to reevaluate their existing expectations of women, work, and family.

In addition to the CDU-FU, conservative women's organizations came into contact with western German women through religious organizations. The nuns of the Order of the Good Shepherd from Munich in western Germany opened a battered women's shelter in Erfurt and became active in the Catholic diocese in Erfurt. The head of the order in Erfurt, Sister Benedicta, is a well-known figure around town who was propelled to local stardom in 2004 when German president Horst Köhler awarded her the National Medal of Service. After unification, West German Ursuline Sisters (also Catholic) entered the Ursuline Convent in central Erfurt, adjacent to the Center for Women and Families, a women's organization that focuses on service provision and has a family-oriented bent. The mission of the Ursuline Sisters is to provide education and care for children. To this end, the nuns manage their own day care, kindergarten, and school. Like the nuns from the Order of the Good Shepherd, the Ursuline Sisters are not politically active, but carry with them an emphasis on family and church that has been transmitted to activists in other organizations.

Catching Up to Western Germany

With such high levels of contact between Erfurt and the West, western German values and norms influence values and norms in Erfurt, both in the feminist movement and elsewhere. The desire to "catch up" to the West has occasionally served to bolster feminist organizations. Efforts at passing legislation on domestic violence profited from this approach as radical and conservative feminists worked together to convince Thuringia's parliamentarians that such legislation was central to westernization. Respondents consistently noted that the public and policymakers quickly accepted domestic violence as a significant social problem in Erfurt in large part because it had been established as such in West Germany. Organizations focused on providing services to survivors of domestic violence received widespread state support, and the state passed legislation to enhance the rights of survivors and provide financial support to shelters for battered women. Service provisioning for women experiencing domestic violence became the largest niche within the local feminist movement.

Appeals to the logic of "catching up" resonate with the spatial alliance between Erfurt and the West through which Erfurt has increasingly claimed a status as a westernized city. Being western rests on both a rejection of the socialist past and embracing a history as German. Both election results and public discourse reflected the denunciation of the GDR immediately after unification. The poor showing of the PDS in early polls after unification, and the refusal of the SPD to work in coalition with the PDS out of fear of being aligned with the SED in the public eye, reflected a desire to move away from the SED and the GDR in the 1990s. Public discourse on the GDR in Erfurt also emphasizes the negative, repressive components of the state, with little, if any, attention to the positive aspects of life in the GDR.

Simultaneously, public discourse pointed to Erfurt's history as German to find cultural and historic ties to the West. Erfurt has been closely connected with western Germany historically, comprising part of the Mainz empires in the tenth and nineteenth centuries. By the beginning of the nineteenth century, many of the border regions of Thuringia were more culturally and linguistically identifiable as parts of Bavaria and Hesse, both states that became part of West Germany, than as distinctively part of Thuringia. Like Erfurt, these areas were remapped as Prussian, then French, and then Prussian again through the Napoleonic wars and beyond. Erfurt is near Weimar, the birthplace of the modern German state. At the close of the Second World War in the spring of 1945, American forces liberated the region. However, Allied troops stayed only for a brief period before trading Thuringia for part of Berlin. In June 1945, thousands of refugees fled from and through Thuringia as the Red Army advanced, arriving in Erfurt in July.

The Allies' brief stay heightened fears about, and resistance to, occupation by the Red Army in Erfurt. More than fifty years later, older Erfurter still talk about the withdrawal of Allied troops and the occupation by the Red Army as parallel to being switched at birth. In the local imagination, Erfurt was never meant to be part of the Communist East. During the GDR, the strength of religion and religious institutions in both the city and the region fortified resistance to the SED. It is no great surprise then that jubilance about unification in Erfurt translated into a public push to "catch up" with western Germany.

The view from the outside is also important. National discourses about locales view Erfurt and Thuringia as central to German history and as making uniquely German contributions to national identity. Thuringia has a signature bratwurst that, following the Bavarian white sausage, is the most coveted of local sausages in Germany. The Thuringian Forest is not quite the Black Forest, but this landscape is famous across Germany and is seen as part of the German landscape ideal. Thuringia is a major destination for domestic tourists who come to see the best and worst of German history: the Wartburg, a renowned feudal castle that was home to Martin Luther as he translated the New Testament into German and that was the birthplace of the formal movement for German unification after the Napoleonic wars; Weimar, the charming small city where Goethe, Bach, Schiller, and Liszt worked, where the Weimar Republic was born, and which was designated the 1999 European Capital of Culture (Roth 2003); and Buchenwald, one of the largest Nazi concentration camps on German soil where 250,000 people were imprisoned and at least 50,000 lost their lives during the Holocaust. Western Germany has embraced Erfurt and Thuringia as a long-lost piece of itself.

Given Thuringia's proximity to western Germany, its ties westward, and the push within the state's dominant political party, the CDU, to embrace westernization, welcome free-market capitalism, and shun the history of the GDR as a tragedy best forgotten, state leaders have sought to build a western city. Rejecting the GDR and embracing free-market democracy, the CDU successfully pushed to officially rename the state the Free State of Thuringia, or Freistaat Thüringen, in 1990. Reflecting on the importance of Erfurt's desire to be like western Germany, one activist from Erfurt concluded, "We may be in the new German states, but we're not so much like other easterners. In Erfurt, we look westward . . . we feel western."

In this climate, appeals by women's organizations based on the "catching up" mentality, especially with regard to the creation of democratic institutions outside of the state, resonated among the city and the public.[3] In rejecting the gender ideology of the GDR and instead embracing very different, but nonetheless both nonindigenous, feminist ideologies, feminists in Erfurt rebuffed identification as East or eastern German, and instead see themselves as moving westward. Yet while cashing in on the "catching up" rhetoric can sometimes work to the benefit of women's organizations in Erfurt, the western influence and the desire to be western have also proven problematic. Had women activists from western Germany offered a more cohesive or monolithic ideology to their counterparts in Erfurt, the feminist movement in Erfurt might have evolved quite differently. Instead, divisiveness inhibited effective coalitions and meaningful cooperation between activists and policymakers with differing visions of gender relations. Simultaneously, public and political support for free-market liberalism that is seen locally as part of westernization undermines feminists' claims for state interventions into inequalities.

Hostile Encounters: Feminism in Thuringia

The city of Erfurt is a place that has presented few opportunities for feminists to pursue their interests. The politics of the state of Thuringia also reflect the traditionalism, conservatism, and religiosity of the region with limited political or discursive opportunities for successful feminist mobilizations. At both the level of the city and the state, the discourse of westernization and the emergent place character as western have occasionally presented possibilities for feminists to align themselves with the spatial alliance with western Germany, which allows them to make claims of the state. However, the dominant trend remains that feminists are shut out of the project of making place within the city and across the state. Jumping scales can sometimes increase opportunities for social movements to engage with place and become part of place. If, for example, one place is dependent on its relationship with another place for resources, social movements can leap across places to find allies outside of their own place who have the clout and authority to effect change. The city of Erfurt and the state of Thuringia are so closely linked and so similar that jumping scales has not proven beneficial to feminists in this context. The state presents no alternative discourses or opportunities from the city, making the jumping of scales fruitless because the same obstacles are present at both the municipal and state levels, and they are even somewhat amplified at the state level.

Still, feminists in Erfurt have sought to influence the statewide level of governance and to make their concerns known to policymakers and the public across Thuringia. In 1993, representatives from women's organizations throughout the state came together to form the Landesfrauenrat Thuringia (State Women's Council of Thuringia, or LFR-TH), which has since served as the broadest network of women's organizations throughout the state and represents the interests of women—and women's organizations—in state politics. Founded largely in response to the creation of a statewide Frauenbüro (Office of Women's Affairs, analogous to GBs) that same year, the LFR-TH, like its counterparts in the other German states, focuses on state-level politics. Members are organizations rather than individuals. Approximately one-quarter of its member organizations operate solely in Erfurt; the remainder are either statewide organizations, most with chapters or headquarters in Erfurt, or are located in one of Thuringia's smaller cities, such as Gera, Jena, or Weimar.

In 2003, I met several times with Hannelore, a leader of the LFR-TH. Hannelore has been involved with women's organizations in both Erfurt and its environs since unification, and she is well aware of the conflicts between some of the women's organizations in Erfurt from her many years of service at the LFR-TH. Already at its inception in May 1993, women involved with the LFR-TH became embroiled in the larger political debate about Germany's abortion law. Some founding members, especially those active in the women's groups of the PDS and radical feminist organizations, wanted to specify their disapproval for this law in the mission statement of the LFR-TH, while others, most notably women active in the CDU-FU, did not think such a statement was appropriate. To help ease tensions between competing groups since her tenure as director began in 1997, Hannelore has urged the LFR-TH to elect boards of directors comprised of women not just from different organizations, but from organizations with differing ideologies; recent members of the board include women involved with the CDU-FU, the Arbeitsgemeinschaft Sozialdemokratischen Frauen (Working Society of Social Democratic Women, or ASF, the women's lobby of the SPD), the Arbeitsgemeinschaft Weiberwirtschaft DIE LINKE (Women's Working Group of the Left in Thuringia), the radical feminist Feministische Partei DIE FRAUEN (the Feminist Party THE WOMEN), the statewide organization of municipal Gender Equity Representatives, and women working with battered women's shelters, women's employment centers, and religious organizations.[4]

Hannelore has tried to promote cooperation across ideological groupings in part because she feels a united front is necessary to cope with the limited resources within the movement. A key problem for the feminist movement in Erfurt and Thuringia is the chronic shortage of funds for women's organizations and the competition for such funds between groups, some of which were already positioned as ideological rivals. Through the creation of a statewide Office of Women's Affairs in 1993, new state funds became available to women's organizations in 1994. Furthermore, as in other states, the statewide GB who headed this office was granted certain political rights that helped women's organizations find a political voice at the state level.

The longest-reigning GB in Thuringia, who assumed the post upon its inception and remained there into the new millennium, was often ineffectual. She maintained a relatively low profile, eschewing frequent public appearances, failing to materialize at legislative committee meetings, and rarely taking on the role of an active lobbyist. As part of the governor's cabinet (*Staatskanzlei*) and carrying the title of state secretary (*Staatssekretärin*), governors appoint state-wide GBs, generally along party lines. Reflecting the general constellation of political power in the state government of Thuringia, all appointees to this post have been members of the CDU, and the first GB was at the conservative end of the CDU with no prior experience with feminism, gender, or women's issues.

The diligent work of her staff members often compensated for the GB's lack of competence and commitment. During the course of the mid- and late 1990s, staff created and maintained an active network of battered women's shelters, secured state funding for various organizations, most especially those working to combat violence against women, developed various educational materials for the public, and hosted regular conferences that brought women from different organizations into frequent and repeated contact with key political leaders. Naturally, certain processes were slowed due to the lack of leadership; for example, in 1998 Thuringia became the last of the new eastern German states to pass a statewide gender-equity law (*Gleichstellungsgesetz*). The lack of commitment of the GB further weakened the position of the feminist movement within a hostile political environment. This ultimately resulted in a stunted, rather than expanded, feminist policy machinery at the state level in the 1990s and early 2000s.

Most organizations, however, did benefit from the presence of a state cabinet officially devoted to women's issues, particularly insofar as the Office of Women's Affairs was tied to the availability of funds. Still, the Office of Women's Affairs had guidelines for funding, and not all organizations in Erfurt satisfied specific criteria. In addition, funds were distributed at different rates to organizations with different goals and services. For example, in the funding guidelines established in 1994 and which remained in effect beyond the end of the decade, the state could pay up to 90 percent of personnel costs and 30 percent of overhead costs for battered women's shelters with the remaining 20 percent of revenue coming from city funds, ABM-subsidized salaries, and private donations. Organizations like Brennessel, which offer services to battered women, but which do not operate a shelter, are not entitled to this level of funding, nor were any funds earmarked for services for survivors of sexual violence against women.

Similarly, the new Office of Women's Affairs would set specific funding parameters for educational and job-training programs, child-care cooperatives, and other types of organizations. During the mid-1990s, one organization, Tiamat, a feminist health center that offered gynecological, holistic, and alternative health services to women and that was, by all accounts, extremely popular in the city, was, in the words of one woman indirectly involved with its funding, "starved out" by the state. The GB in the 1990s was herself a medical doctor and unsympathetic to holistic and homeopathic medicine, as well as to midwifery; activists believe that at her urging, the governor's cabinet set the parameters of the funding guidelines for health centers to exclude Tiamat, which closed in 2000 due to bankruptcy.

Through contacts with political leaders in the municipality and state, as well as through lobbying organizations, nonprofit, nonpartisan women's organizations tried to work throughout the 1990s to secure their own funding, to increase public awareness about a variety of women's issues, and to incorporate their interests into the goals of the state. These efforts were not unilaterally successful, but instead were undercut by a number of different factors. First, because of the internal problems within the Office of Women's Affairs, this office remained relatively marginalized within state politics through the end of the decade, and respondents widely describe it as being far less effective than activists in the nonprofit sector had hoped when the office first opened. Although many women's organizations were able to bypass direct contact with the GB by dealing instead with the staff in the office and with elected state representatives, the Office of Women's Affairs in the 1990s was not a major player in the state cabinet, or in the feminist movement. While it could have been a hub of networks between different women's organizations and politicians, the Office of Women's Affairs became, in the eyes of some activists, a funding agency with little to offer the feminist movement in the realm of networking, contacts, or political clout.

Second, while the presence of women's organizations reinforced the legitimacy of political leaders addressing women's issues, as well as special offices created to attend to these issues, the underrepresentation of women and feminists among elected leaders, especially at the state level, hindered legislative progress. Especially in the dominant CDU, women's issues continued to be relegated to the arena of nonessential social issues. Women involved with the CDU and the CDU-FU are generally very cognizant of this problem and spoke with me at length about the resistance they experienced among their male colleagues in trying to draw attention to women's issues. The marginalization of women leaders was problematic outside of the CDU, as well; even Birgit Adamek, who has served as the GB in Erfurt for more than a decade, reported frequent problems with male council members and other city officials who simply didn't understand the value of women's organizations and who avoided addressing difficult topics like battering and sexual violence.

Third, the ideological divisions within the women's movement meant that elected leaders seeking change on women's issues could not point to a broad base of support among women's organizations. Disagreements between women's organizations and between women politicians from different parties over the age guidelines for guaranteed child care hampered efforts at reinstating state guarantees of child care. Several policymakers I met noted that they didn't pay much attention to the feminist movement because they couldn't identify who it represents, or if it even represents anyone.

Taken together, these three issues undercut the legitimacy of the women's movement and efforts by women in elected and appointed office to increase attention to women's issues in politics. Although activists and femocrats were often able to make do in the absence of cohesiveness and solidarity between organizations, and of legitimate, respected political leadership, many activists continued to feel that their organizations lived on the financial edge and were not able to effect social policy changes. The pervasiveness of these problems—and their effects on specific women's organizations—tended to wax and wane during the late 1990s with some years seemingly better than others, but most leaders in the women's movement approached the new millennium with grave concerns about the longevity of feminist social services and political action in Erfurt.

While every activist I spoke with in Erfurt complained about a shortage of funds for the organization with which she worked, the effects of reduced funding played out differently across organizational contexts. Only the two battered women's shelters seemed financially healthy because they received church funds if other funding sources fell short. Among other organizations, the financial picture featured various shades of pink, with a few running in the red. Given the complex constellation of women's organizations and political actors in Erfurt, some alliances ultimately emerged as more powerful than others. Specifically, those organizations that aligned themselves with conservative feminist ideology and the CDU were more likely to receive municipal and state funding and to be viewed favorably by policymakers and the public. The state was less likely to fund organizations espousing radical or neosocialist feminist ideologies and aligned with the SPD or the PDS, the two opposition parties in the state government, and public support for these organizations also appears lower.[5]

Overall, those organizations with a diversified funding base, or which were supported by a religious institution, fared better financially than those with a narrow funding base. Organizations that received funds from not just the city and state GBs but also from other state offices, such as the Office of Youth, the Office of Families, or state offices like those devoted to employment, human development, and justice, tended to weather the city and state's financial problems better than those organizations that had come to rely on only one or two state agencies for funding. The city's GB recognizes that, in hindsight, she should have done more to push women's organizations in the city toward diversifying their funding sources. Birgit worries that she did a disservice to women's organizations in Erfurt—including the Municipal Women's Center—by encouraging and helping them to apply for ABM and SAM funds through the Employment Office and by helping them navigate statewide funding opportunities through the GB. She laments that, "In these many projects, we moved away from regular financing and used all of the aid money first. That way, a landscape of women's projects developed that was quite large and diverse, but which actually has an insecure foundation, which is what we're feeling today. When these aid programs fall apart—and that trend keeps getting stronger—the women's projects will be hurt because they turned to aid programs first, because they made the most sense and because I urged them to."

Here, Birgit differentiates between regular financing and aid. Regular financing includes money that is permanently legislated for specific issues and aid refers to temporary programs created to support redevelopment in the new eastern German states. ABM and SAM, for example, are considered aid programs. Similarly, the funds municipal and statewide GBs disburse often came through federal funding pools earmarked for the redevelopment of eastern Germany rather than through more permanent, tax-funded pools collected and administered by the local state. The German federal government pumped an estimated US$1.5 trillion into eastern Germany between 1990 and 2003 (Regierungskommission Aufbau Ost 2004); while only a minute fraction of that trickled down into the grant budgets of municipal and statewide GBs, much of their money came from these impermanent, postunification funds, rather than from permanent, legislated accounts. Birgit suggests that perhaps women's organizations should have focused on pushing for permanent, binding funding guidelines instead of piecing together their annual budgets from shorter-term resources and consenting to time-limited funding guidelines set by the GB's office and the state legislature. Had such an alternate approach been successful, state funding for women's organizations would have been institutionalized and less susceptible to funding problems created by the steadily dropping amount of aid money made available through the federal government. Financial commitments, of course, are also symbolically important, and securing state resources would suggest that the state is committed to feminist organizations and the development and maintenance of feminist civil society and social service organizations.

Instead, women's organizations did not attempt to push for permanent funding mandates for any type of women's organization. Retrospectively, some activists now acknowledge that they would have been wise to lobby for such measures, and they also realize that, in many cases, reliance on ABM funds has been especially damaging, not only because some organizations never prepared for being able to fund their own employees, but also because ABM funding resulted in relatively rapid employee turnover and occasionally created conflicts between women working at the same organization as they vied for a limited number of ABM positions. Yet many women's organizations did not look beyond ABM positions and funds from the municipal and statewide GBs, even though funds were often available for women's organizations from other sources.

Eschewing the EU

Feminist organizations in Erfurt have had limited success securing municipal or state funds to support their work. The federal government in Germany does not subsidize local organizations and thus was not an alternate source of financial support, nor did it offer any symbolic support for feminist goals. Another possible resource did exist, however: the European Union. Yet with the exception of the Women's Technical Center, women's organizations in Erfurt have overwhelmingly eschewed funding through the European Union (EU) even as the EU increased the number and size of funding programs available to women's organizations, especially those in underdeveloped regions in Europe, such as the new eastern German states.

Some organizations are functionally ineligible for EU funding. At Brennessel, for example, the programmatic offerings do not fit the funding guidelines set by the EU particularly well, and, as such, the organization would be unlikely to succeed in applying for EU funds. As EU funding directives are almost always geared toward organizations that address economic issues, the emphasis at Brennessel on personal safety and enrichment—rather than on employment and improving human capital—limits its capacity to obtain EU funds. Because activists at Brennessel are ideologically wedded to radical feminism and are therefore unwilling to alter their programmatic and service offerings to fit either the EU's emphasis on employment or on gender mainstreaming, the organiza- tion is ineligible for most types of funding through the EU.

While most activists and policymakers in Erfurt offered positive assessments of the EU generally, few saw any direct relationship between the goals and pro- grams of the EU and their own work. Indeed, most women's organizations in Erfurt have little to no direct contact with the EU and its agencies. Although as a state capitol, the city of Erfurt is home to an EU satellite office, activists and femocrats tend to view the EU as a distant and abstract institution. In discussing the EU with me, respondents would often make spatial references that high- lighted how distanced the EU is from everyday life in Erfurt. Comments about the EU routinely began with phrases like, "Way up there in Brussels. . . ." Such rhetoric reflects the general idea among respondents that the EU is not relevant for Erfurt, is removed from local concerns, and that EU policymakers are far detached from the local experiences of people in Erfurt.

Gender mainstreaming is arguably the most relevant EU policy initiative for local feminist movements, but it does not resonate in Erfurt. Most activists were familiar with the EU's agenda for gender mainstreaming, but they were generally uncomfortable with the idea (Guenther 2008). Reservations about the EU's agenda for gender mainstreaming stem from multiple, interrelated issues that ultimately eliminated the capacity of the feminist movement in Erfurt to implement or otherwise employ gender mainstreaming. In many cases, gen- der mainstreaming, what it means, and what its effects may be for women's organizations are misunderstood. Feminist leaders in Erfurt are afraid that the implementation of gender mainstreaming will have negative consequences for the local feminist movement and local women's organizations. Activists at Brennessel, as well as women I spoke with who work at battered women's shel- ters and who had been employed at the former Municipal Women's Center, expressed concern that the implementation of gender mainstreaming would undercut funding, resources, and public support for organizations and institu- tions that focus on women's disadvantages relative to men.

Although not unilaterally opposed to the concept of gender mainstreaming, most respondents were uncomfortable with the idea of paying equal attention to the effects of gender inequality on women and men. As a group of women I spoke with at Brennessel argued, doing so would veil the fact that gender in- equality has more serious repercussions for women than for men. From their point of view, victims of battering, rape, and incest are overwhelmingly women, and experiences with these forms of violence are far more detrimental to an individual's mental and physical well-being than the more typically male experience with gender inequality, such as being positioned as a secondary caregiver to children or as the breadwinner for a family. What emerged most clearly from this conversation is that gender mainstreaming obscures the power men have over women.

The reception of gender mainstreaming among more centrist and conservative women's organizations has been somewhat warmer, although here, too, some activists primarily expressed confusion about the concept of gender mainstreaming. One upper-level employee at the Center for Women and Families stated that she had heard the term and knew that many of her colleagues were working on it in the state government, but she conceded that she could neither pronounce nor define it. A nun at the battered women's shelter run by the Order of the Good Shepherd relayed that she was familiar with the idea and found it interesting, but she wasn't convinced it had any bearing on her work with battered women: "It is very complicated, this idea, and I'm not really clear how it's relevant for our work with victimized women."

To some degree, ambivalence and concerns about gender mainstreaming among participants in this study seem to stem from misinformation about gender mainstreaming. The approach is not intended as a substitute for feminism. However, as some critics in Erfurt rightly note, even if the EU intends for gender mainstreaming to augment feminist efforts, local constraints on funding and resources could mean that pursuing gender mainstreaming and feminism would become an either/or question.

Gender mainstreaming horror stories from the western German states further heighten these anxieties. Many respondents told me about stories they had heard about women's organizations in western Germany suffering from reduced funding because of the implementation of gender mainstreaming. Others relayed that western German municipalities closed the offices of GBs in cities in western Germany when those municipalities adopted gender mainstreaming.

Even more commonly, respondents, especially those with radical feminist beliefs, drew on the reservations of colleagues in the West to justify their own lack of support for gender mainstreaming. Given the close connections between eastern and western German feminist activists in Erfurt, transmission of gender mainstreaming horror stories, as well as of anti-gender mainstreaming opinions, has been rapid. Furthermore, although there is an absence of research on the reception of gender mainstreaming among western German feminists, the more radical feminist ideology common among western German women working in autonomous feminist organizations there, as well as the specific history of the West German feminist movement and anecdotal evidence from this research, suggests that western German feminists are less likely to support gender mainstreaming than their peers in the eastern German states. With repeated exposure to western German feminists who are critical of, and fearful about, gender mainstreaming, activists in Erfurt have had little opportunity to reach their own conclusions about gender mainstreaming.

The strongest proponents of gender mainstreaming in Erfurt are women politicians from the CDU. These are women who are well received within conservative feminist organizations, but who have limited credibility with radical feminists, like those at Brennessel. Well aware of the lack of support they receive from certain corners in the local women's movement, these proponents of gender mainstreaming have not even attempted to broach gender mainstreaming as a cause that could be taken up by a coalition of activists within and outside of the state.

These women are also seemingly unlikely supporters of gender mainstreaming. The idea does not ostensibly resonate with conservative feminism and its emphasis on women's differences from men as caregivers and nurturers. Yet some conservative feminists have sought to draw attention to the concept, asserting that its utility lies in the fact that gender mainstreaming is less radical than radical feminists' conceptualizations of gender relations and therefore is less likely to threaten male colleagues. However, because gender mainstreaming is not inherently congruent with the beliefs of conservative feminists, conservative feminist proponents report mixed responses to the idea.

Even among state policymakers, interpretations of and enthusiasm for gender mainstreaming vary, and confusion about the meaning of the term abounds. As one conservative femocrat in the state Office of the Equality Representative muses, reflecting the weariness and wariness she and many of her colleagues in state policymaking bring to discussions of gender mainstreaming:

> Already the wording of it makes it almost impossible to translate into German. Maybe it works in England, but here it just doesn't make any sense. And then you can't even explain it in one sentence. You have to use ten sentences and attend a seminar. You have to explain so much about it, and that simply makes it difficult. I think positive action for women was already difficult enough to jus-

tify. It's my feeling that, well, in the last few years, we really started to notice that we were making progress. Things got better. One started to feel accepted, and it was certainly the case that we were integrated. But now with this new gender agenda, or gender mainstreaming, this is again something that, in my view, is difficult, because it's something new again and not a soul understands it and no one wants to hear about it.

In this account, gender mainstreaming is a cause for concern because it is difficult to explain and to comprehend. The danger of confusion and apprehension about gender mainstreaming, as identified by this respondent, is that it creates the risk of losing hard-won ground. This official feels that her office has been successful in making inroads in the last few years, and she worries that attempting to introduce a new concept—and such a complex one at that—will undermine their progress.

Maria, the state representative from the CDU and a longtime member and former head of the Equality Committee of the state legislature, supports the implementation of gender mainstreaming in the state legislature, but she also has concerns about it. Like most other politicians, she sees gender mainstreaming as most important in the legislative arena because one of the primary goals of gender mainstreaming is to evaluate if and how proposed or passed legislation will affect women and men differently. To increase support for gender mainstreaming, Maria pushed the state parliament to discuss the concept on the floor and organized educational events to provide legislators with detailed information about gender mainstreaming. Although, as of 2009, the state government had not instituted any formal procedures for implementing gender mainstreaming, the statewide GB employs the approach in analyzing proposed legislation.

Nevertheless, Maria is aware that integrating gender mainstreaming into state policymaking poses specific challenges. She has witnessed how resistant her male colleagues in particular are to the term, even within the Equality Committee. She notes that the term is not self-explanatory, and that in her party especially, it offends those who advocate the maintenance of the German language.[6] She is also concerned that introducing this new concept will be the proverbial straw that breaks the camel's back in that some male policymakers have, in her view, had enough of all the different demands made by feminist politicians and the women's movement.

Yet Maria is still optimistic that with sufficient pressure from the EU and the federal government, gender mainstreaming could be implemented at the level of statewide governance in Thuringia. She discusses some of the problems she has experienced with gender mainstreaming:

> When one meets a state representative outside of the parliament—the men, anyway—they approach me and say, "Gender mainstreaming! Now you've really cooked up something new, you women. Isn't it enough for you that you're already involved everywhere?" Because they don't understand it. Only the SPD and the PDS—they are the opposition here—don't concede anything about their own problems with men in their party, but I can say that this idea is often met with resistance. I'm someone who is stubborn and I don't let myself get discouraged. The first time we brought up the issue of violence against women, they all laughed, "Now she shows up with this issue in which no one is interested. It's all bunk. That only happens in the lower social classes, in the asocial milieu; normal people don't beat each other up." But now we've achieved that and everyone says, "OK, you were actually right. When you really look around, this does happen." So I hope the same will happen [with gender mainstreaming], only it is a process that will take a long time.

Here, Maria reports that male colleagues see gender mainstreaming as the latest in a string of feminist concoctions. Critical of women in the two opposition parties, the SPD and PDS, for being less open about problems with men and gender inequality in their parties than she is, Maria assures me that she is being totally frank in conceding that men in the CDU can respond less than favorably to the interests of women. While aware of male resistance to gender mainstreaming, she is simultaneously cognizant of the fact that change takes time. Reflecting on her experiences advocating for increased attention to violence against women, Maria remembers how her colleagues in the state parliament responded by claiming that it was a minor problem limited to the underclass and asocial types. Over time, however, they came to recognize that domestic violence occurs in all social groups and is a significant social problem. Maria's hope is that resistance to the idea of gender mainstreaming will erode over time, just as resistance to addressing violence against women did.

Rosa, a state representative from the SPD, also supports gender mainstreaming. For her, the concept goes beyond legislative issues as she sees gender mainstreaming as applicable to various dimensions of social life. In explaining to me why she supports gender mainstreaming, Rosa drew on an example from the experiences of an old friend, Robert. Robert was married to a school teacher who was killed in the massacre at the Gutenburg High School in Erfurt in 2002. Suddenly a single father, he became the primary caregiver to the couple's young children. In discussing the loss of his wife and how he is coping with it, Robert told Rosa that while he would give anything to have his wife back, being a single father also allowed him to experience caring for, and loving, his children in a whole new way. Freed from the social expectation that his wife be primarily responsible for the children, he discovered tremendous joy in parenting. As Rosa tells me this story, she asserts that when applied not just to laws and governments, but also to the entire social system, gender mainstreaming would free both women and men from the constraints of traditional expectations about gender.

That Rosa sees gender mainstreaming as promising in presenting both women and men with new opportunities is tied to her own exposure to gender mainstreaming. As a member of the Equality Committee of the state legislature, Rosa is one of few policymakers in Thuringia who has witnessed gender mainstreaming in action through an educational trip to Sweden in 2002. During this trip, the members of the Equality Committee—which included representatives from the CDU, SPD, and PDS, almost all of whom were female—spent a week in Sweden meeting with experts on gender mainstreaming there, participating in educational events about gender mainstreaming, and touring institutions that have implemented gender mainstreaming. Rosa was impressed with what she saw in Sweden, and while not entirely certain if all aspects of the Swedish model would function effectively in Thuringia, the trip persuaded her to take a more active role in pushing for consideration of the gendered effects of new legislation.

Tatiana, a state representative for the PDS, a leader in the Equality Committee since 2000, and a participant in the trip to Sweden in 2002, is not enamored with gender mainstreaming. She worries that gender mainstreaming will be used to weaken support for women's issues and women's organizations. She is highly critical of the governor and the state legislature for failing to take meaningful action to implement gender mainstreaming. She feels that in order to be a consequential new tool for equalizing gender relations, gender mainstreaming must receive extensive attention at the state level through a minister devoted solely to this issue, specific, legislated guidelines for implementation, and a demonstrated commitment among policymakers to follow through with gender mainstreaming. Tatiana does not see such steps being taken; in fact, she repeatedly mentioned during our conversation how the male-dominated CDU largely resists the idea. While recognizing the work of women within the CDU, and in other political parties, to increase awareness about gender mainstreaming, Tatiana also believes that the CDU is largely paying lip service to gender mainstreaming, rather than taking active, permanent steps toward institutionalizing it.

Tatiana explains, "I also have big concerns about it, that there is little readiness for real change. Right now, I see more of the dangers of gender mainstreaming, that through it we can find a justification for weakening support for women, but without any possibility for replacing women's politics with something new. In that sense, I am a bit ambivalent about it; although I see the positive possibilities of this concept, it also naturally seems dangerous." Tatiana is not unilaterally opposed to gender mainstreaming; in fact, here she describes herself as ambivalent toward the concept. She recognizes that gender mainstreaming holds promise for creating and maintaining real change, but she thinks it is risky because, in her view, it can be twisted to undermine support for women's politics.

In the absence of evidence that gender mainstreaming is being taken seriously by the state government, Tatiana suspects that proponents of gender mainstreaming intend to use the concept to undercut women's politics without replacing it with a useful alternative. Because gender mainstreaming had not, at the time of our conversation, been implemented in Thuringia in any far-reaching way, the proponents of gender mainstreaming, including Maria, Rosa, and a small group of women legislators, mostly from the CDU, have little to point to in the way of concrete examples of change when faced with skeptics like Tatiana. As of late 2003, the only efforts at implementing gender mainstreaming at the state level were in a series of small pilot projects sponsored by the state, one of which sought to put gender mainstreaming into practice at a university in Gotha, and another of which sought to apply gender mainstreaming to village revitalization, or *Dorferneuerung*, programs. The statewide GB's office also partially dedicated one of its officials to oversee issues of gender mainstreaming, and this official became a clearinghouse for information about gender mainstreaming. These steps are not sufficient for Tatiana to think that gender mainstreaming is developing as a viable alternative to feminist politics in the state.

Birgit, the GB of Erfurt, shares Tatiana's concerns. She has heard stories about the effects of gender mainstreaming in western German cities and is afraid that its implementation in Erfurt could lead to the dissolution of her office. She tells me:

> In many cities in the old German states, the concept of gender mainstreaming was used to close Women's Offices, or to throw GBs out of their jobs. I am

especially aware of that happening in another city where a particularly great colleague became a victim because everyone has their own definition of gender mainstreaming. Many women have different definitions, and men certainly do. It's difficult after a time—equality, equal opportunity, plans to support women— now all of a sudden . . . to add gender mainstreaming. I haven't gotten anywhere with it myself. I brought it up at the Women's Political Round Table, and every- one sat up and said, "You have to explain that to us more clearly. We can't even pronounce it. . . ." But the world won't break apart if, today and tomorrow, I'm not the person who brings gender mainstreaming to life for the city of Erfurt.

Here, Birgit expresses direct concern about the safety of her position, which is important to her not just so long as she fills the post, but because she feels strongly that the city needs a GB. Well connected to GBs in other cities through a network of municipal GBs, Birgit had heard stories about GBs in other cities, and especially in the western German states, whose offices were closed under the auspices that having a city official dedicated to women's issues directly con- tradicted the premise of gender mainstreaming. Birgit was especially shaken by the story of a GB whom she held in very high regard. In my own efforts to find out what happened to the displaced GBs of cities invoked by opponents of gender mainstreaming in Erfurt, including not just Birgit, but a number of other women, most of whom are oriented toward radical feminism, I was un- able to find solid evidence to suggest that gender mainstreaming played a role. In the two most oft-cited cases, the cities closed the GB's offices, along with other "nonessential" offices, when they went bankrupt. Neither municipality had formally introduced or implemented gender mainstreaming at the time of these changes.

Nevertheless, stories from the West about the effects of gender mainstream- ing shape attitudes toward gender mainstreaming among both policymakers and activists in Erfurt. While a seemingly greater proportion of government of- ficials support gender mainstreaming than activists, the concept is contentious in both groups. Concerns about gender mainstreaming are also justified with the same logic: that gender mainstreaming is confusing could undermine the progress of the women's movement and may place certain organizations and agencies at risk for closure.

Because of the lack of cohesive support for gender mainstreaming, the state government had taken only minimal steps to comply with EU directives on gender mainstreaming by early 2004. While women in the CDU advocated gender mainstreaming at the state level, their minority position within the party and the lack of visible support from social movement actors outside of the state hampered their efforts. The only nongovernmental women's organization to incorporate gender mainstreaming into its agenda has been the LFR-TH, but even this move has been largely symbolic. The LFR-TH has not integrated gender mainstreaming into its mission statement, but instead makes clear in its publicity materials that "gender mainstreaming and support for women are understood as a dual strategy." Although some members of the LFR-TH had agitated for the implementation of such a group, as of 2003, the LFR-TH had not even created a working group on gender mainstreaming.

Thus, several factors underlie reservations about gender mainstreaming. Because it creates confusion and adds to an already complex list of demands made by women's organizations and agencies, gender mainstreaming could detract attention from other issues. A more frightening possibility is that if gender mainstreaming is fully implemented, many activists feel that it could be used to justify eliminating GBs or funding for organizations that focus on women rather than on gender. The stories advocacy networks with western German feminists transmit heighten such fears. These reservations about gender mainstreaming are strong enough to push feminist organizations in Erfurt away from the EU as a possible resource and ally. Coupled with the feminist movement's relative political weakness in the state, it simply lacks the necessary capacity to promote gender mainstreaming successfully.

The Onward Struggle

The feminist movement in Erfurt emerged from a place hostile to feminist interests and where opportunities for feminists to participate in making place—and becoming part of place—were significantly limited. Many of the characteristics of the place of the city, such as conservatism, religiosity, and traditionalism, are echoed at the state level. Feminists thus have had little success making headway within statewide institutions or to a broader statewide public. The local, statewide, and federal levels of governance all present few political or discursive opportunities for feminists in Erfurt who have been shut out of the processes of making policy and of making place.

Ideological divisions within the feminist movement in Erfurt damaged efforts at organizing across scales of governance. Rather than working together, women's organizations in Erfurt continued to go it alone and were unable to push for changes in the state, including in the office of the statewide GB. Consequently, women's organizations did not receive symbolic, political, or financial support from the state of Thuringia. Feminism and feminist interests remained at the periphery of state institutions and largely invisible to the general public across the state.

Ideological conflict contributed to the lack of entrenchment of feminist interests within the city's and state's political apparatus or public discourse. Feminist organizations could not come together to form an effective lobby. State actors fueled conflicts by playing favorites among feminist organizations and creating resource competition. Policymakers at the state level especially maligned radical feminist organizations whose goals and strategies are least congruent with the state's character.

The spatial alliance with western Germany has operated as both an opportunity and constraint for feminists. Feminists have occasionally been able to legitimize their work by positioning it as part of catching up with western Germany. Specific social services commonly available for women in western Germany— such as shelters for battered for women—have garnered support in Erfurt and in the state of Thuringia in part because of successful claims by feminists that these services are part of westernization. Not all claims at being part of catching up resonate, however. Radical feminists in particular have occasionally tried to inject the idea that autonomous organizations are an important part of developing a western-style civil society into local discourses about catching up. They have also asserted that their ideology is widespread within the western German feminist movement. These arguments do not seem to have taken hold and have had no notable effect on increasing support for radical feminist organizations.

Coalition work with western German feminists also played a part in shaping the relationship between the local feminist movement in Erfurt and the place of the city and state. On the one hand, feminist organizations from western Germany provided valuable logistical support and encouragement to the young feminist movement in Erfurt. On the other hand, feminists from western Germany carried their own ideologies with them, thereby reinforcing rifts between camps of feminists in Erfurt.

Although the EU is a potential site for feminist action and legitimization, feminists in Erfurt view it as a distant and unrelated governing body and source of identity. Alignment with the EU could potentially undermine feminist goals, even if it increases financial security. Reservations about the EU's agenda for gender mainstreaming, which most feminists in Erfurt perceive as threatening the limited gains they have made, retard feminists' willingness to align with the EU. While a small group of women, mostly from the CDU, has sought to promote gender mainstreaming in local governance, the implementation of the concept has been minimal, increasing worries among some other feminist policymakers that gender mainstreaming will become a smokescreen for dismantling support structures for women and women's organizations without a meaningful, effective substitute.

These worries ultimately proved to be well founded. In a surprise move in July 2004, the governor of Thuringia determined that the office of the state-wide GB would be dismantled as a state secretariat and instead would become a suboffice within the Ministry for Social Issues, Family, and Health. This was a major setback in that the GB's office is no longer an independent secretariat, but rather is subsumed under the rubric of social issues and family. Potentially even more damaging, the GB no longer has speaking rights in the state legislature, and rather than reporting directly to the governor, she reports to the minister of social issues, family, and health, who then reports to the governor. State legislator Katja Wolf (PDS), the chair of the Equality Committee, stated in a press release that subsuming the GB's office within the Ministry of Social Issues, Family and Health "exemplifies the typical conservative image of women: women should define themselves solely and completely through their family."

While the move to dismantle the GB's office as a state secretariat was in itself disturbing, even more so is that the change was made virtually without warning and with no input from any women's organization, the Equality Committee of the state legislature, or, reportedly, the sitting GB herself. That such a decision could be made in the absence of any discussion with the effected parties demonstrates the lack of integration of the feminist movement into state politics and just how shaky the ground is under the feet of women's organizations and agencies—including those within the state—in Thuringia.

Other news from Erfurt is no happier. In April 2005, women's organizations criticized the governor's office after it cited financial problems as the explanation for delaying its usual payments to women's centers and battered women's shelters. An initial panic that all funding for women's centers and battered women's shelters would be suspended proved unfounded. Still, many organizations experienced deep and unexpected cuts in their budgets, as well as lengthy payment delays that created problems with vendors and creditors. After weeks of negotiation, the Ministry for Social Issues, Health, and Family announced in May 2005 that it was cutting the annual budget of the State Women's Council from €49,000 to €38,000, a reduction of more than 20 percent. The chair of the

Equality Committee, a member of the PDS, made the following statements in a press release:

> Thuringia is getting rid of its State Women's Council, so now all that will be left are the Gender Representatives in the ministries and equality based on the "Swedish model" left to the boss. Or is it actually about pushing women in Thuringia back in front of the stove!? There, they don't steal jobs from men and there they can take care of their many children. Incidentally, those kids have yet to be born, which seems unlikely in the increasingly misogynist climate in the Free State [of Thuringia]. (PDS Faktion im Thüringer Landtag 2005)

While the LFR-TH will not likely close its doors due to this cut in funding, the decrease in state funds in the immediate aftermath of doing away with the statewide GB does not auger well for the LFR-TH, or for other women's organizations.

In spite of these setbacks, the feminist movement in Erfurt has enjoyed many successes. It has drawn public and political attention to critical social problems, including domestic violence, balancing work and family, un- and underemployment, and sexual discrimination in the workplace. The organizational field remains diverse, if not so vibrant, offering women a range of services from diverse ideological perspectives. Activists accomplished all of this even in the presence of a conservative majority party in city and state governance, and a cultural legacy in the region built on traditional, religious values and an intense resentment of the SED. As I completed my fieldwork during the holiday season, I walked through the city's idyllic Christmas market at least once a day in the weeks leading up to my departure. Yet in spite of the good cheer around me, I felt decidedly un-jolly, bothered by an aching feeling that when I returned to Erfurt, the organizations I had come to admire and respect could be gone.

A Bridge Between Places

Through the course of participating in my research, respondents learned that I was studying the feminist movements in two cities. The former GDR is quite small with a landmass roughly equal to that of the state of Tennessee in the United States, but with significantly better transportation options. Yet virtually no one I met in Rostock had ever been to Erfurt or vice versa. National networks of feminists in Germany are also quite weak and, with the exception of leaders in the shelter movement for battered women, few organizational leaders participate in broader coalitions or networks on a national scale. Thus, local feminist movements in eastern Germany operate in isolation from one another.

Given this lack of visitation or communication, I was not surprised that many activists in each of the cities asked questions about what was happening in the other locale. Feminist activists were curious to know what was going on in the other city and what they might learn from the activities and strategies of feminists elsewhere. I became a conduit of information, sharing my impressions of each place and its feminist organizations with women from the other city.

I sometimes ended up correcting misconceptions women from one city held about those in the other. Many women in Erfurt assumed there was no feminist movement in Rostock or Mecklenburg-West Pomerania. After learning that I was studying feminist organizing in Rostock, one woman I interviewed in Erfurt asked incredulously, "Don't you have to use a magnifying glass just to find any women's organizations up there?" Another woman in Erfurt responded to my report of roughly equal numbers of feminist organizations in both cities disbelievingly, insisting it "just couldn't be possible that there are women's organizations up there." Reflecting characterizations of northeastern Germans as reserved and deliberate, *some wondered if women in Rostock would have the motivation and commitment to organize into projects or organizations.*

While activists in Erfurt often presumed that feminist organizing in Rostock was rare, those in Rostock typically associated feminism in Erfurt and Thuringia with western German radical feminism. Several women in Rostock speculated that women's organizing in Erfurt would be anti-men and focused largely on self-actualization. One leader in the feminist movement in Rostock asked if women in Erfurt practiced, "Hocus-pocus yoga feminism." Several other women there speculated that feminism in Erfurt would be predominantly "cultural" or "lifestyle" feminism that emphasizes ecological living, uninhibited sexuality, and building feminist friendships.

In spite of some undertones of judgment or suspicion, I typically sensed curiosity rather than competition in my conversations about the two cases. Women in both places wanted to understand the parallels and differences between their strategies and experiences. They also wanted to know about the everyday lived experience in the other city. I was frequently asked to describe the physicality and character of the cities, as well as what I personally liked and disliked about each place.

Although I routinely noted various differences between the two places on aspects as diverse as the weather and the nightlife, what struck me most about women's reactions to the information I would convey about the other city is how easily and quickly they would reinterpret my narratives of difference as narratives of similarity. Hearing about feminist organizing in another place was like looking into a distant mirror. Feminists in Rostock and Erfurt could see each other in the stories and assessments I shared. They saw shared struggles around issues like building community, securing funding, and drawing attention to a range of problems facing women. They found common ground in anecdotes about dealing with government bureaucracies, funding issues, and members of the public who assume feminists hate men and/or are lesbians. They laughed about similar annoyances and frustrations with ABM. They always conveyed their good wishes to the other movement. Their enthusiasm for learning about feminism in other contexts reminded me that in spite of the localization and decentralization of German feminism, the structural barriers to mass feminist mobilization at the national level, and the many differences I noticed as an analyst of these two movements, a more unified feminist identity—and even a more unified feminist movement—remains within the realm of possibility in eastern Germany.

7 Claiming Their Places?

The Feminist Movements in Rostock and Erfurt in Comparative Perspective

AFTER MORE THAN A YEAR AWAY, I returned to Rostock to conduct additional and follow-up interviews in the autumn of 2005. In meeting with staff members of the LFR-MV, I heard reports about various new initiatives to help women's organizations expand their funding bases and of the growing emphasis on gender mainstreaming. Many women's organizations continued to prosper and grow. The Women's Educational Network was bustling in preparation for new courses. The Beginenhof was undergoing a fresh round of renovations to improve and expand the office space of Women Helping Women, the parent organization of the city's battered women's shelter, rape-crisis center, and shelter and counseling program for abused girls.

The picture in Rostock was quite different from that in Erfurt, where, when I left the field in 2004, and as I heard through continuing reports from respondents later, women's organizations faced an increasingly uphill battle in securing resources to fund their work. To its credit, the local feminist movement in Erfurt succeeded in creating and maintaining as many women's organizations as in Rostock that offer an array of services to women there, contributed to the passage of several pieces of statewide legislation that offer women increased protection from workplace discrimination and violent partners, and spearheaded a visible public education campaign drawing attention to violence against women. Yet the movement there seemed to be struggling more and more to retain its foothold among public-funding agencies and policymakers. In addition to further reductions in the political power of the statewide GB, many organizations face mounting financial pressures as the local state reduces its commitments to women's organizations.

The current endpoints of these two feminist movements prompted the relatively simple question with which I began this book: How can two feminist movements born out of the same historical transformation from socialism to democratic capitalism and sharing the same national context evolve so differently? The answer is grounded in the places from which these movements emerged. The specific characteristics and mechanisms of these places facilitated the growth of certain types of feminisms and of particular relationships between local feminist movements and the places in which they developed. In this concluding chapter, I put the cases of the local feminist movements in Rostock and Erfurt in direct relief to illuminate the similarities and differences between them and to explore how the contours of feminism and the politics of place in these two cities might point to broader patterns in relationships between social movements and place. Analyzing the histories of these two local feminist movements reveals how the places from which these movements emerged contributed to their differences and explains why the movements themselves participated in making place to varying degrees.

My central argument—that place matters—is easy to take for granted. Yet sociologists interested in social movements have largely avoided thinking about place in favor of focusing more narrowly on the state, thereby limiting their scope to certain kinds of movements and to particular types of movement organizing. Certainly, the state has played a key, albeit variable, role in the development of the feminist movements in Rostock and Erfurt, but a complete understanding of these movements requires looking beyond the state to other dimensions of place, including local culture and ties to other scales of activity and identity.

A framework focused on place incorporates diverse social, structural, and symbolic arrangements into understandings of movement development and outcome. Considering place improves upon more narrow conceptualizations of political opportunities and political fields, both of which largely focus on political structures and distributions of power at the expense of culture and forces outside of a social movement's immediate environment. Political opportunities refer to features in a political environment that render it amenable to movement pressure, such as openness in a polity, divisions among elites, or the presence of allies. A political field may be conceptualized as "a structured, unequal, and socially constructed environment *within* which organizations are embedded and *to* which organizations and activists respond" (Ray 1999: 6, emphasis in original).

Evidence from Rostock and Erfurt clearly demonstrates that political opportunities and political fields are important in shaping state-movement interactions. However, other forces that fall outside of the purview of these political dimensions are also at play. Utilizing a political process perspective to analyze the feminist movements in Rostock and Erfurt would leave out the important traditions, legacies, and spatial dimensions of the cities that have produced and supported specific understandings of gender and particular movement pathways and outcomes. Likewise, while focusing on political fields would potentially provide a broader view than an exclusive emphasis on political opportunities by incorporating political culture, the concept of political fields also requires expansion to recognize culture outside of the political realm, to incorporate the historicity of political fields, and to address the temporal and multiscalar dimensions of movement activism in a globalizing world. Attention to place broadens the lens of analysis to include cultural, historical, and spatial pressures and opportunities and considers the webs to which both places and the movements they contain belong.

Parallel Developments, Divergent Outcomes: Feminism in Rostock and Erfurt

Twenty years after the collapse of state socialism in eastern Germany, the feminist movements in Rostock and Erfurt continue to work for women's improved status and integration into economic and political life. However, the movement in Rostock has been more successful in establishing its centrality to the identity of the city than that in Erfurt, which remains largely illegitimate in the eyes of the public and policymakers. The movement in Rostock also has had greater success in shaping local policy outcomes.

The feminist movements in Rostock and Erfurt arrived at different outcomes in spite of parallel developments in their early histories. Both feminist movements were born out of the reform and dissident movements that led to the collapse of the GDR, although these ties were stronger in Erfurt than in Rostock. The local feminist movements in the two cities were called into action by the massive upheavals during the collapse of the GDR in the autumn of 1989 and the spring of 1990. The unification process created new political opportunities for public protest and civic engagement, and women in these two cities seized the momentum of German unification to bring women's issues to light.

In the immediate unification period of 1989–90, activists in the two cities founded many similar organizations, such as shelters for battered women, crisis services for survivors of sexual violence, and women's technical schools.

Contrary to the findings of other comparative studies of local women's movements (for example, Desai 2002; Hellman 1987; Ray 1999), the issues these feminist movements have sought to address are largely the same: women's employment, balancing work and family, and violence against women. *How and to what degree* the movements in Rostock and Erfurt addressed these issues is where most of the variation arises. In Rostock, feminists emphasize women's economic independence and the importance of women and men working together to reduce gender inequality for everyone's benefit. In contrast, feminists in Erfurt generally either focus on violence against women and target only women, or target both women and men and underscore the importance supporting women within the context of families.

The feminist movement in Rostock has a long list of achievements. Building on the velocity and energy of the unification period, feminists in Rostock who had originally organized through the UFV created more than a dozen women's organizations addressing a range of issues, most visibly women's employment and job preparation and violence against women and girls. While the number of service recipients varies significantly across organizations, tracking reports from the organizations suggest that almost one in ten women in Rostock receive some type of service through these organizations annually.

The overwhelming majority of activists in Rostock, as well as the organizations with which they work, quickly came to adopt a neosocialist feminist ideology. As practiced in Rostock, this ideology stresses women's economic dependence as the basis for gender inequality and values men as important actors in combating this inequality. According to neosocialist feminists, the key to improving women's welfare lies in achieving financial independence for women. Reflecting this ideology, a large number of women's organizations in Rostock aim to improve women's chances in the labor market through employment training and antidiscrimination laws and through day-care services and support for single parents. In addition, the movement has established a number of services for women and girls who experience gendered violence, such as rape and battering. Bringing violence against women to light after decades of stigmatization in the GDR, the rape-crisis center and battered women's shelter view violence against women as a by-product of women's economic powerlessness and provide clients with services that emphasize the importance of women achieving financial independence as individuals and economic equality as a group. Table 7.1 provides an overview of the services available through feminist organizations in Rostock and Erfurt.

Table 7.1 Services women's organizations in Rostock and Erfurt offer by feminist ideology of organization and whether women or women and men are target group*

	Neosocialist	Radical	Conservative
Rostock	Battered women's shelter; Rape-crisis counseling; Shelter for abused girls; Café; Housing collective (single mothers); Support for entrepreneurs; Social events; *Debt counseling; Personal fitness; Day care; Art studio; Job training; Political training; Gender mainstreaming training*	Women's cultural center; Social events	
Erfurt	Job training	Counseling for battered women; Rape-crisis counseling; Job training; Social events; Café; Art studio; Feminist library; Housing collective (30km from Erfurt); Sexuality support/social events	Battered women's shelter; Political training; Unemployment support; *Day care; Job training; Social events; Pregnancy counseling; Art studio/classes*

* Services targeting women and men are in *italics*.

In the feminist movement in Rostock, women are understood as a trinity: mother, survivor, and worker. However, this last component of their identity is most stressed, and their statuses as mothers and/or survivors are important primarily as they relate to their experiences as workers. Women's empowerment—which involves the equal distribution of household responsibilities with male partners and their freedom from violence—hinges on their ability to earn income. To this end, even in organizations that do not explicitly focus on improving women's chances in the labor market, staff infuse clients with the idea that women must achieve economic self-sufficiency.

In the process of developing services for women and building a feminist political lobby, women's organizations and individual activists also established effective working relationships with policymakers at various levels, including the municipal and statewide GBs. With consistent cooperation between women's organizations and the GBs, policymakers outside of the arena of women's issues soon came to recognize the importance of women as constituents and the salience of women's concerns in the transformation from socialism to capitalism. This, in turn, led to the increased capacity of the municipal and statewide GBs, who, with the cooperation and lobbying of women's organizations in Rostock, have been able to introduce and pass new laws and initiatives on domestic violence, gender discrimination in the workplace, and gender mainstreaming.

The feminist movement in Rostock benefits from an entrenched feminist policy machinery. The expanded capacity of the municipal and statewide GBs led to a secure funding base for women's organizations in Rostock. When shrinking state coffers translated into budget shortfalls for women's organizations, the statewide GB started funding a program in Rostock that specifically aims to help women's organizations secure resources by supporting efforts at professionalization, grant writing, and development.

Simultaneously, by the early 2000s, many women's organizations in Rostock received funds through the EU. In diversifying their funding bases to draw on monies from the city of Rostock, the state of Mecklenburg-West Pomerania, and the EU, many women's organizations continued to expand the size of their staffs and the range of their services. Building new projects around the concept of gender mainstreaming has been especially lucrative, and activists and policymakers in Rostock and Mecklenburg-West Pomerania have largely embraced this young idea. New funding directives geared specifically toward gender mainstreaming projects have further increased the flow of funds into the coffers of the local state and local women's organizations. While not all organizations in Rostock are able to access EU funds, the development of a diversified funding base among several organizations reduced competition between organizations for local funds, allowing local state agencies and branches to increase their financial commitments to those organizations that are not eligible for EU support.

In Erfurt, the endpoint has been quite different. As in Rostock, the local feminist movement in Erfurt was born out of the energy of the East German reform movement, although that movement was more visible and powerful in Erfurt than in Rostock. The city's leading women's organization, Women for Change, was one of the most publicly visible women's organizations in Germany during the winter of 1989 when it stormed the local Stasi barracks. Shortly after it gained notoriety as a promising new women's organization, members splintered along ideological lines, founding several separate groups in the winter and spring of 1989–90. In a brief window of opportunity before the first democratic election for city council, the city of Erfurt affirmed its support for women's organizations, and specifically for Women for Change, when the Round Table government voted to incorporate the young women's center as a municipal institution.

Although the Municipal Women's Center enjoyed the most funding and visibility among women's organizations in Erfurt, by the end of 1990, numerous other organizations also emerged. As a whole, these organizations offered women—and occasionally men—a range of services including computer courses, counseling for survivors of sexual assault and domestic violence, and social opportunities. Beyond referring clients to one another, however, activists within these organizations had minimal contact with each other.

Instead, activists within individual organizations developed specific feminist ideologies, including radical, neosocialist, and conservative feminist ideologies. Radical feminists support feminist separatism and view gender inequality as a multifaceted problem rooted in patriarchal institutions like the state, the law, the heterosexual family, and the economy. With their emphasis on women's experiences struggling in a patriarchal society, these organizations privilege women's statuses as survivors. Neosocialist feminists, who are few and far between in Erfurt, tend to see the road to women's equality as paved with jobs. Finally, conservative feminists work to support women's roles in the family, encouraging interactions between women and their children, and the introduction of women into elected office to temper what they see as the impersonal and sometimes uncivilized tendencies of men if left unchecked by women's compassionate, nurturing presence. As such, the work of conservative feminists centers of women's positions as mothers.

Organizations adopting each of these three ideologies convey competing messages about gender to their clients and volunteers and to the public. Radical feminists push women to examine the detrimental effects of patriarchal institutions in their own lives and urge women to embrace a feminist lifestyle, which involves separation from men and male institutions (or at least a significant reevaluation of how to maintain these relationships while making them more equitable), a higher degree of understanding of their own sexuality, body, and psychology, and a commitment to improving women's status locally and globally through mutual assistance and support. Only one organization in Erfurt, the Women's Technical School (which closed in 2008), has a neosocialist feminist orientation. Here, like neosocialist feminists in Rostock, staff members emphasize the importance of financial stability in achieving women's equality and attempt to bring to light how the exclusion of women in some professional fields comes as a disservice not only to women but to those fields and the communities that such professionals serve. Conservative feminists offer a different view of women and gender relations, stressing women's proper place as in the home if they have young children while otherwise promoting women's employment and political participation. Women are encouraged to maintain marriages and the nuclear family. Conservative feminists view the family, rather than the state or the community, as the best protector from social ills and market forces and thus endorse efforts at supporting families.

Activists from these different camps were often unwilling—or unable—to work with women with competing ideologies. In addition, tensions developed between activists with the same general ideological beliefs, but who held differing opinions on specific issues. State funding decisions, which consistently favored organizations with certain practices, ideological orientations, and public personas more than others, heightened these tensions. Ultimately, the conflicts between activists from different organizations and ideological corners inhibited effective cooperation and collaboration within and beyond the women's movement. Rifts within the movement limited cooperative efforts through networks, umbrella organizations, and lobbies and stalled the possibility of a cohesive feminist identity. While in Rostock, women's organizations joined together through RFI, the LFR-MV, and, in the late 1990s, through a new building downtown in which several women's organizations have their offices, women's organizations in Erfurt remained physically, psychologically, and organizationally isolated from one another.

Ideological differences, and the attendant lack of cohesion and coalition within the feminist movement in Erfurt, became especially problematic as funding pools available through the city of Erfurt and the state of Thuringia became smaller during the course of the 1990s and into the 2000s. Without an effective political lobby, the feminist movement was unable to ensure the capacity of the statewide GB, thereby further reducing the long-term probability of continuing state funding for women's organizations. Policy conversations excluded feminist voices, and feminist organizations were unsuccessful in attempting to secure adequate funding from the state, leading to financial struggle. Conservative feminist organizations that more closely fit into the place character of the city fared better financially than the city's primary radical feminist organization. By 2005, the financial fate of even the LFR-TH itself was uncertain.

In comparing the internal logics of the feminist movements in Rostock and Erfurt, three primary ideological and strategic differences emerge. First, neosocialist feminism became the dominant ideology and the primary source of collective identity among women activists in Rostock, whereas in Erfurt, activists split along ideological lines, creating discord between radical and conservative feminists. Second, while the feminist movement in Rostock from the outset worked cooperatively with both the municipal and statewide governments, only some organizations and activists in Erfurt sought, or were able, to forge positive relationships with local policymakers. Third, because of its ideological rifts and divergent approaches to the state, the feminist movement in Erfurt did not develop a cohesive formal or informal lobbying organization, reflecting an inability within the movement to achieve—or even to attempt to achieve—consensus and establishing its outsider status vis-à-vis local government. In contrast, women's organizations in Rostock and throughout the state of Mecklenburg-West Pomerania formally joined forces in building an effective women's lobby at the state level through the LFR-MV, worked together through both formal and informal coalitions and umbrella organizations at the municipal level, and generally prize cohesion and consensus within the movement.

Table 7.2 lays out the core differences in the endpoints of these two women's movements. Although the feminist movements in Rostock and Erfurt share several similarities in their early histories and in their goals, they are differentiated by their relationships with the state, their adoptions of specific ideologies, and, ultimately, their progress in securing funds for programs that improve women's welfare. Both movements succeeded in pushing for the passage of key pieces of statewide legislation (although such legislation was passed earlier in Mecklenburg-West Pomerania than in Thuringia), and both movements continue to involve large numbers of women in a range of organizations addressing diverse issues. However, the feminist movement in Rostock has succeeded in co-opting key state agencies and expanding their capacity, while in Erfurt, the statewide and municipal GBs both witnessed the curtailing of their capacity over the course of the 1990s and into the 2000s. This difference has had significant implications for the level of funding made available to women's organizations through municipal and state coffers and for the degree of public support for the work of these organizations.

Three primary and highly interrelated dimensions of place shaped the strategies and ideologies of the women's movements in Rostock and Erfurt, which in turn influenced their ability to participate in redefining the places of these cities after German unification. First, political forces encompass the political climates and distributions of power in the two cities, which presented specific opportunities and constraints with which women's organizations had to grapple and which also influenced the willingness and ability of activists and organizations to adopt strategies that would be potentially successful in these climates. Second, cultural forces include the presence of specific local histories and cultural repertoires that created different possibilities for the feminist movements in these two cities to build on, or to come into conflict with, existing traditions and institutions. Finally, spatial forces involve the geopolitical positioning and spatial alliances of the two cities, which contributed to the adoption and adaptation of specific ideologies and practices among both social movement and state actors. Political, cultural, and spatial dimensions of place are often overlapping and mutually constitutive, and they not only determine the contours of women's organizing but are also determined by it. In the next three sections, I discuss each of these three interrelated forces in detail to demonstrate how attention to these core aspects of place illuminates feminist formations.

Table 7.2 Successes and setbacks in Rostock and Erfurt

Successes		Setbacks	
Rostock	Erfurt	Rostock	Erfurt
Laws on violence against women	Laws on violence against women	Ideological homogeneity provides clients/public with limited models	Noncooperative relationship with statewide GB
Antidiscrimination law for state employees	Antidiscrimination law for state employees		Financial struggle for many women's organizations
Visible, active women's movement	Visible, active women's movement		Limited capacity of statewide and municipal GBs
Gender mainstreaming law at municipal level	Ideological diversity provides clients/public with multiple models		Weak lobbying organization
Cooperative relationship with municipal and statewide GBs			
Powerful lobbying organization			
Increased capacity of statewide and municipal GBs			
Financial health of women's organizations			

The Politics of Place in Rostock and Erfurt

Since unification, the feminist movements in Rostock and Erfurt have operated in different political environments and respond to different political forces within those environments. Election results, and subsequent elected and appointed leadership, reflect this variation, as do political discourse and rhetoric. Rostock is a left-leaning city in which it is acceptable to support the PDS and where inequality is a recognized social issue. Although not formalized at the state level until 1999, a red-red coalition comprised of members of the SPD and the PDS ruled both the city of Rostock and the state of Mecklenburg-West Pomerania from 1990 to 2006, with the CDU in the role of the opposition party. Erfurt is a right-leaning city where the PDS was maligned after unification and where free markets and families are central. In Erfurt and Thuringia, municipal and state governance has been in the hands of the CDU since unification with the SPD and PDS functioning as opposition parties, but not in a formal coalition.

Formal ties to political parties do not seem necessary for movement success in these cases; in fact, the feminist movement in Rostock has far fewer connections to party leaders than that in Erfurt. What is important is the general political orientation toward state interventions in inequalities. The strength of left-leaning politics in Rostock and Mecklenburg-West Pomerania created opportunities for women's organizations that activists in Erfurt often did not have. These leftist governments recognize the need to preserve state responsibility for social issues and service provisioning after unification, and thus are amenable to claims by feminists for support for women. Congruence between the goals and political orientation of the municipal and statewide governments allowed the feminist movement in Rostock to move across these scales easily and effectively. Because of the stability of the political field (the combined power of the SPD and PDS, as measured by voting percentages and seats in city councils and state legislatures, did not change substantially between 1990 and 2006) and the left's general interest in maintaining or expanding the responsibilities of the state to its populace, women's organizations in Rostock were able to position themselves as deserving recipients of state support and as representatives of a key constituency.

In contrast, the rightist governments of Erfurt and Thuringia approached the expansion of state responsibilities skeptically. Both the municipal and statewide levels of government have resisted claims that women are important constituents, assertions that appear weak given that, until recently, the CDU could clearly win elections with or without the support of women's organizations.

The city and state share similar political orientations that exclude feminists and make jumping between these two scales fruitless. The specific constellation of political power has further hampered the feminist movement by marginalizing both women politicians and feminist actors outside of the state. Feminists' underrepresentation within the CDU and their lack of external support from women's organizations renders them ineffective spokespeople for the feminist movement or feminist issues. (Table 7.3 provides an overview of election results among the major parties in state legislatures for Mecklenburg-West Pomerania and Thuringia.)

At the municipal level, both Rostock and Erfurt support the political left in elections to a greater degree than their respective states. Support for the CDU has consistently been slightly lower in the cities than in their home states. Still, since unification, the mayor of Erfurt, who directly oversees the office of the city's GB, has been a representative of the CDU. In Rostock, the mayor has been from the SPD.[1] Unlike statewide GBs, municipal GBs are not explicitly appointed along party lines, such that which party controls the mayor's office is arguably not as important for women's organizations as which party controls the governor's office where GB's are always appointed along party lines. However, mayors do have considerable discretion in how much they choose to support the municipal GB, and by all accounts the CDU mayors of Erfurt have not provided the same level of rhetorical or financial support for the GB there as the SPD mayors in Rostock have.

Table 7.3 Election results among the major parties for state legislatures in Mecklenburg-West Pomerania and Thuringia, 1990–2006, by percent and seats won

Party	2006	2002/4*		1998/9*		1994		1990**	
	M-V	M-V	Th.	M-V	Th.	M-V	Th.	M-V	Th.
CDU	31% (25)	32% (25)	43% (45)	32% (24)	51% (49)	38% (30)	42% (42)	39% (29)	45% (44)
SPD	30% (33)	40% (33)	14% (15)	36% (27)	19% (18)	30% (23)	29% (29)	25% (21)	22% (21)
PDS	18%*** (13)	17% (13)	26% (28)	25% (20)	21% (21)	23% (18)	16% (17)	16% (12)	9% (9)

* State elections were held in Mecklenburg-West Pomerania in 1998, 2002, and 2006, and in Thuringia in 1999 and 2004.

**In the 1990 elections, the Greens and the FDP also earned enough votes for seats in the state legislature in both states. The PDS in Mecklenburg-West Pomerania also shared the ballot with the Linke Liste, or Leftist List, for this election only.

***The PDS was renamed Die Linke, or The Left, prior to the 2006 election.

Overall, the left is dominant in Rostock and Mecklenburg-West Pomerania and the right is dominant in Erfurt and Thuringia. In both cases, however, the distribution of power is somewhat dispersed because the opposition party or parties remain strong, creating a pluralist system of governance. Conventional wisdom would hold that a left-leaning political climate, like that in Rostock, should be especially favorable to feminist interests, whereas a right-leaning climate would retard feminist progress. In fact, political groups of the left have been widely criticized in a variety of contexts, ranging from labor unions to political parties, for excluding women and resisting a gendered analysis of inequality (for example, Ferree and Mueller 2004; Sen 1989), and feminist movements have attained successes in hostile climates (for example, Gelb and Hart 1999). That the feminist movement in Rostock has been successful in establishing its legitimacy is not merely a function of the strength of the left in the city of Rostock and the state of Mecklenburg-West Pomerania, nor are the challenges for feminists in Erfurt the sole outcome of the dominance of the CDU. Other characteristics of these places, including postunification responses to the end of socialism, broadened or narrowed the scope of possibility to include the concerns of women and women's organizations.

The Legacies of Socialism in Feminism

In postsocialist Europe, socialist legacies are important components of contemporary political cultures, or "the range of possible actions (political or otherwise) that a group or individual can undertake in society. More particularly, a political culture can be thought of as defining the limits of the possible in political life." (Agnew 2002: 114). Socialist experiences and the collective memory of the socialist era shape current attitudes about gender and the state. The legacy of the SED and the GDR informs which political parties and interest groups are acceptable contenders and which social issues are legitimate areas for state intervention. Far from static, this legacy, and the political cultures it contributes to, is constantly evolving in response to exogenous and endogenous pressures. How Rostock, Erfurt, and their respective local states negotiate and remember their socialist histories has significant implications for feminist mobilizations and their outcomes.

Mixed feelings about the socialist past, the unification process, and the rate of change in Rostock and Mecklenburg-West Pomerania since unification have increased support for the political left there, as well as for community-based efforts to mirror or re-create aspects of life in the GDR. The gender ideology of the GDR continues as the basic model for gender relations. The role of the state there is that of protector of its citizens, and the state is expected to intervene to ensure the welfare of its people. Feminist organizations counter the sense of loss of community and solidarity by creating spaces for women to meet each other, form friendships, and feel cared about by others. In tapping into women's unemployment and the balancing of work and family life as key issues, the feminist movement in Rostock continues to recognize women's roles as workers and mothers, just like the GDR. While moving beyond the *Muttipolitik* of the GDR, women's organizations in Rostock capitalize on the GDR's idea that women should be valued as both workers and as mothers. In a local environment where policymakers and the public seem to reflect on their lives in the GDR with conflicted emotions, often dominated by fondness and nostalgia, this approach resonates with the local preference for building on and improving the socialist past, rather than rejecting it completely.

Warm memories about the SED are hard to come by in Erfurt. Here, respondents were far more critical of life in the GDR and remembered the history of the GDR with anger and bitterness. New, western models of gender relations, welfare, and governance have greater appeal. The public rejected the socialist left and its goals and instead embraced the principles of free markets, leading to the dominance of the CDU, which supports a small state that remains outside of the private sphere and civil society, and a gender ideology distinctly different from that of the GDR in emphasizing women's roles as wives and mothers. While some women fondly recalled feeling secure in their jobs and actively involved in their communities, most also commented on the feelings of repression in the GDR.

With the vast majority of Stasi files still in disarray, it is impossible to know if Stasi activity was truly higher in Erfurt than in Rostock, but the accounts of respondents in this sample certainly suggest that, at a minimum, activists in Erfurt perceived the Stasi threat much more than those in Rostock.[2] The presence of so many churches in Erfurt, the primary refuge for dissidents, likely contributed to this perception and may well have contributed to greater Stasi surveillance altogether. Church leaders and active members rarely saw eye-to-eye with the SED, and anti-SED sentiment in Erfurt appears to have been higher than in Rostock before unification because of the greater role of organized religion there.

Reflecting the more negative assessments of life in the GDR there, Erfurt and Thuringia have sought to distance themselves from their socialist past. In

Erfurt, the PDS was, in the words of one respondent, "vilified as the old red," and there was a strong push to unseat the SED. As the postunification reincarnation of the SED, the PDS did not present itself as a reasonable contender for a coalition partner in the eyes of the SPD in Erfurt because the SED was tremendously maligned there during the immediate unification period. The public desire in Erfurt and Thuringia to purge the government of communists meant that the SPD could not risk cooperating with the PDS and opening themselves to accusations of supporting the SED. In Rostock, where citizens were more ambivalent about the SED, in part because of the SED's devotion to Rostock in developing it as a major city and because of the relative absence of religious infrastructure to shelter dissidents, the risk to the SPD of aligning with the PDS was not nearly as great as in Erfurt. The degree of legitimacy of the PDS has been important for feminist organizing because of these coalition dynamics. Feminists in Rostock had powerful allies in the SPD/PDS coalition, but feminists in Erfurt faced a divided left that could not provide them with significant strategic assistance.

State leaders, public figures, and residents in Erfurt have sought to bury the history of the GDR. This tendency created challenges for the feminist movement there. In rejecting the GDR, the climate in Erfurt and Thuringia promotes a small state—namely one that does not interfere in civil society or in private matters, like the family. Thus, while there is support for the creation and maintenance of civil society, the state largely is excluded from participating in civil society, including feminist organizations, or from engaging with many issues feminists focus on that pertain to the family, like intrafamilial violence and child care.

These variations across places within the former GDR serve as a cogent reminder of the heterogeneity of socialist and postsocialist experiences across space. Especially among western scholars and in the western imagination, there has been a marked tendency to view socialism as monolithic, or to recognize variations in socialism only across nation-states. More recently, scholars have begun to identify variations within socialist systems of governance across time (see, for example, Gal and Kligman 2000b; Haney 2002; Verdery 1996). Differences across space are also central in determining postsocialist experiences. Even within the same nation, interpretations and understandings of socialism since its collapse diverge precisely because experiences during the socialist era did. These interpretations and understandings have significant implications for feminist organizing because they shape public and policy attitudes about gender and public interventions in inequality.

In the West, a socialist past is typically viewed as a postsocialist hindrance. Countless empirical examples in eastern and central Europe, including those of organized crime, extreme poverty, the spread of HIV/AIDS, ethnic conflict, political disengagement, and the slow growth of civil society suggest danger lurks in the disruptions after socialism. Yet these problems are neither predetermined nor unilateral. A closer examination of life on the ground in postsocialist eastern Germany demonstrates how the process of remembering and reconciling the socialist era can serve as a powerful foundation for positive social action. In Rostock, for example, feminists have successfully mobilized GDR-era understandings of gender to legitimize their goals and to gain public and political support.

The local feminist movements in both Rostock and Erfurt have created fields of feminist activity and service provisioning that far exceed what is available in similarly sized cities in western Germany. This suggests that a history of socialism is no more a retardant to the development of feminist organizing and the achievement of women's equality and an active civil society than a history of democratic capitalism. The diligent work of the eastern German feminists reminds us that socialist experiences and legacies can be a critical source of strength.

Building on Local Traditions, Community Identities, and Histories

Historically grounded cultural features of places beyond socialist legacies also present opportunities and constraints for local social movements. Feminists in Rostock were able to capitalize on multiple aspects of the city's history and culture to secure their participation in making place. In Rostock, the historic presence of the Beguines in the city, which was kept alive through oral history and the names of public places, provided another kind of legacy that women activists could seize to legitimize their activities and increase their acceptance in the community. While feminists invoke the name of the Beguines in other settings in Germany (including near Erfurt), few cities can actually claim to have hosted Beguine communities. In Rostock, the actual presence of the Beguines in the city adds authenticity to claims by activists that they are building on, rather than departing from, the city's history.

Furthermore, as a port city long organized around seafaring, women's ability to provide critical labor and leadership has an extended history there (Norling 1991, 1992; Porter 1985; Thompson 1985). This history contributes to the public's contemporary support for economic development that provides equal employment opportunities for women and men. Women are valued in Rostock as active in political, economic, social, and family life. Dominant discourses and images present local women as strong and independent.

Activists in Erfurt do not have the same historic and cultural resources to draw on to support their claims that gender equality should be part of the fabric of the city. The history most often cited now as justification for continued state and public support for women's organizations is that of Women for Change, which was such a public and vital source of energy during the collapse of the GDR. Certainly, that Women for Change was born out of the dissident movement helped it establish an early foothold in the city as exemplified through the incorporation of the Municipal Women's Center. However, since the city has no obvious and resonant history of women's organizing or women's autonomy, cultural resources are more limited in this setting than in Rostock.

By contrast, religious institutions have played a significant role in the history of the city of Erfurt and the state of Thuringia. The strength of organized religion contributed to resistance to the SED, which religious critics argued was too repressive and too secular. In Rostock and Mecklenburg-West Pomerania, low levels of religious participation inhibited church-based solidarity and social action. Here, workplace unions and SED-sponsored community organizations were most salient for community building. In Erfurt, respondents—even those who don't identify themselves as strongly religious—pointed to the church as the place where they could find friendship and a sense of community in the GDR. The history of animosity between the SED and religious institutions, especially Protestant churches, promoted negative assessments of the SED.

The number and strength of churches in Erfurt led to a greater number of women's groups there before unification than in Rostock, such that during the fall of 1989 and the winter of 1990, the field of women's social movement activity in Erfurt was broader than in Rostock. The Protestant denominations in particular presented critical opportunities for women's organizations to form and develop, even in the repressive GDR. Yet after unification, the churches that gave birth to the young feminist movement became its greatest retardants through encouragement of nuclear-family models and restrictive gender roles, particularly within the Catholic Church. In addition, given that groups operated within different churches, sometimes across theological paradigms, and in almost total isolation from one another, multiple, competing feminist ideologies emerged, resulting in limited agreement on the overarching goals of feminism. A lack of centralization before unification contributed to the splintering of the movement after unification.

With the collapse of the GDR, the conservative, religious slant of the city presented the local feminist movement with an inhospitable climate in which to pursue many issues salient for women, including women's employment prospects and sexual victimization. Radical feminists couldn't find a strong following in this environment, while some conservative feminists felt constrained by the sudden emphasis on the nuclear-family model with a stay-at-home mother. Certainly, conservative feminists were better able to integrate their ideologies about gender with those of a generally traditional, conservative public, to find ways to frame their campaigns to resonate in this setting, and to develop social service organizations that could compete with the growing number of church-based service providers. Still, conservative feminists harbor mixed feelings about women's roles in church, state, and society. The reorientation from seeing women as workers to viewing them primarily as mothers and wives came as a surprise even to these more religious, traditional women. The culture of the city excluded feminists who believe in women's centrality in both work and family life.

Cutting Across Space:
Regionalization in Rostock and Erfurt

The politics and culture of places are part of spatial networks that involve multiple places and scales of activity. Influences from other regions and the creation and maintenance of spatial alliances constitute significant components of place in Rostock and Erfurt. In Rostock, the desire to differentiate the city and local state from the dominant political practices and ideologies of the unified German state characterized all but the first few months of the postsocialist period. While in the immediate unification period of 1989–90, women's organizations and other political actors tapped into the rhetoric of trying to "catch up" with western Germany, the desire to emulate the old German states soon waned. In spite of joy about the new freedoms stemming from unification, the sense of relative deprivation between Mecklenburg-West Pomerania and the rest of the nation, in particular the old German states, grew as more time elapsed after unification without significant improvements in the economy and the employment market. In the debacle over the state capitol, and in the public western German imagination, western Germany and the unified German government seemed to shun the city.

The rapid postunification shift away from wanting to catch up to western Germany is also partially a historically embedded phenomenon stemming both from the region's centuries-old ties to Scandinavia and its ambivalence toward its socialist past. Stung by the federal state's failed promises to the region, residents, policymakers, and activists alike turned to the city's and region's historic ties with various Scandinavian nations, building a spatial alliance with Scandinavia and distancing themselves from western Germany. By the mid-1990s, women activists, political leaders, and everyday citizens were increasingly looking northward in search of both relevant policy models and sources of identity. Although cognizant of the region's historic and contemporary position as German and its status as part of the German federal state, political and public rhetoric began to emphasize the region's dissimilarities from western Germany and its ties to the North. Women's organizations in Rostock tied into this new spatial alliance by framing their work as in opposition to the federal government's models for gender and, beginning in the late 1990s, as instead based on Swedish models of gender policy. With the introduction of gender mainstreaming in the European Union in 1996, activists had further external validation through the spatial alliance with Sweden, a major proponent of gender mainstreaming. Gender mainstreaming became a major focal point of women's activism in Rostock by the late 1990s. Women's organizations were able to take advantage of the desire for autonomy from the national state and for identification with the socialist democratic North by positioning themselves as part of a broader, collective effort to redefine Rostock and Mecklenburg-West Pomerania as un-German in their recognition of, and attention to, women's issues and gender inequality.

Just as Rostock and Mecklenburg-West Pomerania increasingly identified with their northern neighbors, policymakers and activists in Erfurt and Thuringia focused on emulating western Germany. Like Rostock's spatial alliance with Scandinavia, Erfurt's spatial alliance with western Germany predated unification. Closer and better connected to the West than Rostock, residents of Erfurt had frequent contact with western Germans after unification. The feminist movement especially experienced an influx of feminists from the West who were interested in helping organizations there after hearing about the dramatic efforts of Women for Change in storming the Stasi barracks. Simultaneously, policymakers, especially those from the CDU, sought ways to expedite Erfurt's and Thuringia's redevelopment, laying to rest the history of the GDR and pushing the region toward rapid development following a neoliberal corporatist model.

Unlike in Rostock, where the goal of catching up was quite short-lived, in Erfurt and Thuringia, achieving western German standards has remained a dominant feature since unification. This can be attributed to the region's greater exposure to, and exchange with, western Germany, both historically and since unification. Thuringia has identified as Germanic for centuries, whereas both insiders and outsiders regard Mecklenburg-West Pomerania as historically Slavic and Scandinavian.

Women's organizations sought to capitalize on this spatial alliance by building on the idea of "catching up" with the West. Although the rhetoric of catching up provided some support to both radical and conservative feminists in Erfurt because both groups could make limited claims to be engaged in developing a western-style civil society, this popular narrative has overall excluded feminist interests. Feminists could easily frame a few specific feminist issues— like domestic violence—as relevant to the desire for westernization because these issues were widely accepted as social problems in the West. Other issues, like gender mainstreaming, were sidelined in Erfurt at least in part because they did not reflect the input of western German feminists in Erfurt or the priorities of the unified federal government. On the whole, catching up involves reducing state responsibility for public welfare and instead finding private solutions for social problems. This logic undercuts state responsibilities to support feminist organizations financially and limits interest in state interventions in the marketplace. Since promoting feminist goals was also not central to the national identity of West Germany, feminists in Erfurt have found it difficult to assert that support for feminism and the achievement of feminist aims is part of westernization.

Rostock and Erfurt have moved in almost opposite directions in developing their spatial alliances. Rostock and Mecklenburg-West Pomerania reject the federal German state and embrace Scandinavian models of social life and policy. Feminists in Rostock benefit from this spatial alliance because their interests in neosocialist feminism and, more recently, gender mainstreaming, resonate with Scandinavian models. Feminists in Rostock utilize identification with Scandinavian gender norms to reinforce the place of the city. In this way, they participate in place in Rostock and contribute to the city's sense of itself.

In contrast, in Erfurt and Thuringia, western Germany is the central model and point of identification and aspiration. Here, activists and policymakers have tried to ride the push to catch up to the old German states by stressing how their work will help the city in its mission to become western. This effort has not been successful, however, because catching up with western Germany does not involve public or state support for most feminist goals. Instead, the way the rhetoric of catching up plays out in Erfurt and Thuringia actually supports the exclusion of feminists from place because their claims for state resources and attention to gender inequalities challenge the identities of the city and region as traditional, religious, and western. EU gender policies, which are largely discordant with those of neighboring western German states, the unified German government, and the local government, appear more threatening than helpful.

The spatial aspects of place, including spatial alliances, thus can present both constraints and opportunities for social movements. Local places continue to serve as lenses through which local actors interpret larger social processes, like unification, and supranational agendas, like the EU's gender mainstreaming agenda. Everyday actors understand broader social changes, including political, economic, and social transformations and processes of regionalization and globalization, through their refraction in the local. Social movements can attempt to manipulate spatial resources to their benefit by jumping scales or contributing to spatial alliances. However, such opportunities are not always present, and in some cases, alternate scales of activity and spatial alliances constrain the possibilities social movements have for effecting social change.

Claiming Their Place

The collapse of state socialism and the unification of East and West Germany presented eastern German communities with the opportunity to reimagine and redefine place. Feminists attempted to participate in this process of making place in the hopes of establishing the centrality of feminist goals for the identity and success of their cities. This involved reaching out to both the local state and the local public. Neosocialist feminists in Rostock have been largely successful in assuring their integration into place where their efforts resulted in the institutionalization of myriad women's organizations, the inclusion of GBs and the LFR-MV in processes of political decision making, and the acceptance of several issues as social problems that require redress through state and public attention. The feminist movement feeds back into the city's identity as progressive, equitable, and Baltic. The feminist movement in Rostock has succeeded in entrenching itself in the place of the city and in aligning its work with the broader goals of the community.

In Erfurt, place was closed to feminist activists because they did not have the political, spatial, or cultural traction to claim participation rights in making place. A conservative, traditional local culture that stresses private solutions and a small state was not amenable to feminist involvement. Coupled with institutional features of the local feminist movement, most notably the ideological divisions within the movement, feminists in Erfurt have been largely unsuccessful in shaping place and becoming a key part of it.

The unique local historical legacies in Rostock and Erfurt, as well as their different geopolitical positions within Germany, influenced the place characters of those cities. In turn, these specific understandings of place gave rise to particular feminist ideologies. While a left-leaning political climate that prizes autonomy from the national state and identification with Scandinavian states has supported the growth of neosocialist feminism in Rostock, a conservative political culture and strong religious institutions and traditional attitudes toward women, work, and family have pushed the women's movement in Erfurt toward two conflicting ideologies, radical feminism and conservative feminism. Radical feminism rejects the place of the city, while conservative feminism seeks to bring limited feminist insights into an environment generally hostile to feminist concerns.

This book has explored two local feminist movements within the framework of place and has advanced a schema for thinking about place as involving political, cultural, and spatial dimensions that interact with local feminist movements. Figures 7.1 and 7.2 provide a visual map of the interactive and mutually constitutive processes at work in making place in Rostock and Erfurt. Here, the general political orientations of the two cities and their respective states, their spatial alliances, local responses to socialism and unification, and unique, local histories created and reinforce specific feminisms, which in turn often contribute to the features of place. (Note that radical feminism does not ostensibly support the continued dominance of the right in Erfurt, or the religiosity of the city and region.) Each of the key aspects of the places of the cities are mutually reinforcing over time and have functioned to entrench these interactive cycles as relatively stable features of the places in Rostock and Erfurt.

Local places offer divergent possibilities and limitations for women's organizations that provide services and function as public advocates for women's issues. The possibilities are more than just political: they involve opportunities and constraints across multiple, interlocking realms, including the political and cultural arenas cutting across scales. The place of Rostock was conducive to the emergence of neosocialist feminism and a strong political and public interest

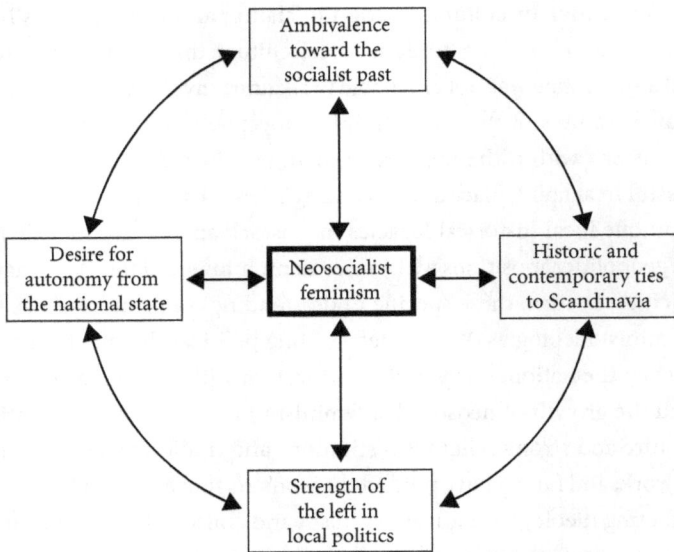

Figure 7.1 Interactions Between Aspects of Place and the Feminist Movement in Rostock

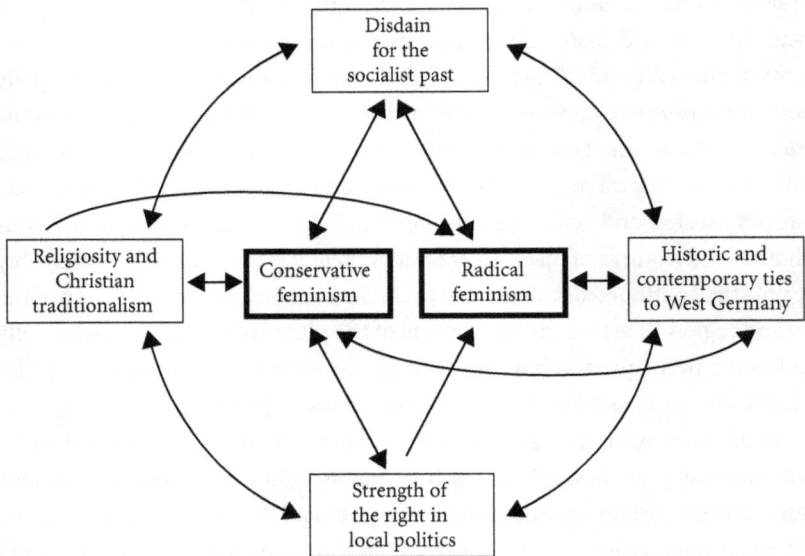

Figure 7.2 Interactions Between Aspects of Place and the Feminist Movement in Erfurt

in women's issues. Feminists were also able to participate effectively as part of place by positioning themselves as central to the city's identity as un-German and instead Scandinavian in its focus on gender equality. The place of Erfurt, by contrast, was less penetrable for feminist activists. In spite of their efforts at positioning themselves as contributing to the effort of catching up with western Germany, the feminist movement has not successfully influenced place in Erfurt, nor has any ideological camp of feminists established themselves as part of place in Erfurt.

Local feminist movements can best be understood through the lens of place because this framework provides attention to multiple arenas of social movement activity and recognizes the importance of nested scales of action. Even movements that primarily target their local states and local communities engage with other levels of activity, sometimes as reinforcement, sometimes as opponents. My analysis has devoted a good deal of attention to interactions between the feminist movements in Rostock and Erfurt and different levels of the state because these movements primarily target the state. However, unlike the two dominant perspectives for understanding social movements, namely political process perspectives and culturally oriented perspectives, a framework sensitive to place does not automatically privilege the political over the cultural, or vice versa. Instead, place deliberately highlights the empirical specificity of particular contexts.

Over time, as additional studies examine social movements through the lens of place, it will become increasingly possible to develop classification schema to identify generalizable patterns across places that share particular features and to refine the analysis of these components. This analysis of the local feminist movements in Rostock and Erfurt reveals that several aspects of place are especially salient for local feminist mobilizations and have specific effects on such mobilizations. First, leftist political cultures are more supportive of claims for state interventions in inequalities. Second, spatial alliances with leftist regions and positive collective memories about strong state interventions reinforce claims for present and future state interventions. Third, strong Christian institutions and ideologies promote traditional gender relations and give rise to public attitudes that separate the public and private, thereby creating challenges for feminist movements.[3] Finally, place-specific histories and local cultures—like the legacy of the Beguines in Rostock, or that city's seafaring tradition—can serve to support or thwart feminist efforts by contributing to specific, localized understandings of gender.

Developing Feminist Civil Society After Socialism

A frequent criticism of feminist organizing since the early 1990s both in post-socialist eastern and central Europe and elsewhere has been the overwhelming tendency of feminist movements to eschew mass protest outside of the state in favor of focusing on institutionalizing feminism within the state and providing social services for women. The phenomenon, alternately described as "NGO feminism," "the civil society trap," and "market feminism" (Alvarez 1999; Einhorn and Sever 2003; Lang 1997), involves the development of gender experts with technocratic knowledge and the primacy of service provisioning over political advocacy, coupled with the receipt of extensive state funding. Feminist critiques link NGO-ization to neoliberalism's interests in promoting specific organizational forms, co-opting dissent, and offloading state responsibilities onto nonstate actors. A core concern about NGO feminism is that dependence on the state presumably renders feminist organizations less able to alter the structures of the state because these are the very structures upon which they depend for survival. Other concerns center on the nondemocratic structure of NGOs and the co-optation of feminist expertise into state bureaucracies.

Discussion about the relationship between feminist movements and the state has been central and prolonged in feminist debates. Nor are these concerns singular to feminism; the experiences of other rights-based movements have raised similar questions. Can social movements transform the state if they depend on it for resources? Are professional, hierarchical organizational forms antithetical to goals of feminist social justice? Through processes of offloading responsibilities for public welfare to social service organizations, is the state simultaneously reducing its responsibilities and expanding its power?

Most feminist activists and scholars recognize both benefits and challenges stemming from NGO feminism (Alvarez 2009; Hemment 2004, 2007; Sloat 2005). In her reevaluation of the NGO-ization debates, Sonia E. Alvarez (2009) notes that feminist NGOs importantly produce and disseminate feminist knowledge and discourse and thus are far from useless or neutral as NGOs. State feminism in particular can increase women's political representation and attention to women's policy issues.[4] Working on the inside has had demonstrably positive effects for women in many cases, although the evidence on this point in Germany in particular is unclear. Many state-funded nonprofit organizations engage in political advocacy work, and recent evidence suggests that state funding does not lead directly to less effective or less powerful advocacy (Chaves, Stephens, and Galaskiewicz 2004; Landriscina 2006).

This debate is not easily resolved as both autonomy and co-optation present advantages and constraints. This study reveals how, in practice, such discussions vary across both time and space for feminist activists. In Rostock, activists consistently understood the municipality and the regional state as allies with a responsibility for ensuring women's welfare and increased gender equality in the home and in the workplace. Over time, distrust of the federal state and faith in the local state and the supranational governance of the EU increased. These sentiments were grounded in the specific spatial and temporal experiences of women in Rostock, including the continued strength of the left in local politics, the emerging spatial alliance with Scandinavia, and evolving feelings of negativity toward the consequences of unification.

In Erfurt, activists developed feminist ideologies that competed on many points, but which largely saw the state as an entity that should not be permanently involved in women's welfare. Radical feminists understand municipal, local, federal, and supranational forms of governance as inherently patriarchal and, rather than seeking out participation in these institutions, attempt to develop separate alternatives, thereby creating "safe" spaces for women and rejecting hierarchical and bureaucratic modes of organization in favor of nonhierarchical, consensus-driven arrangements. Conservative feminists, who associate state intervention with the repressive practices of the SED and GDR, are skeptical about the value of state-supported feminism because of their belief in the primacy of a small state and the autonomy of institutions free from state coercion. As the family was one of few realms free from state intervention in the GDR, their interest in promoting families as primarily responsible for the welfare of individuals also reflects lessons from the socialist past.[5] Consequently, conservative feminists maintain that civil society and the family should both exist without state involvement.

Although radical and conservative feminists share an opposition to state intervention in civil society, organizations representing both groups attempt to secure state funding and the integration of women's interests into the state. In this sense, while their attitudes toward the state are very much distinct from those of neosocialist feminists, their practices are not. Women in all three ideological camps agitated for state funding and the creation and maintenance of state offices dedicated specifically to women's issues, as well as for direct state sponsorship of a women's center and battered women's shelter in Erfurt. In fact, all but two of the women's organizations represented in this study operate with the majority of their funds coming from the state, and women in both cities loudly supported the continued presence of municipal and statewide GBs.[6]

The disjuncture between the expressed ideologies and actual behaviors of feminists in Erfurt reflects the daily realties of life in eastern Germany. Private charitable giving has never been a core part of life in western Germany and was unheard of in the GDR. While a handful of private foundations fund nonprofit organizations in Germany, these funds are few and far between. The women active in these movements also rely on their own employment within women's organizations for their survival, such that volunteerism, which is atypical in eastern Germany given the high value placed on paid labor in the GDR, is not viable for most of them. Because they are dependent on their work for income, and in the absence of other funding sources, they have no alternative but to rely on the state. The decision among activists in both cases to pursue state support and the institutionalization of women's interests through femocratic state positions thus reflects the pragmatic consideration of survival.

Consequently, women's organizations in Rostock and Erfurt have tried to develop relationships with the state that they think will be most beneficial to the women in their communities. As many respondents in both cities noted, no state is free of gender; the struggle in eastern Germany then has been to shape state messages about, and practices of, gender. Feminists across the ideological spectrum view the state as a source of gender inequality and as a site for redress.

Concerns about NGO-ization also problematize how states offload and outsource their responsibilities to the private and nonprofit sectors. Yet the domains of responsibility assumed by feminist organizations rarely overlap with the traditional welfare provisioning of the state. States have not historically recognized most of the services offered by feminist organizations as falling under their purview, and few feminists in fact would advocate that the state be responsible for them. For example, although many rape-crisis centers and battered women's shelters in western Europe and the United States receive state funding, these are newer, not historical, areas of welfare provisioning, and feminists do not typically push for the state to take over responsibility for providing these services. Offering feminist social services is a core goal of many feminist movements, including those in Rostock and Erfurt.

The relationship between local levels and branches of the state in Rostock and Erfurt and the feminist movements there can perhaps best be understood by thinking about the state and nonprofits as engaged in coregulation (Giugini and Passy 1998). The city governments of Rostock and Erfurt have acknowledged—albeit to varying degrees—that feminist organizations make a contribution to their cities and also recognize that feminist organizations desire some autonomy, particularly in how services are rendered. The state has turned to feminist organizations for their expertise on gender issues and relies on these organizations to identify service needs and to provide services the state is poorly prepared to. The state also turns to feminist activists for their expert knowledge on gender issues.

Looking closely at these two movements also reveals that feminist movements can be service oriented and remain political. The feminist movements in Rostock and Erfurt are both state-centered, yet they still engage in actions outside of the state and agitate for agendas set by activists, not by state actors. States are not the only targets of social movements (Van Dyke, Soule, and Taylor 2004), nor should movement success be measured solely as changes in the state. Feminism has long involved the creation of spaces where women find solidarity and empowerment through their relationships with other women. The feminist movements in Rostock and Erfurt offer such spaces. The organizations that comprise these movements cover a range of issues and collectively are highly inclusive. They offer different organizational models, including consensus-driven, nonhierarchical structures. They also offer women a number of different avenues through which to participate in feminist politics including noninstitutional and institutional modes of protest. In Erfurt in particular, the feminist movement also incorporates diverse ideologies.

Across activities and ideologies, feminist organizations in the two cities challenge women's subordinate status and gender inequalities. What alternate models for gender relations they endorse varies across feminist ideology, but the feminist movements in Rostock and Erfurt encourage discussion and debate about gender roles and women's roles in society. Radical feminist organizations in Erfurt are especially dedicated to consciousness-raising, yet even those groups that do not explicitly focus on consciousness-raising are engaged in similar, if more subtle, efforts at encouraging women to think about how their gender shapes their experiences. Service provisioning involves imparting clients and participants with new ways of interrogating gender in their own lives.

While their organizational forms and accomplishments may differ from the mass-based western European and North American feminist mobilizations of the 1970s, local feminist movements in postsocialist Europe are nonetheless making important contributions to building new understandings of gender. Given the specific history of interactions with the state under socialism, it is hardly surprising that feminist movements in eastern Germany often look to the state for protection and redress from inequality. At the same time, the history of extensive state involvement in the private sphere motivates feminist organizations to maintain some distance from the state. Under capitalism, feminist organizations have discovered important opportunities for working with the state, as well as limitations, particularly insofar as state support necessitates professionalization. The relationships between these movements and the states with which they interact are thus a balancing act, one that cannot be understood without considering the specific histories, institutions, and cultures at play.

Western feminists' sense of disappointment in feminism in postsocialist Europe—and especially in eastern Germany, which was, in 1989, the seemingly most viable feminist movement in the former Soviet bloc—is not surprising, but it is unfair. Holding a western feminist lens to eastern feminist movements simply doesn't work. As Nanette Funk (2004) has cogently argued in her discussion of why western feminists' critiques of liberalism don't resonate in postsocialist Europe, "One can construct arguments and analyses 'from the outside' in categories developed by Western feminists from within their liberal traditions, but other issues may be primary, 'from the inside,' from within the region" (718). Projecting their own interests into the post-Soviet world, western feminists have especially expressed disappointment about the failure of eastern feminists to mobilize effectively to preserve abortion rights. Such disappointment reflects western histories and priorities and fails to recognize the important differences between women's experiences and priorities across the former Iron Curtain. Future analyses of feminist formations after socialism should explore the specificity of such formations without resorting to western standards. Setting aside western lenses brings to light how specific histories shape contemporary patterns and challenges and expands western understandings of feminism.

Future Prospects for Feminism After Socialism

Eastern German women did not retreat to the domestic sphere after German unification in 1990. Instead, they have held onto their identities as workers and as key participants in fields of action in the public sphere, including politics. Although no longer visible as feminists in the arena of national politics, eastern German feminist activists continue to advance their agenda at local levels, serving as important resources within their communities in providing valuable social services and in challenging gender inequalities.

The form of postsocialist feminist organizing varies in accordance with specific, localized dynamics. Although feminist movements in eastern Germany have largely mobilized around the same core issues, namely women's employment opportunities, violence against women, and access to child care, feminist strategies, ideologies, and outcomes vary notably. Place matters, and in order to understand the causes and consequences of feminist social movements, we must come to understand place better.

Situating the women's movements in Rostock and Erfurt within their specific locales throughout this analysis has revealed the critical importance of place for local social movements. Places are both targets of social movement activity and important influences on social movement formation, development, and outcome. Dimensions of place are exogenous to these two feminist movements, and yet they are also permeable and flexible. Places, and the webs between them, are not easily altered, but they are susceptible to change, and feminists in Rostock and Erfurt will continue to push for changes.

Local feminist movements need to find ways to embed themselves in place, to render themselves indispensable. In a conservative, religious, traditional context like that in Erfurt, this is challenging, but it may not be impossible. Feminists there need to have open dialogues about strategy. Developing a long-term strategy is particularly difficult for those organizations living hand-to-mouth because they often do not have the time or other resources to dedicate to strategizing. However, in order to ensure their long-term survival, time must be set aside for this. Finding routes for building a more cohesive presence would especially increase the movement's legitimacy among the public and policymakers.

More open recognition of state-movement dynamics could help feminist organizations advocate for their interests more effectively. Feminist activists and organizations should foster open dialogue about their political agendas, how to achieve them, and how to interact with state offices and agencies. At present, there is very little debate or discussion about these issues in either Rostock or Erfurt. This is unfortunate because certain dependencies—like those on the state—become reified, and feminists fail to take a step back to consider the broader picture of which they are a part.

Local feminist movements also must continue with recent efforts to build bridges across places such as through regional and national coalitions between women's organizations working in different areas of eastern Germany. While a few such coalitions exist, including a nationwide coalition of State Women's Councils and a national conference of battered women's shelters, communication between feminists working in different political fields remains erratic, and when it does occur, it is often laden with judgment. Internet communication can increase flows of information between women otherwise focused exclusively on their immediate communities. Such contacts would enrich local feminist projects by bringing women with often competing perspectives into direct dialogue with one another and would enable the exchange of innovative ideas and strategies, many of which can be adapted from one setting into another.

Issues internal to the movement are important, as are external forces. While many of the factors I have identified as salient for the development of feminist movements are exogenous to these movements, they are also permeable, flexible, and susceptible to change. Strategic policy and movement decisions in both cities, and elsewhere, can contribute to movement longevity and ability to positively contribute to their cities. Improving women's social and economic capital, as feminist organizations in Rostock and Erfurt strive to do, can only stand to benefit these communities. The publics and policymakers in these locales and others should support such efforts.

The European Union could also serve as an important supranational resource for feminist goals in eastern Germany (Roth 2008). In order to become such a resource, EU policymakers need to more thoroughly consider the intended and unintended consequences of gender policies, which in turn necessitates greater attention to how EU agendas may conflict or align with local contexts (Weiner 2009). Most critically, EU policymakers need to evaluate not only how national member states receive and implement gender mainstreaming but also how subnational levels of governance and the relevant actors at those levels do. Especially because the German national state has been slow to accept and implement gender mainstreaming, local support for this agenda may be crucial for the overall success of gender mainstreaming in Germany. However, this success is unlikely to be forthcoming in the absence of more concerted efforts on the part of the EU or other supporters to educate relevant social actors about gender mainstreaming and to demystify what the term means, how the concept can be implemented, and what its effects may be. Highlighting cases where gender mainstreaming has been successfully implemented without reducing an interest specifically on women and women's issues, as in Rostock, could further increase empirical credibility. In addition, EU policymakers should evaluate their efforts at propagating this agenda with attention to criticisms of the gender mainstreaming agenda and to the possibly unintended consequences of pushing a new policy idea, such as contributing to conflict within feminist movements or undermining feminist efforts.

The redevelopment of eastern Germany remains a top policy priority in Germany. The German public and the German government need to recognize that this redevelopment cannot and should not happen without women. Eastern German women are deeply committed workers and citizens, and they represent an untapped resource in Germany. In trying to access this resource, German policymakers at all levels of governance would be wise to reconsider the dominant attitude that everything about East Germany was undesirable. Reinstating policies that better enable women to combine work and parenting will contribute to greater productivity and a more satisfied populace. As the PDS (now The Left, or Die Linke) makes a surprising comeback in German politics—even in Thuringia, the PDS netted almost one-third of the vote in the 2006 election cycle—political leaders should become more attuned to dissatisfaction in eastern Germany about the current fate of that region. One core strategy for remedying the poor integration of eastern Germany into the unified Germany would be to restore the principle, and introduce the practice, of gender equality so that the unified Germany might become a model of gender egalitarianism more recognizable to eastern Germans and more beneficial for all Germans.

Reference Matter

Methodological Appendix

Integrating Comparative, Narrative, and Feminist Approaches

To unravel the complex relationships between place and feminist movements in eastern Germany, I utilized a hybrid of methodological approaches. A multisited, comparative strategy allowed for identification of how differences in local environments interact with the goals, strategies, and organization of local feminist movements. In adopting a comparative approach, I was also able to examine how overlapping scales of governance (city, state, national, international) interact in different settings (Martin and Miller 2003).

Social struggle is spatial struggle, and space not only contains activism but also is alive with the networks, cultures, traditions, identities, and categories that create and sustain social movements. This analysis includes multiple units of analysis, many of which have nested relationships, such as individuals, organizations, political fields, cities, states, and international institutions. By selecting cities as the core basis for comparison while also attending to issues of scale, I am able to examine the geographic differentiation of political, legal, and cultural opportunities. This application of the comparative method in turn reveals how the local state (that is, the city) is at once a contested site and a mediator between women's organizations and other levels of both governance and social life.

When I initially began working on this project as a case study in 2000, I selected Rostock because the university there was offering a course in which I was interested. As logistics supported continuing in Rostock, the city became the de facto starting point. In moving beyond a case-study approach to a comparative approach, I sought a second case that would constitute a strategically matched pair with Rostock (Paulsen 2004). I developed a list of all eastern German cities similar in size and other demographics to Rostock that could serve as second cases. Ultimately, I selected Erfurt because it presented key similarities and differences. Virtually indistinguishable from Rostock in terms of its size and the demographic characteristics of its population (age, racial, and ethnic composition; rates of education, unemployment, welfare receipt, and crime;

average household income), Erfurt nonetheless had an apparently very different feminist movement. While the local feminist movement in Rostock was largely unknown until well into the 1990s, that in Erfurt entered the national spotlight in December 1989, but struggled throughout the 1990s. I therefore selected cases with contrasting outcomes in anticipation of discovering both hidden similarities and why the feminist movements in these two cities developed differently.

An emphasis on narratives adds a temporal dimension to the research design, focusing on the sequencing and relationships that, taken together and over time, constitute the focus of inquiry (Griffin and Stryker 2000). I adopt Robin Stryker's (1996) strategic narrative approach, which "requires the narrator to focus on individuals, institutional or collective actors; the actions they take; and when, where, why, how, and with what consequences they take them" (305). As Stryker notes, the emphasis on eventful time in narrativist accounts highlights how structures are reproduced or transformed through actors' use of the rules and resources created by those structures. The period since unification has not been static, but instead is characterized by ongoing changes and transformations that can best be captured through attention to structural changes over time, and how these changes create or limit subsequent opportunities for social action.

The narratives of the social actors involved in this research also play a key role. Francesca Poletta (1998) has observed that in anomic periods when established institutions and dominant ideologies are absent or in the midst of upheaval, as in postsocialist periods, social actors may use narratives to transform confusing events into logical stories, or may reformulate threatened or fragmented social identities into powerfully mobilizing identities. These narratives become most evident through the collection of stories. A guiding mission of this project has been to compile such narratives and arrange them in a theoretically meaningful and contextually specific way.

Feminist epistemology also informs the research strategy. Feminist methods go beyond even the antipositivist methods used by most scholars of social movements by developing situated knowledge. Feminist methods focus on gender, gender inequality, and how expectations of gender are played out in everyday life (DeVault 1999; Naples 2003). In emphasizing participation and reflexivity, feminist methods are useful in obtaining insider knowledge that can illuminate the logic and strategies of social movement actors within their particular structural location.

Data and Fieldwork

I initially entered the field in Rostock in 2000 intending to engage primarily in the ethnographic work of participant observation. Ethnography involves the study of people in their social worlds (Burawoy 1991). Feminist ethnographers have pushed the boundaries of ethnography to ensure that fieldwork involves recognition of the experiences of women and others who are less powerful (DeVault 1999). Borrowing from the tradition of institutional ethnography (Smith 1990), I wanted to engage in research that would uncover the organization of social relations within feminist movements and between feminist movements and outside actors and power-holders.

Shortly after beginning my fieldwork, it became apparent to me that in order to understand women's experiences as feminists after socialism, I needed to be able to hear their voices in a more direct manner than participant observation alone would allow. I thus decided that while participant observation should continue as an important research tool, interviews would be key to learning about the processes in which I was interested, namely the development of local feminist movements and their interactions with place and scale. Thus, in conducting fieldwork in Rostock and Erfurt during multiple periods since 2000, I have drawn on a range of sociological research tools, including interviews, observations, and archival research to reveal how the story lines—the plots and outcomes—of these two local feminist movements have changed and evolved since unification.

In this book, I draw on data from interviews I conducted with sixty-three women— thirty-two in Rostock and thirty-one in Erfurt—between 2000 and 2004. Because I interviewed some respondents at multiple time points, the total number of interviews is seventy-four. The sole criterion for participation by activists was involvement in feminist organizations during or since unification. Although I did not exclude men from the sample, none emerged as appropriate interview subjects. I recruited state officials based on the relevance of their position for women's organizations in each city, or because of their involvement both in feminist organizations and formal political life. In Rostock, participants represented a total of thirteen organizations, while in Erfurt they represented twelve organizations, including one that no longer existed at the time of the interview. While in Rostock, all of the interviewees were actively involved in women's organizations at the time of the interview, two respondents in Erfurt had worked with feminist organizations, but no longer did so when I met them.

In Rostock, the sample included one currently appointed government official, one formerly elected government official, and three current employees of government agencies (see Table A.1). Of these employees, one was also elected into a specific position

Table A.1 Comparison of sample composition in Rostock and Erfurt by primary occupational status

	Rostock	Erfurt
Elected government official	1	4
Appointed government official	1	2
Government employee	3	2
Activist outside of government	27	23
Total	32	31

by coworkers. The remaining twenty-seven respondents were activists. In both Rostock and Erfurt, most femocrats work both in state offices and in the nonprofit sector. I classify respondents as either officials or activists based on their primary place of employment at the time I met them.

Because Erfurt is also the state capital of Thuringia, the sample in Erfurt includes a greater number of government employees and leaders: four were elected officials, two were appointed officials, and two were employees at government agencies. Of the elected officials, two represented the CDU and one each represented the SPD and PDS. As in Rostock, one of the government workers was also elected by coworkers for a specific position. All state officials and employees in this sample work primarily at the city or state level, although the elected and appointed officials in particular are also extremely familiar with national and EU politics and policies, as well as with the platforms of their parties. Twenty-three respondents in Erfurt were activists.

Activists in the sample were and/or had been volunteers and/or employees at women's organizations. These individuals were identified for possible participation either directly by me or by suggestion from other participants. At the conclusion of interviews, I asked participants to suggest other activists I should speak with; these often-overlapping lists quickly produced a second round of interviews and helped me establish a sense of the social and professional networks among feminist activists in the city. Since I was interested not only in the "star" organizations but also in more subordinate groups, I relied on a municipal list of all women's organizations to ensure that I reached as many different types of groups as possible. In addition, I drew on the suggestions of one of my earlier informants with whom I could candidly discuss the power dynamics between groups in Rostock. I spoke with at least one woman from every women's organization that has existed in either city since 1989, including now-defunct groups.

In Erfurt, the first round of interviews relied heavily on cold calls to women's organizations listed in the phone book or with a presence on the Internet. A few weeks into the research, the GB's office provided me with a list of all incorporated women's organizations in Erfurt. As in Rostock, I relied on informants to provide suggestions for further interviews.

With few exceptions, the participants were extremely friendly and eager to speak with me. While I had been warned about the antiwestern attitudes of eastern Germans, the participants in this study were overwhelmingly generous with their time and insights. I began fieldwork when I was twenty-five years old, and I suspect my youth was an advantage as most women were about my mother's age and tended to treat me like a daughter or a daughter's good friend. An additional advantage was that while I am of West German origin, I spent most of my life living in the United States, providing me with a unique insider/outsider status through which I possessed both linguistic and cultural fluency as well as separation from the West Germans that many easterners have learned to regard with suspicion. Respondents routinely inquired with curiosity about my unmistakably German name and my German-language skills, and sometimes they seemed notably relieved when I advised them I had not been raised in West Germany. Perhaps most influential in encouraging their openness with me was the fact that these women were eager to tell their stories. Normally silenced and marginalized as women and as eastern Germans, they welcomed my interest in their lives and work and enthusiastically shared and asked questions of me.

I did experience gate-keeping in attempting to interview two higher-level government officials, the statewide GBs in Mecklenburg-West Pomerania and in Thuringia. In both cases, I made appointments with the representatives themselves, but, at the time of the interview, was instead routed to lower-ranked staff members. While initially disappointed by my inability to meet directly with these officials, I found that their associates provided tremendous insight. In Mecklenburg-West Pomerania the staff member I interviewed had worked in the office since its inception in 1993; in Thuringia, she had worked there since 1996. Unlike the representatives, who serve for appointed terms only, the assistants had experienced the growth of these offices since their inception and were therefore better able to provide information on how these ministries had changed and evolved over time.

Demographic questionnaires completed by activists prior to the interviews reveal that activists included in this sample in Rostock and Erfurt share much in common. In Rostock, the average age of respondents was just under forty-nine years old, with a range of thirty-five to sixty-seven. In Erfurt, the average age of respondents was just under fifty-two years old, with a range of twenty-eight to eighty. Women activists who are native to Rostock appear to be slightly more educated than women native to Erfurt. The sample in Rostock included six women with doctoral degrees, four with master's degrees, five with advanced vocational degrees, just one who had only completed the high school *Abitur* exam, which allows students to pursue a university degree, and none who had only completed high school without *Abitur*. In Erfurt, none of the women held doctorates, three had master's degrees, six had advanced vocational degrees, and four had completed high school without *Abitur*. All but six women activists are or have been married and have children, although many of those children are now adults. A total of six respondents live with partners, and three specified that they are in lesbian relationships.

For almost all of the participants, their current work represents a significant shift from their preunification careers. The sample includes a biologist, a ships' engineer, a linguistics professor, a large-animal veterinarian, a geologist, a sociologist, a music professor, several early childhood and elementary school teachers, a public health expert, a shipyard worker, a bookbinder, a dairy worker, a fashion designer, a portrait photographer, a secretary, and an agricultural worker. A few of these women have retrained since unification, often into "helping" professions such as social work, counseling, and psychology. Even more, however, have made the leap into feminist organizing without any additional training and simply learn by doing.

Participating in social movement organizations is largely a new experience for these women. Only sixteen women (eight in Rostock and eight in Erfurt) reported involvement with any type of voluntary, civic, or political organization before unification. Their involvement was often with state-sponsored organizations like workplace unions, neighborhood associations, the SED, the Society for German-Soviet Friendship, professional organizations, and the DFD. Outside of the realm of activities that the SED would smile upon, one woman in Erfurt was active in the politics of the CDU before unification, and another woman in Erfurt participated in a political discussion group for women organized under the auspices of the Lutheran Church. One woman in Rostock who was married to a minister worked with peace groups through the church. The remaining women only joined women's organizations during or after unification.

While most of the participants were born and raised in East Germany, almost always in or near Rostock and Erfurt, five participants, four in Erfurt and one in Rostock, are West German. Three of the West Germans in the sample are government employees, one of whom followed her husband eastward and two who were recruited from the West for their expertise in specific domains. Two other western Germans are nuns whose order established a shelter for battered women in Erfurt. In addition, one woman from Erfurt is an American citizen born to a German mother and an American father on a U.S. Army base in West Germany and who has lived in Erfurt since unification. Only one respondent, originally from Russia, migrated before unification, arriving in Erfurt in 1982.

When first faced with the possibility of interviewing western Germans, I debated whether I should exclude them from the study. Ultimately, I decided against such exclusion for several reasons. First, western German women, while a minority among women activists in eastern Germany, are active in women's organizations in the cities under consideration, especially in Erfurt. While their experiences and interpretations are different from those of women raised in the GDR, I felt this outsider status could provide a new angle and might offer me different ways of thinking about women's activism in eastern Germany since unification. Second, the role of western German women in eastern German feminist organizations is highly contested. In addition to the ideological conflicts that often emerge between eastern and western German women, eastern German women are also sometimes wary of westerners who come to the eastern states and arguably take jobs that would otherwise be filled by eastern German women. Speaking with western German women allowed me to hear the other side of these debates and to better understand how conflicts between eastern and western women are negotiated in the workplace and in the organizational field. Third, western German women in eastern Germany often came with specializations in specific areas. Hearing about their successes and challenges in transmitting certain ideas within their fields further illuminates what kinds of framing strategies resonate in the eastern context.

During the interviews, which generally lasted at least ninety minutes, but which were often as long as three to four hours, women answered questions about their careers and interests before unification, how and why they joined the organization(s) with which they work, and what they view as the most positive and negative consequences of unification. They described their perceptions of the local community, local politics, and the field of women's organizations in their cities and nationally. We also discussed which problems their organizations attempted to deal with and how they approached these problems, what the costs and benefits of participating in their organization(s) were, who else participates, and what they see as possibilities and challenges in the future.

The interview guide for government officials was slightly different than that used for women activists. In these interviews, I focused more heavily on how well feminist political work is received by political leaders, the evolution, power, and influence of specific offices, the state's overall view of the women's movement, and the overall political climate in the city and state. I also asked government officials to discuss how they thought their city or state was different from, or similar to, other cities and states in eastern Germany in terms of its support for women's issues. Because most government officials also had specific areas of expertise, such as women's unemployment or gender mainstreaming, the interview questions were tailored to tap into these areas of knowledge. Interviews with government officials generally lasted ninety minutes to two hours in length.

Importantly, with one exception that was largely accidental, I did not interview government officials who work outside of the feminist movement. Undoubtedly, the perceptions of state leaders who are not directly involved with women's issues would have brought additional nuance to the question of how well policymakers understand and respond to demands made within the feminist movement. I excluded these individuals partially for logistical reasons: a reasonable sample of government officials outside of the movement would have added a great deal of time to the project timeline and government officials were, as a rule, already the most difficult group to access. Rather than expending my resources on those individuals whose stories and interpretations are largely part of the public record, I wanted to devote my time and energy to recording the stories of women whose experiences are rarely heard. The overall response of policymakers to the goals of the feminist movements in Rostock and Erfurt could be more than adequately captured through legislative and financial records and decisions. Hearing their justifications for these decisions would certainly have been interesting, but I wanted to focus on the decisions themselves and on the perceptions social movement actors have of those decisions.

Although I structured the interview guides around a specific set of questions, I attempted to maintain an informal environment in which participants would feel comfortable elaborating beyond the specified questions. Before, during, and after the interview, respondents were encouraged to share their thoughts on other themes and topics they felt were important, and most did so, often sharing with me great detail about their personal histories and providing richly detailed and nuanced stories of their lives in the

GDR and today. I also frequently asked follow-up questions to elicit more information or for clarification.

As has been well documented (DeVault 1999; Wolf 1996a), the research process is fraught with complexities of power and status. Diane Wolf (1996b) identifies three dimensions of power in fieldwork: (1) power differences that generally stem from different positions of the researcher and the researched along axes of inequality; (2) power exerted through the research relationship, such as unequal exchange, exploitation, and the researcher's control over the research relationship; and (3) power exerted after the completion of fieldwork through writing and representation. As a highly educated West German-American, I come from a position of privilege relative to many of the respondents. As a researcher, I am also situated as someone possessing expert knowledge and who ultimately passes some type of judgment on the people and organizations I encounter. These positions are relevant for my research insofar as they influence my perceptions, as well as the degree of access and trust respondents offer me.

Ultimately, the most problematic aspect of the project came down to naming. As I have discussed elsewhere (Guenther 2009), I was troubled by the need to honor confidentiality without silencing respondents, who often wanted to speak on the record. I found myself in an ethical gray area that I suspect is not uncommon to fieldworkers, even if it is not routinely discussed (see Scheper-Hughes 2000, for a notable exception). Because any effort at complete confidentiality would require changing the names and details of the cities under consideration, I realized early on that I could not assure full confidentiality. Many women and the organizations with which they work also wanted to speak on the record. As women and as eastern Germans, they are typically silenced, and they welcomed the opportunity to be heard. Ultimately, I decided to use real place and organization names. I have, however, used pseudonyms for all respondents except for those who are public officials or lobbyists and who typically speak on the record. In cases where a respondent's comments might damage relationships with funding organizations or other resources, I disengaged individual voices from specific organizations and identities.

With their consent, I tape recorded interviews and later transcribed them for data analysis with the help of two research assistants. Three activists, all in Erfurt, felt uncomfortable being recorded, and I instead took notes. In addition, two interviews, one in Rostock and one in Erfurt, were conducted by telephone. As I did not have the necessary equipment to record on the telephone, here I took copious notes. Finally, equipment failure during one interview in Rostock required note-taking during the latter portion of that interview.

Interview data was augmented by nonparticipant and participant observation, as well as by tours of facilities and informal conversations with employees, volunteers, and clients who were not formally interviewed. Often, at the completion of the interview, activists would show me around their offices, explaining how different physical spaces were used and how and why these spaces had changed over time. For example, during a tour of a battered women's shelter, the director and her colleague showed me how the rooms had been renovated, how these renovations influenced client and staff morale, and who had funded the renovations. While I was unable to meet any current residents because of concerns about confidentiality, the director invited me to join her, her colleague, a former client, and the client's young daughter for a prescheduled coffee date. By chance, another former client joined us, and I was then able to hear about their experiences as residents of the shelter.

During tours, I was also often introduced to coworkers who would then describe their roles within the organization. In many cases, these introductions led me to invite coworkers to participate in the interview process, but I often found it more convenient and less intimidating for the employees simply to speak with them when I met them. These nonsupervisory employees, many of whom were accidental activists sent over by the Employment Office, were the most difficult to recruit and the most difficult to interview formally because their self-deprecating tendencies and possible fear of violating workplace norms of hierarchy led them to refer me to their bosses.

However, while perhaps not possessing the same type of expert knowledge as women who had been involved with an organization since its inception and who were truly career activists, it was important to include their knowledge for several reasons. Such women provided invaluably sobering assessments of the role of organizations in the community. While directors sometimes took on a preacher's aura in regaling me with their accomplishments, lower-level employees were more candid about who the organization did and did not reach and what they accomplished and, just as importantly, failed to accomplish. Similarly, these women, who generally did not participate in women's mobilizations during unification, could comment on the attraction of women's organizations in the postunification period. Since they were themselves drawn into the movement after the period of the most significant movement activity, they may also represent a new generation of women activists. These newer recruits were also in and of themselves representations of the organizations' successes and failures insofar as they presented me with an opportunity to assess how well an organization was transmitting organizational goals, values, collective identities, and ideologies to its workers.

After the interviews, tours, and introductions, I often was able to spend more time at organizations. As many of the women's organizations have public spaces, such as informal cafés or feminist libraries, I often received invitations to hang around, read their materials, or chat with other employees, volunteers, and clients. I was also able to come back to these public spaces at other times to see who might be around to talk for a bit, or to see who was using the space and how. I did not formally interview clients at organizations that provide services because my core questions rest neither on the outcomes of service provisioning, nor on the differences in motivation between activists and nonactivists.

Participant observation at special events also allows me to consider the roles of non-activists and of women who are only peripherally involved with women's social movement activity. These events included the monthly Women's Political Roundtables held in Rostock and Erfurt, events related to Violence Against Women Awareness Week in Erfurt, attendance at readings and film screenings sponsored by women's organizations, and the annual convention of the CDU's Women's Union (CDU-FU) in Weimar, a city near Erfurt. I also observed routine activities at women's cafés and open studios. In these settings, my presence was generally unobtrusive. In Erfurt in particular, I frequently crossed paths with the same women from one event to the next, and soon I was treated like just another attendee rather than as a novelty.

Finally, my analysis draws on archival resources. Many of the organizations I visited maintain archives, whether of minutes from meetings, newsletters, fliers, letters to elected officials, posters, and/or brochures. Whenever conducting interviews at an organization, I inquired about the existence and availability of such documents and was usually generously rewarded. While some organizations had virtually no such documentation, most at a minimum were able to provide fliers and posters dating back to the inception of their organization. A few women also shared their personal mementos with me, offering copies of photographs, fliers, and banners. Brennessel, the radical feminist group in Erfurt, also produces a monthly newspaper, and I was able to collect a solid archive of this publication. Many organizations, especially in Rostock, have an Internet presence, and information from Web pages is included. The Internet also presented me with the opportunity to maintain contact with participants after leaving the field, and e-mail has aided in clarifying confusing or unclear points made during interviews and in keeping me abreast of more recent developments in Rostock and Erfurt.

Government officials and offices also provided me with relevant documents. Most noteworthy here were documents relating to debates about gender issues in local governance, as well as local legal statutes, internal memos, and position papers. The Office of Gender Equity in Rostock and Erfurt, as well as the Office of Gender Equity and Equality Between Men and Women in Thuringia and the Office of Gender Equity in Mecklenburg-West Pomerania provided collections of brochures, fliers, legal statutes, and calendars of events.

Collectively, interviews, observations, and archival data provided rich information into the development of the feminist movements in Rostock and Erfurt. Using Atlas.ti, computer software that helps researchers organize qualitative data, I coded interviews and a selection of field notes and archival documents. Through coding, I was able to identify themes and rhetorical strategies. I built timelines of shifts within the movements and traced the evolution of specific issues. I mapped networks and relationships between organizations and other actors, such as state agencies. My conceptualization of feminism as grounded in the dynamics of place emerged from my immersion in the voices of respondents and my own voice from the field.

Notes

Chapter 1

1. The literature on "glocalization" spans various disciplines and has become quite vast. For a pioneering sociological perspective, see Robertson (1994).

2. The Berlin Wall fell on November 9, 1989, after the East German government responded to weeks of protests by announcing that visits to West Germany and West Berlin would be permitted. East Germans participated in free elections on March 18, 1990, in which a coalition of conservative parties, the Alliance for Germany, which supported rapid unification with West Germany was victorious. On October 3, 1990, five eastern German states and the reconstituted state of Berlin, now incorporating East and West Berlin, joined the Federal Republic of Germany, and the GDR was formally dissolved. October 3, the Day of German Unity, is now a national holiday.

3. Reacting in large part to the dropping fertility rate in Germany, in 2007, the Federal Minister for Family Affairs, Seniors, Women, and Youth, Ursula von der Leyen, began actively promoting the expansion of day-care spaces in Germany. The goal is to triple the number of day-care spots available in Germany to 750,000 by 2013.

4. West and western German women, especially working mothers, are also subject to derision as *Rabenmütter*.

5. Beginning in the mid-1990s, the gender disparity in unemployment began closing. In 2004, the unemployment rate for women in eastern Germany was 20 percent, compared to 22 percent for men and to an overall unemployment rate of 10 percent in the old western German states. However, only individuals registered with the Unemployment Office and actively seeking work are reflected in these statistics. Unemployment among women may in fact be higher than 20 percent, but women are more likely than men to give up on finding work through the Unemployment Office and thus no longer bother to register as unemployed.

6. Under federal law, children ages three to six are guaranteed a place in kindergarten. Not only does this law ignore the needs of working women with children under the age of three, but kindergarten is typically only half of the day in many parts of Germany, leaving parents with a child-care problem for the afternoons.

7. Because I largely concluded fieldwork well before the PDS became The Left, I refer to that party as the PDS throughout this book.

Chapter 2

1. As Lynne Haney (2002) so aptly demonstrates in the Hungarian case, the assumption of homogeneity within socialism is unfounded. Identifying the stages of welfare-state evolution in the GDR is beyond the scope of this project; however, I do not assume that the GDR period had a single, monolithic welfare state.

2. Statistics on women's labor-force participation in East Germany are typically overinflated because the GDR included women in school full time, as well as women on maternity leaves, within the count of full-time workers. Even so, women's participation in the formal labor force in East Germany was extremely high with generous estimates at more than 90 percent and conservative estimates closer to 80 percent.

3. In 1986, this law was expanded to include first-born children and offered eighteen months paid leave for the birth of third and subsequent children.

4. In many respects, West Germany was a more "woman friendly" state than the United States or some other western European nations, primarily because women could benefit from its strong social safety net and worker protections. The focus of comparison in this chapter is only between East and West Germany.

5. For a statement of goals of one group of women participating in the UFV, see DiCaprio (1990).

6. See Maleck-Lewy and Ferree (2000) and Young (1999) for more detailed discussions of the abortion debate.

7. SAM was terminated in 2004 and at that time ABM was merged into the program for distribution of unemployment benefits. ABM was fully terminated as of January 1, 2009.

8. Through the 1990s, statewide GBs were typically part of the state chancellery such that they reported directly to governors. Beginning in the early 2000s, however, many GB's offices were subsumed into other state ministries, such as the Ministry for Family and Social Issues. As of 2008, Mecklenburg-West Pomerania was the only German state with a GB who was still part of the state chancellery. Because these changes occurred after the period under consideration in this book, I do not analyze the implications of these shifts, although they presumably do not have positive effects for local feminist movements.

Chapter 3

1. Neither the UFV nor the official women's party of the GDR earned enough votes for a seat on the city council, but that the women's parties earned any recognizable portion of the vote helped establish that women's concerns needed to be addressed by city politicians.

2. Under German law, cities of ten thousand or more are required to have a GB in place. The impetus for this appointment thus did not come from Rostock or from the women's movement there.

3. I was unfortunately not able to interview the first GB because she retired before I began work on this project and now spends much of her time in Guatemala; however, I was able to speak with her former assistant and several friends and other colleagues.

4. Like many other buildings, ownership of the barracks could not be established as the SED had exercised eminent domain in acquiring it from a private owner.

5. Because of the design of the building, the apartments ultimately included one small studio that is rented to a single woman with no children living with her.

6. For a discussion and detailed analysis of these events, see especially chapter 5 of Karapin (2007).

Chapter 4

1. For the full text of the gender mainstreaming resolution, see Hansestadt Rostock (2001).

2. Whether this is the also the case for gender mainstreaming remains to be seen.

3. In 2013, the EU will be changing its categorization system of need. To date, eastern Germany has been treated as underdeveloped. As of 2013, eastern Germany will be reclassified among more developed regions. This is expected to result in significant budgetary problems for local feminist organizations in Rostock.

Chapter 5

1. Kerstin Schön was no longer living in Erfurt when I conducted fieldwork there, so I was unfortunately unable to interview her.

2. In German, Evangelical (*evangelisch*) refers to Protestantism rather than to evangelism (*evangelikal*). This use should not be confused with the American understanding of evangelical as proselytizing and/or fundamentalist. The Evangelical Lutheran Church in Germany and the Evangelical Church in Germany, a federation of Protestant denominations, are mainstream Protestant institutions.

3. The earliest footprint of the cathedral dates to the mid-700s.

4. After the collapse of the GDR, Stasi records revealed that in fact many church leaders, including priests and ministers, had cooperated as Stasi informants.

5. In 1993, the city council changed the structure of the Frauenamt, as well as its title, consolidating what had previously been three positions into one and renaming the office the Amt für Gleichstellung und Geschlechter. The rhetorical shift from women to equality and gender, which occurred in virtually all eastern German cities in the early 1990s, represented a break from the western German tradition, grounded in radical feminism, of referring to these offices as women's offices, and toward a new, more neutral emphasis on gender and gender inequality.

6. That five of the respondents in Erfurt were uncomfortable about being tape recorded, while none were in Rostock, may reflect concerns about surveillance.

7. Chancellor Merkel was born in West Germany and raised in East Germany.

8. As of 2003, state-funding guidelines established that the state would pay 80 percent of salary costs for social workers at battered women's shelters that employ one social worker per eight beds for battered women. The funding formulas for battered women's shelters are generally far more advantageous to shelters in eastern Germany than in western Germany.

9. In the early 1990s, when the Municipal Women's Center employed twelve women, was still in the process of making equipment purchases, and didn't receive funding from any source but the city, the annual cost to the city was closer to €200,000 (DM400,000).

Chapter 6

1. The city of Mühlhausen, about thirty miles from Erfurt, is the geographic center of Germany.

2. A range of conflicts between eastern and western German feminists have been documented. For some discussions of these conflicts, see Ferree (1995, Forthcoming) and Young (1999).

3. One of the major goals of the reform movement in the GDR was the creation of a civil sphere.

4. Nationally, the women's organization of the PDS is called LISA, or the Socialist Working Group of Women in the Left (Die Sozialistische Arbeitsgemeinschaft der Frauen in der Linkspartei), but in Thuringia, the equivalent organization is called the Women's Working Group of the Left in Thuringia (Arbeitsgemeinschaft Weiberwirtschaft DIE LINKE Thüringen) (*Weiberwirtschaft* is a term, often used as a derogatory, for a female-headed household or female-dominated business).

5. In 1994 the SPD and CDU fractions in the state parliament formed a short-lived official coalition.

6. The late 1990s and early 2000s in Germany witnessed extensive discussion about German orthography because of the growing use of English words and greater attention to regional variations in the German language. A federal commission was established to set specific guidelines for German spelling, grammar, and punctua-

tion. The federal Ministry of Culture released its completed guidelines—which must be used in schools and government institutions—in June 2004, although several sets of guidelines were released earlier. One of the major debates that emerged through the new "correct spelling" (*Rechtschreibung*) guidelines was if and how to integrate non-German words, such as "highlighter," "flyer," "know-how," and "Handy" (mobile phone). Public debate about the "Englification" of German, as represented by the media, suggests that a not insignificant number of Germans opposed the formal admission of English words into the German language, as determined by the Council for German Orthography.

Chapter 7

1. In March 2005, the city elected a nonpartisan mayor from a year-old informal voter's group called Bündnis für Rostock. This independent candidate who pioneered the city's popular annual sailing regatta, the Hansesail, represents himself as a political progressive committed to fiscal responsibility. He took office in April 2005.

2. See Funder (2003) for an interesting account of the process of restoring these files.

3. The relationship between religion and women's rights is highly complex. Not all Christian perspectives will necessarily endorse traditional approaches toward gender, but this has been the case in Erfurt and especially in heavily Catholic Thuringia.

4. See, for example, Banaszak, Beckwith, and Rucht (2003a, 2003b), Stetson (2000), and Stetson and Mazur (1995).

5. See especially chapter 4 of Gal and Kligman (2000b) for an interesting discussion of the role of the family during and after socialism.

6. The two exceptions include an organization called Frauenbrücke Ost-West (Women's Bridge East-West) in Rostock, the local chapter of a national organization committed to increasing contact between women from across the former border, and the Convent Group in Erfurt. Neither group is officially incorporated as a nonprofit, nor does either group have office space, paid staff, or any other financial obligations.

Works Cited

Adler, Marina A., and April Brayfield. 1997. Women's work values in unified Germany: Regional differences and remnants of the past. *Work and Occupations* 24 (2):245–66.

Agnew, John A. 2002. *Place and politics in modern Italy.* Chicago: University of Chicago Press.

Althausen, Gudrun, Angela Berlis, Christine Busch, Brigitte Enzner-Probst, Erika Godel, Karin Held, Regine Hildebrandt, Renate Höppner, Johanna Jäger-Sommer, and Margot Kässman. 2000. *Kinder, Kirche, und Karriere: Von der berufstätigen Mutter im Dienst des Herrn Erfahrungsberichte.* Berlin: Wichern-Verlag.

Alvarez, Sonia E. 1999. Advocating feminism: The Latin American feminist NGO "boom." *International Feminist Journal of Politics* 1 (2):181–209.

———. 2009. Beyond NGO-ization? Reflections from Latin America. *Development* 52 (2):175–84.

Amt für Statistik und Wahlen der Stadt Erfurt. 1990. *Endgültiges gesamtergebnis Erfurt/ Stadt.* Erfurt: Stadt Erfurt.

Aronson, Pamela. 2003. Feminists or "Postfeminists"? Young women's attitudes toward feminism and gender relations. *Gender & Society* 17 (6):902–22.

Bach, Jonathan. 2002. "The taste remains": Consumption, (n)ostalgia, and the production of East Germany. *Public Culture* 14 (3):545.

Banaszak, Lee Ann, Karen Beckwith, and Dieter Rucht. 2003a. When power relocates: Interactive changes in women's movements and states. Pp. 1–29 in *Women's movements facing the reconfigured state,* edited by Lee Ann Banaszak, Karen Beckwith, and Dieter Rucht. Cambridge: Cambridge University Press.

———, eds. 2003b. *Women's movements facing the reconfigured state.* Cambridge: Cambridge University Press.

Beckwith, Karen. 2001. Women's movements at century's end: Excavation and advances in political science. *Annual Review of Political Science* 4:371–90.

Benford, Robert D., and David A. Snow. 2000. Framing processes and social movements: An overview and assessment. *Annual Review of Sociology* 26:611–39.

Berdahl, Daphne. 2000a. An anthropology of postsocialism. Pp. 1–13 in *Altering states: Ethnographies of transition in eastern Europe and the former Soviet Union*, edited by Daphne Berdahl, Matti Bunzl, and Martha Lampland. Ann Arbor: University of Michigan Press.

———. 2000b. "Go, Trabi, go!": Reflections on a car and its symbolization over time. *Anthropology & Humanism* 25 (2):131–41.

Beveridge, Fiona, Sue Nott, and Kylie Stephen. 2000a. Mainstreaming and the engendering of policy-making: A means to an end? *Journal of European Public Policy* 7 (3):385–405.

———. 2000b. Addressing gender in national and community law and policy making. Pp. 135–55 in *Social law and policy in an evolving European Union*, edited by Jo Shaw. Oxford: Hart Publishing.

Booth, Christine, and Cinnamon Bennett. 2002. Gender mainstreaming in the European Union: Towards a new conception and practice of equal opportunities? *European Journal of Women's Studies* 9 (4):430–46.

Boston Women's Health Book Collective. 1979. *Our bodies, ourselves.* New York: Simon & Schuster.

Brown, Annalies, Gerda Jasper, and Ursula Schröter, eds. 1995. *Rolling back the gender status of East German women.* London: Pluto Press.

Bundesarbeitsgemeinschaft kommunaler Frauenbüros. 2003. Available at www.frauen-beauftragte.de.

Burawoy, Michael. 1991. Teaching participant observation. Pp. 291–300 in *Ethnography unbound: Power and resistance in the modern metropolis*, edited by Michael Burawoy, Alice Burton, Ann Arnett Ferguson, and Kathryn J. Fox. Los Angeles: University of California Press.

Chaves, Mark, Laura Stephens, and Joseph Galaskiewicz. 2004. Does government funding suppress non-profits' political activity? *American Sociological Review* 69 (2):292–316.

Clemens, Elisabeth S. 1993. Organizational repertoires and institutional change: Women's groups and the transformation of us politics. *American Journal of Sociology* 98 (4):755–98.

Daly, Mary. 2000. *The gender division of welfare: The impact of the British and German welfare states.* Cambridge: Cambridge University Press.

Desai, Manisha. 2002. Multiple mediations: The state and women's movements in India. Pp. 66–84 in *Social movements: Identity, culture, and the state*, edited by David S. Meyer, Nancy Whittier, and Belinda Robnett. Oxford: Oxford University Press.

Deutsche Bundesregierung. 2003. *Jahresbericht der Bundesregierung zum Stand der deutschen Einheit 2003.* Berlin: Deutsche Bundesregierung.

————. 2004. Jahresbericht der Bundesregierung zum Stand der deutschen Einheit 2001. Available at http://www.bundesregierung.de/Anlage766722/Jahresbericht+zum+Stand+der+Deutschen+Einheit+2004.pdf.

DeVault, Marjorie. 1999. *Liberating method: Feminism and social research*. Philadelphia, PA: Temple University.

DiCaprio, Lisa. 1990. East German feminists: The Lila manifesto. *Feminist Studies* 16 (3):621–34.

Dodds, Dinah, and Pam Allen-Thompson, eds. 1994. *The Wall in my backyard: East German women in transition*. Amherst: University of Massachusetts Press.

Dölling, Irene, Daphne Hahn, and Sylka Scholz. 2000. Birth strike in the new federal states: Is sterilization an act of resistance? Pp. 118–47 in *Reproducing gender: Politics, publics, and everyday life after socialism*, edited by Susan Gal and Gail Kligman. Princeton, NJ: Princeton University Press.

Duggan, Lynn. 2003. East and West German family policy compared: The distribution of childrearing costs. *Comparative Economic Studies* 45:63–86.

Einhorn, Barbara. 1992. German Democratic Republic: Emancipated women or hard-working mothers? Pp. 125–54 in *Superwoman and the double burden*, edited by Chris Corrin. Toronto: Second Story Press.

Einhorn, Barbara, and Charlotte Sever. 2003. Gender and civil society in central and eastern Europe. *International Feminist Journal of Politics* 5 (2):163–90.

Elshtain, Jean Bethke. 1992. *Public man, private woman: Women in social and political thought*. Princeton, NJ: Princeton University Press.

Eschle, Catherine. 2000. *Democracy, social movements, and feminism*. Boulder, CO: Westview Press.

Ferree, Myra Marx. 1993. The rise of "Mommy politics": Feminism and unification in (East) Germany. *Feminist Studies* 19 (1):89–115.

————. 1994. "The time of chaos was best": Feminist mobilization and demobilization in East Germany. *Gender and Politics* 8 (4):597–623.

————. 1995. Patriarchies and feminisms: Two women's movements in post-unification Germany. *Social Politics* (spring):10–24.

————. 1996. Institutionalization, identity, and the political participation of women in the new Bundesländer. *Research on Russia and Eastern Europe* 2:19–34.

————. 2006. Angela Merkel: What does it mean to run as a woman? *German Politics and Society* 24 (1):93–107.

————. Forthcoming. *Sisterhood since the sixties*. Stanford, CA: Stanford University Press.

Ferree, Myra Marx, and Carol McClurg Mueller. 2004. Feminism and the women's movement: A global perspective. Pp. 576–607 in *The Blackwell companion to social movements*, edited by David A. Snow, Sarah A. Soule, and Hanspeter Kriesi. Malden, MA: Blackwell Publishing.

Fraser, Nancy. 1993. *Justice interruptus: Critical reflections on the "postsocialist" condition*. New York: Routledge.

Funder, Anna. 2003. *Stasiland: True stories from behind the Berlin Wall*. New York: Granta Books.

Funk, Nanette. 1993. Abortion and German unification. Pp. 194–200 in *Gender politics and post-communism*, edited by Nanette Funk and Magda Muleller. New York: Routledge.

———. 2004. Feminist critiques of liberalism: Can they travel East? Their relevance in eastern and central Europe and the former Soviet Union. *Signs* 29 (3):695–726.

Gal, Susan, and Gail Kligman. 2000a. *The politics of gender after socialism*. Princeton, NJ: Princeton University Press.

———, eds. 2000b. *Reproducing gender: Politics, publics, and everyday life after socialism*. Princeton, NJ: Princeton University Press.

Gelb, Joyce, and Viviane Hart. 1999. Feminist politics in a hostile environment. Pp. 149–81 in *How social movements matter*, edited by Marco Giugni, Doug McAdam, and Charles Tilly. Minneapolis: University of Minnesota Press.

Ghodsee, Kristen. 2005. *The red Riviera: Gender, tourism, and postsocialism on the Black Sea*. Durham, NC: Duke University Press.

Giugini, Marco, and Florence Passy. 1998. Contentious politics in complex societies: New social movements between conflict and cooperation. Pp. 81–107 in *From contention to democracy*, edited by Marco Giugni, Doug McAdam, and Charles Tilly. New York: Rowman & Littlefield.

Greer, James L. 1986. The political economy of the local state. *Politics & Society* 5 (4):513–38.

Griffin, Larry J., and Robin Stryker. 2000. Comparative and historical sociology. Pp. 382–92 in *Encyclopedia of sociology* (2d ed.), vol. 1, edited by Edgar F. Borgatta and Rhonda J. V. Montgomery. New York: Macmillan.

Group of Specialists on Mainstreaming. 1998. *Gender mainstreaming: Conceptual framework, methodology and presentation of good practice*. Strasbourg Cedex: Council of Europe Publishing.

Guenther, Katja M. 2006. "A bastion of sanity in a crazy world": A local feminist movement and the reconstitution of scale, space, and place in an eastern German city. *Social Politics* 13 (4):551–75.

———. 2008. Understanding policy diffusion across feminist social movements: The case of gender mainstreaming. *Politics & Gender* 4 (4):587–614.

———. 2009. The impact of emotional opportunities on the emotion cultures of feminist organizations. *Gender & Society* 23 (3):337–62.

———. 2009. The politics of names: Rethinking the methodological and ethical significance of naming people, organizations, and places *Qualitative Research* 9: 411–21.

———. Forthcoming. The strength of weak coalitions: Transregional feminism in eastern Germany since unification. In *Strategic alliances: New studies of social movement coalitions*, edited by Nella Van Dyke and Holly J. McCammon. Minneapolis: University of Minnesota Press.

Hampele, Anne. 1993. The organized women's movement in the collapse of the GDR: The Independent Women's Organization (UFV). Pp. 180–93 in *Gender, politics, and post-communism: Reflections from eastern Europe and the former Soviet Union*, edited by Nanette Funk and Magda Mueller. London: Routledge.

Hampele-Ulrich, Anne. 2000. *Der Unabhängige Frauenverband: Ein frauenpolitischen Experiments im deutschen Vereinigungsprozess*. Berlin: Berlin Debatte Wissenschaftsverlag.

Haney, Lynne. 2002. *Inventing the needy: The gender transformation from socialist welfare state to welfare capitalism in Hungary*. Berkeley: University of California Press.

Hansestadt Rostock. 2001. Anwendung des Gender Mainstreaming-Prinzips in der Stadtverwaltung Rostock. *Hansestadt Rostock Bürgerschaft*.

———. 2002. *Statistisches Jahrbuch 2002*. Rostock: Hansestadt Rostock.

———. 2004. Wahlausschuss bestätigte Wahlergebnisse der Europa- und Bürgerschaftswahlen. Available at http://www.rostock.de/Internet/stadtverwaltung/stadt/info.jsp?wohin=/presse/loadPresseFrame.jsp&seq_id=13905. Accessed June 20, 2004.

Harsch, Donna. 1997. Society, the State, and Abortion in East Germany, 1950-1972. *American Historical Review* 102 (1):53–84.

Hartmann, Heidi. 1997. The unhappy marriage of Marxism and feminism: Towards a more progressive union. Pp. 97–122 in *The second wave: A reader in feminist theory*, edited by Linda Nicholson. New York: Routledge.

Heckathorn, Douglas D. 1996. The dynamics and dilemmas of collective action. *American Sociological Review* 61 (April):250–77.

Heinecke, Herbert. 2002. *Konfession und Politik in der DDR: Das Wechselverhaltnis von Kirche und Staat im Vergleich zwischen evangelischer und katholischer Kirche*. Leipzig: Evangelische Verlagsanstalt.

Hellman, Judith Adler. 1987. *Journeys among women: Feminism in five Italian cities*. New York: Oxford University Press.

Hemment, Julie. 2004. Global civil society and the local costs of belonging: Defining violence against women in Russia. *Signs* 29 (3):815–40.

———. 2007. *Empowering women in Russia: Activism, aid, and NGOs*. Bloomington: Indiana University Press.

Jarausch, Konrad. 1994. *The rush to German unity*. New York: Oxford University Press.

Kantola, Johanna. 2006. *Feminists theorize the state*. New York: Palgrave Macmillan.

Karapin, Roger 2007. *Protest politics in Germany: Movements on the left and the right since the 1960s*. University Park: Pennsylvania State University Press.

Keck, Margaret, and Kathryn Sikkink. 1998. *Activists beyond borders: Advocacy networks in international politics*. Ithaca, NY: Cornell University Press.

Kenawi, Samirah. 1995. *Fraungruppen in der DDR der 80er Jahre*. Berlin: Grauzone: Dokumentionsstelle zur nichtstaatlichen Frauenbewegung in der DDR.

Klawiter, Maren. 2008. *The biopolitics of breast cancer: Changing cultures of disease and activism*. Minneapolis: University of Minnesota Press.

Knoke, David. 1988. Incentives in collective action organizations. *American Sociological Review* 53 (June):311–29.

Kolinsky, Eva. 1999. Women, work, and family in the new Länder: Conflicts and experiences. Pp. 101–25 in *Recasting East Germany: Social transformation after the GDR*, edited by Chris Flockton and Eva Kolinsky. London: Frank Cass.

Kriesi, Hanspeter. 1995. The political opportunity structure of new social movements: Its impact on their mobilization. Pp. 167–98 in *The politics of social protest*, edited by J. Craig Jenkins and Bert Klandermans. Minneapolis: University of Minnesota Press.

Landeshauptstadt Erfurt Stadtverwaltung. 2002. *Jahrbuch*. Erfurt: Landeshauptstadt Erfurt Stadtverwaltung.

Landriscina, Mirella. 2006. A calmly disruptive order: The case of an institutionalized advocacy organization at work. *Qualitative Sociology* 29 (4):447–66.

Lane, Christa. 1983. Women in socialist society with special reference to the German Democratic Republic. *Sociology* 17 (4):489–505.

Lang, Sabine. 1997. The NGOization of feminism: Institutionalization and institution building within the German women's movements. Pp. 101–20 in *Transitions, environments, translations: Feminisms in international politics*, edited by Joan W. Scott, Cora Kaplan, and Debra Keates. New York and London: Routledge.

Le Goff, Jean-Marie. 2002. Cohabiting unions in France and West Germany: Transitions to first birth and first marriage. *Demographic Research* 7 (18):593–624.

Liebert, Ulrike. 2002. Europeanising gender mainstreaming: Constraints and opportunities in the multilevel euro-polity. *Feminist Legal Studies* 10:241–56.

Lorber, Judith. 2001. *Gender inequality: Feminist theories and politics*, 2d ed. Los Angeles: Roxbury.

Maier, Charles S. 1997. *Dissolution: The crisis of communism and the end of East Germany*. Princeton, NJ: Princeton University Press.

Maleck-Lewy, Eva. 1995. Between self-determination and state supervision: Women and the abortion law in post-unification Germany. *Social Politics* 2 (1):62–75.

Maleck-Lewy, Eva, and Myra Marx Ferree. 2000. Talking about women and wombs: The discourse of abortion and reproductive rights in the GDR during and after the Wende. Pp. 92–117 in *Reproducing gender: Politics, publics, and everyday life after socialism*, edited by Susan Gal and Gail Kligman. Princeton, NJ: Princeton University Press.

Martin, Deborah G., and Byron Miller. 2003. Space and contentious politics. *Mobilization* 8 (2):143–56.

Martin, Patricia Yancey. 1990. Rethinking feminist organizations. *Gender & Society* 4:182–206.

Massey, Doreen. 1994. *Space, place, and gender*. Minneapolis: University of Minnesota Press.

Masson, Dominique. 2006. Constructing scale/contesting scale: Women's movement and rescaling politics in Québec. *Social Politics* 13 (4):462–86.

Mazey, Sonia. 2001. *Gender mainstreaming in the EU: Principles and practice*. London: London European Research Center.

Mazur-Stommen, Susan. 2003. Church, state, and city: Fighting over the Bäderregulung in Rostock, Germany. Paper presented at the Annual Meeting of the German Studies Association, San Diego.

Melucci, Alberto. 1995. The process of collective identity. Pp. 41–63 in *Social movements and culture*, edited by Hank Johnston and Bert Klandermans. Minneapolis: University of Minnesota Press.

Meyer, Sibylee, and Eva Schulze. 1998. After the fall of the Wall: The impact of the transition on East German women. *Political Psychology* 19:95–116.

Meyers, Marcia K., Janet C. Gornick, and Katherine E. Ross. 1999. Public childcare, parental leave and unemployment. Pp. 117–46 in *Gender and welfare state regimes*, edited by Diane Sainsbury. Oxford: Oxford University Press.

Miethe, Ingrid. 1996. Das Politikverständnis bürgerbewegten Frauen der DDR im Prozess der deutschen Vereinigung. *Zeitschrift für Frauenforschung* 14 (3):87–101.

———. 1999a. *Frauen in der DDR-opposition: Lebens- und kollektivgeschichtliche Verläufe in einer Frauenfriedensgruppe*. Opladen: Leske + Budrich.

———. 1999b. From "Mother of the revolution" to "Fathers of unification": Concepts of politics among women activists following German unification. *Social Politics* 6:1–22.

———. 2008. From "strange sisters" to "Europe's daughters"? European enlargement as a chance for women's movements in East and West Germany. Pp. 118–36 in *Gender politics in the expanding European Union: Mobilization, inclusion, exclusion*, edited by Silke Roth. New York: Berghahn Books.

Miethe, Ingrid, and Anne Ulrich-Hampele. 2001. Preference for informal democracy: The east(ern) German case. Pp. 23–32 in *Pink, purple, green: Women's, religious, environmental, and gay/lesbian movements in central Europe today*, edited by Helena Flam. New York and Boulder, CO: Columbia University and East European Monographs.

Minkoff, Debra C. 1999. Bending with the wind: Strategic change and adaptation by women's and racial minority organizations. *American Journal of Sociology* 104 (6):1,666–1,703.

Mitchell, Juliet. 1971. *Women's estate*. New York: Pantheon.

Naples, Nancy. 2003. *Feminism and method: Ethnography, discourse analysis, and activist research*. New York: Routledge.

Nash, Katherine. 1997. GDR women and German unification: Meanings of paid work and child care. Doctoral thesis, Department of Sociology, University of Minnesota, Twin Cities, Minneapolis.

Norling, Lisa. 1991. The sentimentalization of American seafaring: The case of the New England whalefishery. Pp. 164–78 in *Jack Tar in history: Essays on the history of maritime life and labour*, edited by Colin Howell and Richard Twomey. Fredericton, New Brunswick: Acadiensis Press.

———. 1992. "How fraught with sorrow and heartpangs": Mariners' wives and the ideology of domesticity in New England, 1790–1880. *The New England Quarterly* 65 (3):422–46.

Offe, Claus. 1997. *Varieties of transition*. Cambridge, MA: MIT Press.

Oliver, Pamela E., and Hank Johnston. 2000. What a good idea! Ideologies and frames in social movement research. *Mobilization* 5 (1):37–54.

Ortbals, Candice D. 2008. Subnational politics in spain: New avenues for feminist policymaking and activism. *Politics & Gender* 4 (1):93–119.

Ostner, Ilona. 1994. Back to the fifties: Gender and welfare in unified Germany. *Social Politics* 1:333–58.

Paulsen, Krista E. 2004. Making character concrete: Empirical strategies for studying place distinction. *City & Community* 3 (3):243–62.

PDS Faktion im Thüringer Landtag. 2005. Katja Wolf: Regierung gefährdet Landesfrauenrat. Available at http://www.pds-fraktion-thueringen.de/presse/pm2005/pm190505b.html. Accessed May 23, 2005.

Pfaff, Steven. 1996. Collective identity and informal groups in revolutionary mobilization: East Germany in 1989. *Social Forces* 75 (1):91–117.

Poletta, Francesca. 1998. Contending stories: Narrative in social movements. *Qualitative Sociology* 21 (4):419–46.

Pollack, Mark A., and Emilie Hafner-Burton. 2000. Mainstreaming gender in the European Union. *Journal of European Public Policy* 7 (3):432–55.

Porter, Marilyn. 1985. "She was skipper of the shore-crew": Notes on the sexual division of labour in Newfoundland. *Labour/le Travail* xv:105–23.

Probst, Lothar. 1993. *"Der Norden wacht auf": Zur Geschichte des politischen Umbruchs in Rostock 1989–1991*. Bremen: Edition Temmen.

Quack, Sigrid, and Friederike Maier. 1994. From state socialism to market economy—women's employment in East Germany. *Environment and Planning* 26:1,257–76.

Ray, Raka. 1998. Women's movements and political fields: A comparison of two Indian cities. *Social Problems* 45 (1):21–36.

———. 1999. *Fields of protest: Women's movements in India*. Minneapolis: University of Minnesota Press.

Ray, Raka, and Anna C. Korteweg. 1999. Women's movements in the third world: Identity, mobilization, and autonomy. *Annual Review of Sociology* 25:47–71.

Rees, Teresa. 1998. *Mainstreaming equality in the European Union*. London: Routledge.

Regierungskommission Aufbau Ost. 2004. *Abschlussbericht des Gesprächskreises*. Berlin: Ministerium für Verkehr, Bau- und Wohnungswesen.

Regulska, Joanna, and Magda Grabowska. 2008. Will it make a difference? EU enlargement and women's public discource in Poland. Pp. 137–54 in *Gender politics in the expanding European Union: Mobilization, inclusion, exclusion*, edited by Silke Roth. New York: Berghahn Books.

Rinke, Andrea. 1994. Wende-bilder: Television images of women. Pp. 124–38 in *Women and the Wende: Social and cultural reflections of the German unification process*, edited by Elizabeth Boa and Janet Wharton. Atlanta, GA: Rodolpi.

Robertson, Roland. 1994. Globalisation or glocalisation? *Journal of International Communication* 1 (1):33–52.

Roth, Silke. 2003. Goethe and Buchenwald: Re-constructing German national identity in the Weimar year 1999. Pp. 93–106 in *Why Weimar? Questioning the legacy of Weimar from Goethe to 1999*, edited by Peter M. Daly, Hans Walter Frischkopf, Trudis E. Goldsmith-Reber, and Horst Richter. New York: Peter Lang.

———, eds. 2008. *Gender politics in the expanding European Union: Mobilization, inclusion, exclusion*. New York: Berghahn Books.

Rudd, Elizabeth. 1999. Coping with capitalism: Gender and the transformation of work-family conflicts in former East Germany. Doctoral thesis, Department of Sociology, University of California, Berkeley.

Rueschmeyer, Marilyn. 1998. Women in the politics of eastern Germany: The dilemmas of unification. Pp. 87–116 in *Women in the politics of post-communist eastern Europe*, edited by Marilyn Rueschmeyer. Armonk, NJ: M.E. Sharpe.

Sandole-Staroste, Ingrid. 2002. *Women in transition: Between socialism and capitalism*. Westport, CT: Praeger.

Scheper-Hughes, Nancy. 2000. Ire in Ireland. *Ethnography* 1 (1):117–40.

Schmidt, Verena. 2005. *Gender mainstreaming—an innovation in Europe?* Opladen: Barbara Budrich Publishers.

Schröder, Karsten, ed. 2003. *In deinen Mauren herrschen eintracht und allgemeines Wohlergehen: Eine Geschichte der stadt Rostock von ihren Uhrsprüngen bis zum Jahr 1990*. Rostock: Ingo Koch Verlag.

Schulenberg, Jennifer Lisa. 2000. Neuenbundeslaender: The effects of state and policy reunification on the women and families in the former GDR. Master's thesis, Faculty of Graduate Studies, University of Guelph, Canada.

Schwarzer, Alice. 1975. *Der kleine Unterschied und seine großen Folgen*. Frankfurt: Fischer Verlag.

———. 1984. *Das EMMA-Buch*. München: DTV.

———. 1985. *Lohn Liebe, zum wert der Frauenarbeit*. Frankfurt: Suhrkamp Taschenbuch.

Sen, Ilina. 1989. Feminists, women's movements, and the working class. *Economic and Political Weekly* 24 (29):1,639–41.

Shaw, Jo. 2002. The European Union and gender mainstreaming: Constitutionally embedded or comprehensively marginalized? *Feminist Legal Studies* 10:213–26.

Sloat, Amanda. 2005. The growth of women's NGOs in central and eastern Europe. *European Journal of Women's Studies* 12(4):437–52.

Smith, Dorothy. 1990. *The conceptual practices of power: A feminist sociology of knowledge*. Boston: Northeastern University Press.

Spakes, Patricia. 1995. Women, work, and babies: Family-labor market policies in three European countries. *Affilia* 10 (4):369–97.

Squires, Judith. 2007. *The new politics of gender equality*. Basingstoke, UK: Palgrave Macmillan.

Stetson, Dorothy McBride, and Amy G. Mazur, eds. 1995. *Comparative state feminism*. London: Sage.

———. 2000. Women's movements and the state: Job training policy in France and the US. *Political Research Quarterly* 53 (3):597–623.

Stryker, Robin. 1996. Beyond history versus theory: Strategic narrative and sociological explanation. *Sociological Methods & Research* 24 (3):304–52.

Swidler, Ann. 1995. Cultural power and social movements. Pp. 25–40 in *Social movements and culture*, edited by Hank Johnston and Bert Klandermans. Minneapolis: University of Minnesota Press.

Szepansky, Gerda. 1995. *Die stille Emanzipation: Frauen in der DDR*. Frankfurt: Fischer.

Tarrow, Sidney G. 1994. *Power in movement: Social movements, collective action, and politics*. Cambridge: Cambridge University Press.

———. 1998. *Power in movement: Social movements and contentious politics*. Cambridge: Cambridge University Press.

Taylor, Verta. 1996. *Rock-a-by-baby: Feminism, self-help, and postpartum depression*. New York: Routledge.

———. 1999. Gender and social movements: Gender processes in women's self-help movements. *Gender & Society* 13 (1):8–33.

Taylor, Verta, and Nancy Whittier. 1992. Collective identity in social movements: Lesbian feminist identity. Pp. 104–29 in *Frontiers in social movement theory*, edited by Aldon D. Morris and Carol McClug Mueller. New Haven, CT: Yale University Press.

Terrell, Peter, Veronika Schnorr, Wendy V. A. Morris, and Roland Breitsprecher. 2001. *HarperCollins German unabridged dictionary*. New York: HarperCollins.

Thayer, Millie. 1997. Identity, revolution, and democracy: Lesbian movements in Central America. *Social Problems* 44 (3):386–407.

Thompson, Paul. 1985. Women in the fishing: The roots of power between the sexes. *Comparative Studies in Society and History* 27 (1):3–32.

Trappe, Heike. 1995. *Emanzipation oder Zwang? Frauen in der DDR zwischen Beruf, Familile und Sozialpolitik*. Berlin: Akademie Verlag.

Trappe, Heike, and Rachel A. Rosenfeld. 1998. A comparison of job-shifting patterns in the former East Germany and the former West Germany. *European Sociological Review* 14:343–68.

Trzcinski, Eileen. 1998. Gender and German unification. *Affilia* 13 (1):69–101.

Van Dyke, Nella, Sarah A. Soule, and Verta Taylor. 2004. The targets of social movements: Beyond a focus on the state. *Research in Social Movement, Conflicts, and Change* 25:27–51.

Verdery, Katherine. 1996. *What was socialism, and what comes next?* Princeton, NJ: Princeton University Press.

Weiner, Elaine. 2009. Eastern houses, western bricks? (Re)Constructing gender sensibilities in the European Union's eastward enlargement. *Social Politics* 16 (3):303–26.

Whittier, Nancy. 1995. *Feminist generations: The persistence of the radical women's movement*. Philadelphia, PA: Temple University Press.

Wolf, Diane, ed. 1996a. *Feminist dilemmas in fieldwork*. Boulder, CO: Westview Press.

———. 1996b. Situating feminist dilemmas in fieldwork. Pp. 1–55 in *Feminist dilemmas in fieldwork*, edited by Diane Wolf. Boulder, CO: Westview Press.

Wuerth, Andrea. 1999. National politics/local identities: Abortion rights in post-Wall Berlin. *Feminist Studies* 25 (3):601–31.

Young, Brigitte. 1999. *Triumph of the fatherland: German unification and the marginalization of women*. Ann Arbor: University of Michigan Press.

Zajicek, Anna M., and Toni M. Calasanti. 1998. Patriarchal struggles and state practices: A feminist, political-economic view. *Gender & Society* 12 (5):505–27.

Zippel, Kathrin. 2004. Transnational advocacy networks and policy cycles in the European Union: The case of sexual harassment. *Social Politics* 11 (1):57–85.

Index

The authorized representative in the EU for product safety and compliance is:
Mare Nostrum Group
B.V Doelen 72
4831 GR Breda
The Netherlands

www.ingramcontent.com/pod-product-compliance
Lightning Source LLC
Chambersburg PA
CBHW020344270326
41926CB00007B/309